TWIN REFLECTIONS

International Singers Reflect on God's Providential Care

Janice and Faye Rostvit

LANGMARC
PUBLISHING
AUSTIN, TEXAS

TWIN REFLECTIONS
International Singers Reflect
on God's Providential Care
by Janice and Faye Rostvit
Front Cover Photo by Rostvit Twins, taken at
the Maroon Bells near Aspen, Colorado
Cover Graphics: Michael Qualben

Back Cover Photo: Permission by Apre Photographers,
Colorado Springs, Colorado
Photos on pages 32, 34, 164, 193 with permission from
Stegner Portraits, Colorado Springs, Colorado
Photos on pages 26, 68, 96, 126 with permission from
James E. Ragsdale, Colorado Springs, Colorado
Photos on pages 64 and 65 with permission from Olan Mills

Copyright @ 2002 by Janice and Faye Rostvit

First Printing 2002
Printed in the United States of America

Published by LangMarc Publishing
Box 90488, Austin, Texas 78709
1-800-864-1648

Library of Congress Cataloging-in-Publication Data in process

ISBN: 1-880292-28-9 $16.95

DEDICATION

To our loving parents, Ed and Helga Rostvit.
They have taken us to the airport countless times
and have faithfully upheld us in prayer,
entrusting us to God's protective care.

Dear Readers ∼

Our sole purpose in writing *Twin Reflections* is to give
God glory by following the Scriptural exhortation,
"Declare His glory among the nations, His wondrous
deeds among the people." (I Chron. 16:24 NIV)

Janice and Faye Rostvit

TABLE OF CONTENTS

Foreword vii
Acknowledgments ix

PART I Reflecting on God's Directed PATH

1. Here We Go Again 3
2. Butterflies 9
3. In the Spotlight 19
4. Venturing Out 27

PART II Reflecting on God-Given PROVISIONS

5. A New Direction 35
6. God Knows Our Needs 41
7. Learning to Sing in a Foreign Language 49
8. Empty Pockets Yet Ample Provision 57
9. In Stormy Times 63
10. Bus Ministry 69
11. The Driver with the Open Heart 85

PART III Reflecting on God's PROVIDENTIAL Care

12. Music Around the World 99
13. On the High Seas 109
14. Believe It or Not 119
15. We Pray, Yet Worries Prey 127
16. Impossible 137
17. Norway, Land of Our Heritage 143
18. Twin Incidents 155
19. Music and Nature 165

PART IV Reflecting on God's Solutions to PROBLEMS

20. Stranded 175
21. Not By Our Plan 185
22. Airport Adventures 193

23. Short on Time 203
24. Victor Vega Rodriguez 207
25. In a Restricted Area 211
26. Agents 219
27. Mediterranean Marvels 229
28. Out in the Night 239

PART V Reflecting on God's Answers to PRAYERS

29. Be Still 247
30. Lord, Please Heal Me 259
31. Lost and Found 269
32. Pray for Rain 283
33. Ask for a Sign 293
34. Along the Ramu 299
35. Conflict in the Night 317

PART VI Reflecting on God's Dealings with PEOPLE

36. Two Phone Calls 329
37. Behind Bars 337
38. We See Jesus in a Blue Shirt 341
39. Mountain Top Experience 355
40. God's Timing 361
41. To the Arctic Circle 371
42. Double Curse Double Blessing 381

FOREWORD

Have you ever found yourself in a situation you didn't know how to handle? Then this book is for you.

The Rostvit Twins know what it is like to go to unknown places, with danger at every turn, being short on financial resources, and caught in unusual situations, yet always experiencing the Lord's hand upon them. "The Twins," as they are known in various countries, saw many opportunities to serve their Savior; at times it was risky, but they simply stepped out in faith.

Their ministry has blessed national and missionary alike. If you are wondering how I know, my wife Linda and I, together with our children, Shelley and Tim, served in Africa for twenty years. We hosted Faye and Janice on their first trip in 1968. We were out in "the bush" in an area of Zambia called Kapyanga. We were living in a round mud-brick house that we had built. It had few amenities, but the Twins never complained. They just made themselves at home and helped wherever possible. They encouraged and loved each of us, taking time to play with our children, or to pray with Linda and me. Upon our move to Lilongwe, Malawi, the Twins visited us again at a time when we were pioneering a new work. These sisters again ministered to us in many ways.

The Rostvits have memorized numerous songs in the languages of every country they visit. How the faces of the nationals would light up when they would hear songs of Jesus sung in their own heart language by these American twins.

A colleague of mine, now living in Turkey, saw the Rostvit Twins take center stage at the amphitheater in Ephesus. Since there were tourists from many nations, Janice and Faye sang in the various languages represented: Turkish, Norwegian, French, Russian, Japanese,

Chinese, and others. When one man requested South African, the Twins sang in Zulu complete with the click sounds. The man was astonished. He admitted, "I requested that to stump you. I never thought you could do it." It makes no difference to the Rostvits if they are singing in the amphitheater in Ephesus or under a mango tree in Zambia; to an unknown pauper in the side streets of a city in India, or before heads of state in Taiwan. Their ministry of music has brought joy to the hearts of thousands around the world. Janice and Faye have the unique ministry of assuring people of various nationalities that the God of heaven loves and cares for them.

The vocal harmony, as can only be produced by twins, is something special. Their style is original and unique. As well as singing in the vernacular of various people throughout the world, they have composed many songs as inspired by the Lord. You will read the lyrics of some of their songs in this book.

Every page is filled with true-to-life ministry in the 20th century that will cause you to be in awe at what GOD has wrought. Many are fascinated when seeing these globe-trotting identical twins, but this book does not promote their accomplishments. It has been written in hopes that when reading about God's workings, you will reflect upon His mighty acts, not only in the lives of these twins, but also in your own.

Don Mechem

[Don Mechem, together with his family, served as missionaries for twenty years in Zambia and Malawi, Africa. Since then he has been the field director for Turkish World Outreach, an international mission reaching Turkish people in various nations. His mission trips now take him to various European and middle eastern countries and Australia.]

ACKNOWLEDGMENTS

As this book reflects on God's providential ways, we praise Him for even orchestrating events to provide a computer for us. John and Doreen Halfpenny, longtime friends in Australia, gave us a sizable gift. Then when we gave a concert in Carl Junction, Missouri, the minister, Boyce Mouton, took up a love offering earmarked for a computer. The two gifts totaled $1109. Gordon Clymer, a special brother, got us in contact with a salesman who gave us discounted prices for the model we wanted. To our amazement it totaled exactly $1109.

We are deeply grateful to MTS Travel for the excellent fares and service they have given us over the years for our overseas flights. When we have unusual destinations or last minute changes, Jan Batchelder, our travel agent, cheerfully says, "Not a problem."

We are grateful for our Christian parents, Ed and Helga Rostvit. They have been very supportive, not only in our singing ministry over four decades, but also in our endeavor to write this book. They have critiqued each chapter. Mom, who has published her own life story, gave advice to improve style. Dad, who reads for pleasure, saw the big picture. His comments usually spotlighted problems that meant more revision, but were needful.

Our sisters, Laura Jean Tate and Sharon Foster, have given much prayer support through their families and churches. When we began writing, Laura Jean challenged us, "If you'll finish your book, we will get our basement remodeled." We thought we had plenty of time, but within months their basement was transformed into showcase rooms. That gave us incentive to get busy!

Betty Doebbeling is a cousin who is writing about her experiences as a nurse in Viet Nam. She was a great lift as we critiqued chapters for each other. We appreciate Bill Stephenson for the motivation he gave at times when the writing was "shelved," and we thank his wife Kathy for excellent editing suggestions on many chapters. Their treating us to a week of seclusion helped us to get the manuscript outlined and organized.

We thank Herman Chapman and Mike Lyons who both unselfishly gave of their time to help us with their computer expertise.

There have been many prayer partners, including ones already mentioned. Without prayer support, our service for Christ could be rendered ineffective. In particular we thank Carol Hertzke, Jean Marie Oberly, Jim and Twila Brompton and their family. These dear people prayed specifically and saw the answers at various stages of the writing. We appreciated time at the Brompton's ranch to do much of our final editing. Their Christ-like examples have been a lift to us, keeping us focused on the Author of our salvation.

We also thank God for Lois Qualben for accepting our book for publication. She has been kind, gracious, and thoughtful in every step of the publishing process. Thanks for sharing our aspirations that *Twin Reflections* will glorify God and challenge readers to live by faith.

Janice and Faye Rostvit

PART I

Reflecting on God's Directed PATH

Does God have a certain path for some to take, though it is not what that person had envisioned for his future? Joseph had not planned to go to Egypt, yet despite the humiliation of servitude and incarceration, his moral character and faith in God prevailed, so that eventually he saw God's plan and purpose. When Saul of Tarsus was on the road to Damascus, Jesus steered him onto God's intended path.

> "A man's steps are directed by the Lord. How then can anyone understand his own way?" (Prov. 20:24 NIV)

God's ways are higher than our ways. Do we choose to walk that high road, even if the path at times becomes obscure? Even if our strength gives way to weakness? Even if another path looks easier, more desirable, or more lucrative?

> "Many, O Lord my God are the wonders you have done. The things you planned for us no one can recount to you; were I to speak and tell of them they would be too many to declare." (Ps. 40:5 NIV)

The two of us never intended to become singers, but God had HIS plan. We have marveled as we reflect and see that His plan has been best for our lives.

1962: ROSTVIT SISTERS QUARTET
Standing: Laura Jean and Sharon
Seated: Janice and Faye

1

Here We Go Again

∽ by Janice ∽

The bulging flight bag threatened to slip from my shoulder as I hefted my suitcase and guitar case onto the well-worn step of the Agra airport's transit bus. The pungent aroma of curried *samosas* from a street vendor's stall penetrated my senses. India is unique, providing sufficient cultural shocks on a daily basis. On this particular bus, we were in for another surprise.

I elbowed the flight bag, shifting its weight to my back before grasping the folds of my sari so I could step aboard. Again taking the suitcase and instrument in hand, I muttered, "Here we go again." Faye followed with her equal burden of baggage.

At the top of the steps we both paused, momentarily dumbfounded. The buzz of conversation had ceased. Passengers were straining to see over the seat backs. All eyes were on us. They were curious and fascinated to see American twins in Indian attire. We likewise stared back. All the passengers were Japanese. Japanese! In the middle of India? My attention was diverted as the driver spoke.

"I'm sorry, but your transport bus already left. This is a special charter," he said.

With bewildered apologies, we turned to leave. But the driver, apparently having second thoughts, held out a hand.

"No, Wait! Ride with us. I know the destination of the transport bus. It is not out of our way. We will take you there." Grateful, we found seats.

Noticing our instruments, a man asked if we would sing. When we proceeded to sing Japanese songs, the passengers' expressions registered obvious surprise and delight.

"So you are Christians," a man said. By their request we continued singing, grateful not only for the ride, but also for the opportunity to witness. Later we did wonder what they thought of the Christian songs, as we learned they were on a Buddhist pilgrimage tour.

When the bus arrived at our stop, we thanked the driver and exited. We watched as the bus pulled away.

"Who would have thought we would sing for Japanese Buddhists in India?" Faye asked.

"Who ever thought we'd have a life of singing PERIOD!" To think that years ago it began of all places, on a bus—a school bus!

⸱⸱⸱

It was the spring of 1960. The stubby yellow school bus chugged slowly along the gravel road. I gazed out the window, my eyes fixed on nothing in particular. We were shy country girls growing up in ranch country at the edge of the Rocky Mountains. America's youngest president, John F. Kennedy, had taken office. The Soviet Union under Krushchev's heavy hand was strengthening the Iron Curtain. The Berlin Wall was constructed. There were problems in the world—but not in our world. The only frustration we faced was the time wasted on this school bus.

We always dreaded the long ride home. It wasn't so long in distance but in time. It annoyed us that the driver took the twenty-three miles at such a snail's pace. We had chores to do: slop the hogs, feed the rabbits and calves, and carry water to some newly planted spruce trees. We also needed to saddle our black horse and canter to the neighbor's home to get some milk. Homework took time, too, but above all we wanted some free time to play. At age fourteen we were still kids more than teenagers. Our sister Laura Jean, age eighteen, and sister Sharon, sixteen, were into makeup, fingernail polish, and dreaming about boys. Not us! We still preferred climbing trees, riding a horse, or scratching a sow's belly.

As the bus rounded a bend, Pikes Peak came into view. The mountain was our weather barometer. A cloud on the Peak often gave us a half-hour warning of a coming storm, and in April it could be rain or snow. This day it was clear, which was all the more reason to want to hurry home. Why couldn't this driver speed it up, I wondered. Faye interrupted my thoughts.

"Guess how many fence posts to the Murr's ranch gate," she said. Guessing games had become a daily pastime on the tiring hour-and-a-half ride. If we weren't counting fence posts, we were counting horses in a pasture or antelope in a herd.

For the boys on the bus, boredom naturally led to mischief and chaos. One time they took the bottom cushions from some of the seats and stacked them on top of others, leaving the younger children to sit on empty frames. To add to the commotion, a boy reached into the toolbox behind the backseat to rattle the tire chains. As the noise level increased, the redness on the back of the driver's neck rose like mercury in a thermometer. Then the brakes were applied and, like an explosion from an overdue volcano, the man stood to vent a tirade of angry words. His uncontrolled temper failed to gain respect. Consequently, as soon as the bus had resumed its sluggish pace, bedlam reigned again.

After some weeks, that bus driver could cope no longer. A new driver named Bill Blair was assigned to our route. We liked this rugged-looking man with dark hair, a dimpled chin, and a winning smile. He had an air of authority about him that commanded respect, rather than demanded it. When he set his square jaw and looked through us with penetrating blue eyes, we all sat up and listened.

And the driving! This man knew how to find fourth gear! There would be no more need to entertain ourselves by counting antelope or fence posts. Now even telephone poles sped by in a blur. We did have to stay on guard though for the small humped bridges with their unusually steep approaches. Mr. Blair enjoyed acting the part of a stunt driver, picking up speed before hitting the ramps. When the wheels left the ground, we left our seats. No one wanted to lose this great driver, so for the most part we all were on our good behavior.

The atmosphere on the bus had so improved that we began to sing. We sisters harmonized on well-known popular tunes, folk songs, and gospel music. Sharon was often the one to suggest that everybody sing. The children joined us, enthusiastically clapping and singing, "He's got the whole world in His hands...."

Little did we know we would soon be launched into a singing career. We had never entertained the idea. We assumed we would eventually marry ranchers' sons and live a normal life of having a family, tending a garden, and feeding livestock. That just wasn't GOD'S plan. We have not regretted following His path, although it was difficult at first.

School Superintendent Verne Totten stood to address the faculty meeting. He discussed the upcoming athletic banquet.

"If we are going to hire some entertainment like we've done other years, we need to be booking them now." He paused and scratched his head. "Could we possibly come up with some talent within the student body to save on the school's budget?"

The small rural school had no music or drama classes. What entertainment could they expect to find? The handful of teachers and staff sat shaking their heads, void of ideas. Then Mr. Blair's voice broke the silence.

"How about the Rostvit sisters? They've been singing on my bus."

We found out about the faculty's discussion the following day. During recess, teacher Fern Simpson approached us with record albums in hand and told us to look them over. As she plugged in a portable phonograph, she instructed us to copy the words of some songs. Then she turned to leave. The clicking of her high heels on the hardwood floor matched the pounding of our hearts.

With more dread than enthusiasm, we thumbed through the LPs. From the Chordettes, we chose the popular song "Lollypop," and from the Lennon Sisters, well known for singing on the "Lawrence Welk Show," we chose the song, "How Will I know My Love?" We also worked up arrangements of some choruses we had been singing on the bus, each of us finding our niche in four-part harmony.

Although we practiced diligently, we still were nervous when the day of the banquet arrived. With lips quivering and knees knocking, we performed and then returned to our respective places at the tables.

Whew! That's over, we thought. But it wasn't. There would be more practice sessions, more programs, and more battles with nerves. We had just begun a life of singing.

1963: Sharon, Janice, Faye, and Laura Jean Rostvit

2

Butterflies

∼ by Faye ∼

A microphone! What a threatening object! We all had the same idea—back away as far as possible. Three feet seemed to be the limit as we bumped into pots of decorative potted plants. Their large leaves draped over our shoulders. We stayed there, content to be partially hidden by the shrubbery. Sharon hummed a starting note for the hymn "Let Him In." She pitched it too low, but we kept singing, too embarrassed to start over. Singing didn't come easily, but butterflies did.

Three weeks after the athletic banquet, we were again before the student body, this time for the baccalaureate service. I glanced at the audience. There in the back row sat the older boys leaning back in their chairs. They were smirking!

We finished the first verse, then my mind went blank. I tried to concentrate. I was reaping the consequence of laziness. Since we needed to learn just two songs, we had failed to take our practice sessions seriously. Baccalaureate was nearly upon us before we had memorized the second verse. We hadn't learned it well enough, especially considering the stress we would feel when facing an audience of high school peers.

The words came just in time: the first line, then the second. I didn't know that my sisters were experiencing the same line-by-line panic. Then it happened! We all forgot the words. Seconds ticked by. All was silent, except for the snickers that came from the back row. We returned, red faced, to our seats. Humiliation! How could we possibly find enough courage to sing again at the end of the service? We did, however, perform well on our other number. But for fourteen-year-old girls like us, the embarrassment of the first song was indelibly etched in our memories.

Summer arrived and with it the relaxing family excursions into the mountains. We four girls would ride in the back of our parents' pickup truck, allowing the wind to whip at our hair. The spectacular mountain scenery inspired us to sing at the top of our lungs. Often by the time we had reached a campsite, our voices had been taxed, but we would still enjoy singing around the campfire.

Later that summer, our father's construction work took him to Leadville, an old mining town high in the mountains. For several weeks we lived in a camping trailer beside Turquoise Lake, well named for its aqua waters reflecting Colorado's highest peaks. In the evenings we would go fishing with Dad and Mom and watch the sun set over the snowcapped ranges. While Dad was at work, we girls had all day free to go for

 walks in the forest. The wind whistled through the pines, and aspen leaves shimmered in the sunlight. We walked by the shores of the lake, memorizing the words

of some hymns. A year earlier Janice and I had both accepted Jesus as our Savior. Now these were times of reflection and growth, where God's love and presence engulfed us. Singing in those surroundings became worshipful praise rather than practice sessions, fun rather than work, joy rather than drudgery.

On Friday evenings, when Dad's work had ended, we would all return to Colorado Springs. We hated to leave the mountains where the only butterflies were real ones, those created by God. On Sundays the fluttering of nerves in the stomach would begin again.

Of the four of us, I seemed to have the worst case of stage fright. While we sat in the congregation waiting for our turn to sing, I would be doubled over with stomach pain. I had not yet learned that God's presence could be just as near to me among the crowds as He had been in the mountains.

All too soon summer had ended, and it was time to return to school for tenth grade. Requests for singing increased as teachers arranged programs: PTA meetings, office parties, and luncheons of service organizations. Laura Jean and Sharon looked forward to each singing engagement, as they were more self-confident than Janice and I were. We dreaded performances; the fright showed on our faces. We were becoming accustomed to comments such as, "Nice singing girls, but," pointing to Janice and me, "you two looked scared."

I finally began to pray, but admittedly not for the right solutions. I should have asked God's help in overcoming my shyness. Or I should have prayed "Not my will but Thine be done." Instead, I was praying for snowstorms, car troubles, or for sore throats—anything — in hopes of postponing or, better yet, canceling programs.

One day the Lord answered my selfish prayers. I awoke with a case of laryngitis. I was pleased! We rode to school that morning, confident that the program scheduled for the noon hour would be canceled. Our English teacher, Mrs. Simpson, had arranged to take us into Colorado Springs to sing for a ladies' luncheon. As soon as we arrived at school, we approached her.

"We can't sing today," I explained in a raspy whisper. "I've lost my voice."

Much to our consternation, Mrs. Simpson merely said, "You can't cancel out at this late date. They're counting on you. You must go."

"Then I guess it will have to be a trio." I assumed that my pitiful sound would convince her that at least I had a valid reason to be excused. But she was not to be dissuaded.

"You are coming, too. It is unique for four sisters to sing together, and your harmony and blend are perfect. If you still have no voice by noon, Faye, you can move your lips and pretend to sing. After all, it's only for three songs." Her expression clearly communicated I had no further choice in the matter. Mrs. Simpson was helping to instill within us a sense of responsibility and the importance of fulfilling obligations. Later we learned to appreciate the values she was teaching us.

Twelve o'clock. The room was filled with ladies seated at round tables. They turned their attention toward us as we sang from a low platform. I feared that ladies at the nearby tables could surely detect I was merely moving my lips. I felt foolish! As soon as we had finished the three songs, we headed for the lobby, making our way between the tables. The ladies were all clapping as we passed. The sound seemed only a mockery, exposing my deception—unmerited recognition, at least for me! I had to restrain myself to keep from bolting for the doorway. Once we reached the lobby, Mrs. Simpson encouraged us, speaking loud enough for us to hear over the din of the applause.

"You did a fine job." Excited, she added, "Oh, they want an encore."

"What's an encore?" we all echoed, never having heard the word.

"They want you to sing another song." With a swish of her hand, she urged us back toward the dining room. My nightmare was not yet over. Reluctantly I followed my sisters back to the platform and faked it through another song.

It did nothing for my painfully low self-esteem when one of the ladies came to us afterward and remarked, "I've heard you girls on several occasions, and today you sounded even better."

Needless to say, I never again prayed for laryngitis.

⋘≈≋≋≋⋙

"What have you done with the sheet music, Faye?" Laura Jean demanded. "We have got to learn that song today." I was horrified.

"I must have left it in my desk at school." On short notice, we had been asked to learn "The Lord's Prayer" to sing for a friend's wedding. Mrs. Simpson, always eager to help, had loaned us the sheet music. Now it was Saturday, and we knew there wouldn't be enough time to learn the song if we waited until Monday. Sharon, who needed no excuse to get behind the wheel of a car, volunteered to drive to school and retrieve it. I, feeling at fault, went along.

When we reached the school, we were astonished to find that the front doors were locked. We hadn't counted on that! After all, none of us ranchers ever locked our homes; why should the school doors be locked? We circled the building, trying every door. Everything was locked up tight.

With drooping shoulders, we walked around to where we could see the windows of the room that served as the joint classroom for the ninth and tenth grades. That's where the sheet music should be—so near and yet so far. Then I saw something that gave me a glimmer of hope. One of the windows was cracked open an inch or two. There was only one drawback: the room was on the second floor!

I eyed the massive brick structure built in 1902. A ladder would never reach. Determined to avoid another blunder like baccalaureate, I was desperate to get that sheet music. I could scale the wall. Occasional bricks stuck out more than the others. The pattern of uneven bricks was consistent.

"You can't do that!" Sharon protested when I asked her to give me a boost.

Determination blinded my senses. The wall was only a barrier to overcome, a challenge no more difficult than climbing a tree at home or rock climbing in the mountains. Although reluctant, Sharon gave me a shove. Cautiously I climbed. All my daily chores of carrying buckets of feed to the calves, slop to the hogs, and water to the garden had paid off—my arm muscles were strong. I pulled myself upward from one protruding brick to the next. The most difficult task was to get up onto the window ledge. Though the maneuver was precarious, the fear of being unprepared for a wedding drove fresh adrenaline through my veins.

When at last I was safely on the ledge, I glanced down. Sharon, who had been watching nervously, breathed a sigh of relief.

Kneeling on the wide ledge, I slipped my fingers into the narrow opening beneath the window and gave it a jerk. It wouldn't budge. I glanced around nervously. No one was in sight. I was thankful this was at the back of the building, facing the prairie rather than the road.

"What's the matter? Can't you open it?" Sharon called from below.

"It's stuck," I muttered through gritted teeth while giving the window another yank. Still no give. I tried to jiggle it from side to side. Bits of weathered paint sprinkled onto the ledge. The ancient window was binding in its grooves. I wiggled it some more, then finally felt it give a fraction of an inch. Little by little it moved until the opening was wide enough for me to squeeze through.

With the sheet music in hand, I waved it in the window for Sharon to see, then pulled down on the old frame. It closed as stubbornly as it had opened. Soon I was pushing on the release bar of the front door and exiting the building. We sped homeward and began to practice. We learned the song and, though we were nervous as ever, the wedding went off without incident.

One day Mrs. Simpson introduced us to Collette Divine, a professional singer. She thought we had potential, so this kind lady offered to give us voice lessons weekly. She drilled us on breathing exercises to strengthen the diaphragm, taught us how to run scales, and how to interpret songs using "louds" and "softs" for proper emphasis. For all of her professional help, of which we were deeply grateful, Collette refused to accept payment.

Our sister Laura Jean saw to it that we would maintain the daily routine of vocalizing and working on songs. Despite all the practice, we couldn't learn enough new songs. We were being asked to sing several numbers every Sunday at church. Although we dreaded the weekly drain on our repertoire, it was an effective motivation to keep us practicing.

I remember the time when I tripped on the steps to the platform. In the process, I knocked a flower arrangement from its stand. Then I discovered that I had tennis shoes on, while my sisters were wearing high heels. I tried to sing but my voice cracked. A lump formed in my throat and I began to cry. Then Janice gently shook my shoulder.

"Wake up! Wake up!" I bolted upright in bed, relieved to discover that it was only a dream. Why did the butterflies even follow me to bed?

> "In the morning you will say, 'If only it were evening!' And in the evening, 'If only it were morning!' - because of the terror that will fill your hearts ..."(Deut. 28:67 NIV)

Although by now performances were generally running more smoothly, there were occasional nightmares in real life. I recall one occasion when we attempted a new song in church. It had a lovely message about rising on eagle's wings, based on Isaiah 40:31. We had learned the words, but the harmony was difficult. As we started to sing, we failed to get the harmony parts correct. Only a line or two into the song, we were forced to stop and try again. The second attempt was no better, nor the third. After failing four times, we gave up and sang "The Lord's Prayer."

God was training us and molding our character. Growth at times was painful, but He was leading us. God also provided encouragement along the way. No matter how many mistakes we made at church or how embarrassed we felt, Leroy Hays, the music director, was there to comfort and encourage us. Truly a man of God and a loving person, Leroy was always searching for talent among the young people, urging them to use their abilities for the Lord.

Another dear encourager was Mrs. Peterson, an elderly lady who sat on a hard-backed chair at the side of the auditorium. As we would descend from the platform, she would lovingly pat each of us on the arm. With an angelic smile and soft, nearly inaudible tones, she would whisper, "God bless you." Of course, our parents were always behind us. They did not push us into a singing career, however. I remember when Dad had a serious talk with the four of us and said, "If this singing business ever goes to your heads, I'll put a stop to it!" We appreciated his sense of values.

Downtown Colorado Springs. The City Auditorium. A benefit program for the March of Dimes. From backstage I could hear the constant hum of voices as people entered, filling the seats on the main floor. My stomach churned. Janice and I were seventeen years old. Nearly three years had passed since we had begun to sing. Why was I still such a nervous wreck, especially for big important programs? Why did the fear still show on my face? Would I never overcome stage fright?

I cleared my throat, then took a deep breath. The palms of my hands were wet with perspiration. I paced back and forth in the darkness behind the final set of curtains. I returned to the side of the platform where Laura Jean and Janice stood talking. They seemed to be relaxed and looking forward to this opportunity. Passing them, I pulled aside the curtain to peer out into the audience. Even the balconies were nearly filled.

The knot in my stomach tightened. I retreated to the ladies' dressing room. Sharon was by the mirror combing her hair. One glance in the mirror showed that I, too, needed to primp. That maverick lock of hair was out of place again! The bright lights surrounding the mirror exaggerated the redness of the pimples on my chin.

"May I borrow some more of your makeup, Sharon?"

Soon I was behind stage curtains again, biting my fingernails, clearing my throat for the umpteenth time, and glancing nervously at my watch. It was nearly time for the program to begin. I wished that we were the first ones to perform, so we could be done with our part.

When the Master of Ceremonies took center stage, the murmur of the audience died down. The first group was announced. The closer the time came for our part in the program, the more tense I became. I had not yet learned to cast my every care upon the Lord or to take strength from His Word.

"God has not given us a spirit of fear, but of power, and of love and of a sound mind." (II Tim. 1:7 NIV)

By the time we were finally introduced, I had mixed emotions—an amalgamation of fear and of relief. I took one final deep breath, squared my shoulders, and followed my sisters into the spotlights. Sometimes the actual facing of the enemy is less dreadful than the time of anxiety preceding it.

We stepped up to the microphones. I don't recall which songs we sang that evening, but I do remember one thing: halfway through our portion of the program I felt the fright leave my face. I was elated! There was hope for me yet. The butterflies were still there, but perhaps they were at least beginning to fly in formation.

1963: Four sisters nervous to be up front

3

In the Spotlight

∼ by Janice ∼

───────●───────

The mechanics of it all were coming easier: enunciation, breath control, crescendos, blend, harmony, and stage presentation. With the improvements came an increase in bookings to a variety of places.

The Air Force Academy

Like endless white waters cascading down a mountainside, cadets, erect, dignified, and handsome in their dress uniforms, parade down the marble staircase. Several return our looks of admiration, and we blush under their gaze. They give rapt attention as our harmonic melodies ring through the large hall, echoing with overtones. We are flattered by their whistles, wild applause, and a standing ovation.

Is it recognition and flattery that is important to a singer?

Hootenanny

Ranchers in jeans, boots, and western shirts saunter in, slipping their cowboy hats onto the racks by the door. There is foot stomping and hand clapping to our folk songs and songs of the old west. We include other styles of music: some popular, some barbershop harmony, and some gospel songs. Audience feedback is positive. The atmosphere is light and lively.

We feel at home with the down-to-earth folk; but we also ponder if entertainment is but the means to a shallow, temporary happiness?

Broadmoor International Center

A tuxedo-clad gentleman, with airs of an aristocrat, courteously escorts his fair lady to a table, helps to slip the fur stole from her shoulders, and pulls out her chair. With a swish of her evening gown, head erect, and eyes aloof, the lady gracefully takes her seat. Her diamond necklace glistens in the light from a chandelier.

Feeling out of place, I slip back from my vantage point behind the stage curtain. We give what we consider a good performance but hear a minimal glove-muffled applause as we retreat backstage. We are quick to judge that, for the affluent, it may be below their dignity to react.

In reality, is it not our own pride and immaturity that fails to make allowances for behavioral patterns of another social class?

A Television Talent Contest

In the studio, hot floodlights are switched on. The camera is aimed at us like a threatening weapon. A signal is given, and we burst into song, starting with the bell chord of "Mr. Sandman." All the hours of perfecting the details pay off. We win second place among the sixty contestants in the statewide contest. We sense somewhat how an athlete feels who trains for the Olympics.

Is it the winning that is of chief importance, or is it

the privilege of competing and the attitude with which one competes? Has not a greater prize already been won by the lessons learned through the discipline and training it takes to personally achieve one's best?

A Night Club

Lights are dim and the room is blue with smoke. The twang of country music fills the air. We enter and locate a table where we await our turn to sing. A friend had made the booking for us, so we didn't know what kind of place it was. We squint smoke-irritated eyes to see Buck Owens, a popular country western singer, performing from a low platform. I assume this to be an exclusive restaurant to be hiring famous artists.

It is our turn to perform. As we are singing "Carolina Moon," a couple make their way to the center of the room to dance. We shift, ill at ease, not comfortable with providing dance music. Then a man, a bit tipsy, staggers to the railing near the platform, looks at me, and in slurred speech blurts, "How about the next dance?" I sense a sinking feeling.

We continue our program, but a battle rages within, for we realize then we are in a nightclub. We ride home in silence, feeling guilty. We informed the man who arranged the booking that in the future we didn't want to entertain in bars.

As ones who house the Holy Spirit, should we not be more selective where we perform?

Chicago

An all-expense-paid trip sponsored by the Burlington Railroad takes us to Chicago to sing for the opening of a new hospital. The trip is an adventure as we explore the full length of the train, enjoy free meals in the dining car, and sleep in the unique berths. In Chicago, hotel rooms

and all meals are provided.

Should we be seeking a life of luxury and adventure at someone else's expense?

1963: A trip by train to
Chicago to sing for
a dedication of a
new hospital.

The Tourist Attraction

The aroma of barbecued beef and baked beans permeate the rustic structure at the Flying W Ranch. In the foothills of the Rockies, twelve hundred tourists a night enjoy the chuck wagon suppers with its western entertainment. As a part of the show, we gain experience singing before large crowds and dealing with the public.

During our three summers at Flying W Ranch, we develop a friendship with some Navajo ladies and a new interest in languages surfaces. The Navajo language with its linguistic peculiarities is a challenging language to learn with any semblance of accuracy, but our friends were pleased by our efforts.

Was God also preparing us for a cross-cultural ministry?

1964-1966: Cora Martin, a
Navajo, befriends the
twins, teaching them
many things about her
culture and language.

The Antlers Hotel

We marvel at the antique furnishings and gilded ornate interior of the historic hotel where businessmen, city officials, and politicians gather. Shortly before our program, we learn that the Governor of Colorado is in the audience. Admittedly we are more nervous for this presentation.

Should it matter who is in the audience? In one sense it shouldn't make a difference. We should do our best regardless of who is listening. But in another sense, to consider one's audience can make the difference between merely "performing" and truly "communicating."

A Radio Station

We receive an unusual assignment: to compose and record ten jingles. Some jingles would announce the time, the news, the weather, or sports. Others would give the station's identification or introduce particular programs. Strange as it may seem, Faye and I, though still teenagers, had previously taken little interest in listening to the radio. Now we carried a small transistor in hopes of hearing some of our own jingles.

Were we but feeding our egos?

Annual Street Breakfast

Rostvit Sisters, accompanied by the Flying W Wranglers, sing for the annual Colorado Springs street breakfast.

Streets of downtown Colorado Springs are blocked off. Bales of hay are set around so that the six thousand locals and tourists can be seated for the informal affair. Breakfast is served in the early morning, and we, among other entertainers, perform from a flatbed truck. Many people draw near to snap pictures, and afterward we grow weary of signing autographs.

Is fame and fortune what a singer should delight in?

Christian Groups

Youth rallies, ladies' meetings, conventions, weddings, funerals, revival meetings, youth camp activities, and church services enter into the schedule as frequently as the secular bookings. At one gathering the man who is to introduce us approached us.

"How do you pronounce your surname? Is it Roosterfoot?" It was hard to keep from laughing.

"No, sir, it is Rostvit," Laura Jean said.

"Oh, Rost-vit," he repeats, pronouncing the syllables with care and nodding confidently. He mouths the name repeatedly as he walks toward the platform. "Rostvit, Rostvit, Rostvit." The audience hushes as the man steps up to the mike,

"We have a treat tonight, a quartet from Colorado Springs, the ROOSTERFOOT Sisters."

We were more amused than annoyed. After all, it shouldn't matter whether or not our name be remembered. Are we not to lift up the name of Jesus?

———

Our varied singing bookings gave us opportunities to see people in all walks of life. Perhaps through these experiences God was helping us to mature, to see people from His perspective, to learn important lessons, set standards, make value judgments, and sort out priorities.

"Ponder the path of your feet, and let all your ways be established." (Prov. 4:26)

Our sphere of opportunities widened as K.O. Backstrand, our minister, arranged some tours to churches in other states. Nightly concert tours can be tiring, but we were young, so it was all an exciting new adventure for us.

Rostvit Sisters Quartet Ventures Out

1964: The Rostvit Sisters
were often mistaken as quadruplets.
Clockwise from top: Laura Jean, Janice, Sharon, Faye

4

Venturing Out

∼ by Faye ∼

———————◼———————

SCRE-E-E-CH!! We were startled to hear a car pulling to a sudden stop by the curb. The four of us were dressed alike and had been strolling in Seattle, Washington. Our hair, styled the same, bounced in unison as we turned to look. The driver had an excited expression on his face.

"I've never seen quadruplets before," he yelled through an open window. "This is exciting! I can't wait to tell my wife!" Before we could respond, he was speeding away. We smiled.

One day we were seated in a small cafe in Reno, Nevada. A man approached our table.

"In which casino are you gals performing?" When we told him the address of the church where we were to have a concert, his expression indicated obvious disappointment. "Oh! You won't make any money that way."

"There are things more important than money," Laura Jean said.

"Well, if you ever sing in a casino, let me know." The man turned and left the cafe.

Our gospel concert tours took us throughout forty states. As in these two incidents, people were curious about the four look-a-likes. Yet we realized outward appearance and performance, important though they be, were not to be a primary objective. We were no longer to be entertainers putting on a show. Our songs, as well as our demeanor, were to draw others to Jesus.

In 1963 to 1966 the Rostvit Sisters traveled throughout the United States giving concerts in churches. Left to Right: Sharon, Faye, Janice, Laura Jean

I will share four incidents through which our quartet learned a lesson or saw God's hand intervening to help us.

When Things Don't Go As Planned

On our first concert tour in the fall of 1963, God demonstrated a truth from Proverbs 16:9: "A man's heart plans his way, but the Lord directs his steps."

As excited youth, we had left Colorado and headed for California to make our first recording. Our first stop was to be in Phoenix, Arizona. We thought everything would go as planned but, upon arriving at the church, we were informed our concert was canceled. It was the day of assassinated President John F. Kennedy's funeral, and the preacher had considered it most respectful not to gather a crowd.

There was a lesson for us. Our itinerary, no matter how well planned, may change. We need to let our schedule be flexible in God's hands.

Danger in the Night

I was behind the wheel late one night in a mountainous area of Idaho. Rain added to the already oppressive darkness, making visibility poor. I was eighteen and inexperienced, and I was driving too fast for the conditions. Suddenly my headlights revealed the dim figure of a man standing in the middle of the lane some distance ahead. He was waving his arms, indicating for us to slow down. I eased up on the accelerator while nervously tightening my grip on the steering wheel. Our parents had warned us not to pick up strangers. But would I be heartless to pass by if the man were stranded?

As we drew near, I sensed the man did not desire a ride. He was now motioning me to switch into the left lane. I complied. The road took a sharp turn to the right around a sheer rock face. We were shocked! Just around the corner lay a huge rockslide covering the entire right lane. Had the man not directed us into the other lane, we most certainly would have met with a terrible accident.

As we slowly circumvented the rock pile and continued on our way, we looked for the man's car, but there was none. We wondered where the man had come from. In this wilderness area we had seen neither a house nor a ranch for miles. Why was the man willing to stand in the rain on a cold, dark night?

Or could he have been an angel?

When There's a Breakdown

"Yikes, what do we do now?" The large pool of oil beneath the van was clear evidence even to us non-mechanically-minded girls that we had a major problem. We had just completed a concert in Wichita, Kansas. The church parking lot was almost deserted as we stood by our van.

We had left home three days earlier, beginning a ten thousand-mile tour of the eastern states. In February Laura Jean had married Randy Tate, so he was along on this tour. The van had developed a strange noise. Randy, who knew a great deal about cars, checked the engine. The Greenbriar was an air-cooled Corvair with dual carburetors, a mechanic's nightmare. Randy could not pinpoint the problem.

The gentleman who locked the building approached us. His eyebrows raised at the sight of our obvious dilemma.

"Do you mind if I take this to my shop? It is a government school for mechanics. We've been looking for a Corvair to work on. Since the work is done by students, there will be no labor charge and parts will be half price. We can have the job done in a couple of days." We gladly consented.

The following day we were transported to the repair shop to see how the work was progressing. We were surprised to see the entire engine disassembled. All the parts down to the smallest bolts were arranged on a long counter. The man we had met at church held up one of the pistons.

"Here was your main problem." He revealed a hole about an inch in diameter. The mechanic assured us the engine could be reassembled by the following day. True to his word, the van was back in running order the next day. It ran perfectly the remainder of the tour. For the complete overhaul we were charged a mere $21.

Truly the Lord had orchestrated the circumstances to direct that man to our aid. Considering what exorbitant costs usually accompany car repairs, we praised God for the magnitude of this blessing.

When We Face a Loss

"Oh no! BURGLARS!" The sliding glass door in the dining room had been broken. Mud stained the light carpet. Desk drawers lay open. Shades were drawn. The contents of our suitcases were strewn all over the bedroom. Our money was gone!

On tour we were always pinching pennies, wondering if we would have sufficient funds to reach our next engagement. By the time we had reached Detroit, however, we had been feeling quite secure. Because of our new record album bringing in more income, we had nearly $300 on hand. Then came the burglars who took it all.

The Lord used the experience for good. It took our minds off of our own self-sufficiency and taught us to depend on Him. During the remaining concerts, Bill Gaither's song "Lovest Thou Me?" took on new meaning." While singing the final line, "I love Thee, Lord,... more than fame, more than wealth, more than the world," we would reflect on the memory of the theft and vow anew not to ever strive for worldly gain.

Later that same year, August 1965, Sharon married Tom Foster. On occasion we would still perform locally, but the bookings were limited. Janice and I could relate to the old song, "Wedding Bells Are Breaking Up That Old Gang of Mine." A chapter of our lives—quartet travels—was ending, and at age twenty, we were again facing a dilemma. What do we do now?

" . . . Cause me to know the way in which I should walk,
for I lift up my soul to You." (Ps. 143:8b)

"Wedding Bells Are Breaking Up
That Old Gang of Mine"

February 1965 Laura Jean and Randy Tate marry

August 1965 Sharon marries Tom Foster

PART II
Reflecting on God-Directed PROVISIONS

The Holy Spirit was teaching us through life's circumstances. The following chapters cover our college years. They were lean years materially speaking, yet they were rich in growth as we were learning to trust in an all-sufficient God.

We recount some of the extraordinary ways in which God obviously supplied our needs. Even when needs are provided in very ordinary circumstances, we should give God the glory.

"Oh that men would give thanks to the Lord for His goodness, And for His wonderful works to the children of men!" (Ps. 107:8)

Lord, here I am,
Humbled once again,
You have met my needs according to Your riches
    in glory!
Lord, here I stand,
I've seen Your mighty hand,
For Your ways are higher than our ways!
For this will I praise You, lifting up Your holy
    name,
Telling of Your wondrous works, I will never be
    the same!

(A portion of the song "His Ways are Higher than Our Ways" by the Rostvit Twins)

1966-1967: The twins sing as a trio with Wilma Backstrand
during their freshman year at college.
Left to right: Faye, Wilma, Janice

5

A New Direction

∼ by Janice ∼

I stood watching the car drive out of our ranch gate, the glow of the taillights fading into the night. We had enjoyed the evening with our minister, Kenneth (better known as "K.O.") Backstrand, and his wife Marcia. Then why was I feeling so uneasy? Was it what K.O. had said as he was slipping on his coat? He had suggested that we go to Bible college. We told him we weren't interested, yet Marcia had pressed further. She explained that their daughter, Wilma, and Karen Colner, another girl from church, had plans to enroll in Ozark Bible College in Missouri in August.

"It would be good if you could all go together," she said in her gentle, loving way.

We smiled but shook our heads, not wanting them to get their hopes up. By the time we were beside their car saying our good-byes, I assumed the subject had been dropped. Then K.O., slipping the key into the ignition, turned to us and said, "Pray about it, girls."

The others had returned to the house as soon as the car had pulled away, but I had lingered, mulling over the Backstrands' words. College! The very word chilled me more than the brisk January night air. As I headed to the porch, I paused and took in the view to the west. I never tired of looking at the mountains, now looming ghostlike against the star-studded sky. It was as though I was searching for stability from the majestic snowy range. Was I being like a young bird, hesitant to leave the nest and face the unknown? Doubtless the Holy Spirit was making me uncomfortable. But I couldn't pray. Feeling the bite of the winter air, I turned and retreated into the house.

Within the hour, we were ready for bed. I lingered by the light switch of our upstairs bedroom. Then the words tumbled from my lips.

"Faye, what do you think about it?"

"About what?" Her threatened expression clearly indicated she already anticipated my reply with dread.

"Bible college."

"No, forget it!" She pulled up the covers and turned on her side so as not to face me. She feared that if I wanted to go, she would probably go, too. We had always done everything together.

With no further discussion, I flipped off the light and made my way to bed, feeling relieved that Faye had no more interest than I did.

A strange thing happened the next morning. Before we were out of bed, Faye propped herself up on one elbow and asked, "Well, what about it, Janice?" The question surprised herself as much as it did me. This time it was my turn to react.

"No, forget it." But I couldn't forget it! The Holy Spirit was working overtime to convince us. Within the day our fears diminished in light of the positive aspects. It would be good to have a better knowledge of the Scriptures so that we could witness to our friends. Also since quartet travels were cut to a minimum, we saw the need for a new direction.

In the months that followed, we made our plans for college with growing anticipation.

⟨⟩

"Come look at the sunset." Faye joined me at the dormitory window. The sun hung low, a crimson sphere aglow on the hazy horizon. We had left Colorado before daybreak. After the long tiring trip by car, there were quick good-byes, as Dad would have to get back for his construction job. The farewell was as tough on Mom and Dad as it was for us.

It was our first day at college. We had settled into the dorm amid the discomfort of Missouri's oppressive summer heat. As we stood by the window, we missed the view we had been accustomed to—mountains to the west. Yet we marveled at the rich hues this sunset displayed.

"Hey, Twins." We turned to see Wilma Backstrand in the doorway. "We freshmen girls have been invited to Elaine Mazza's room on third floor." The three of us located the already crowded room and found sufficient space to sit on the floor.

Elaine, also a freshman, wanted us to get acquainted and have a prayer time. She proposed that each in turn give her name and reason for having come to college.

"My name is…and I plan to study for four years, graduate with a degree in Sacred Literature…."

"…I plan to go for the bachelor of Christian education degree and hopefully secure the position of a Christian education director in a church or a Christian school."

"…I would like to get a master's degree with a major in…."

Graduate! This degree! That degree! Each girl related commendable plans, looking four or five years down the road. I wondered what I'd say when it would come my turn. What would the others think when they'd hear that we had no definite plans beyond one year? My racing thoughts came to a screeching halt upon hearing the quiet voice of another girl.

"I haven't really made any plans yet. All I know is I want to study God's Word and seek His will." This girl without reservation had humbly put it into words. I was wrong to have been so worried about what others might think. By the close of the evening we entered into a prayer time with a new resolve to seek God's direction and His approval rather than man's.

The following day brought all the bustle of matriculation. Somewhere from the hubbub of the jostling students and college staff emerged the impressive figure of a middle-aged man in a dark suit. His hair was graying at the temples, and his eyes smiled with a kind, sincere warmth.

"Rostvits, how good to have you here! I'm George King, head of the music department." He explained that he had heard us as a quartet. "We need music groups to travel on weekends to represent the college. Can we count on you?"

"The quartet has broken up. Our sisters are married now," I said.

"That's all right. You have a good repertoire of songs to rearrange as a duet."

Neither of us liked the suggestion. Two-part harmony would seem empty. We could see in Mr. King's eyes that he sensed our apprehension.

"If it would be too much of an adjustment, consider finding someone to join you," he said.

During our freshman year we formed a trio with our hometown friend, Wilma Backstrand. She became like a very special sister, and we truly felt that the Lord, who knew our insecurities, had provided Wilma as a perfect means for weaning us from a quartet to a duet.

There were times during the year when Wilma could not join us on a weekend trip. We missed her, but her absence motivated us to build our repertoire and confidence as a duet. The trio was also destined to break up very naturally at the end of that year as Wilma and her fiance, Ben Waddle, were making plans for a September wedding.

The studies made us hunger for more, so by springtime we were already making plans to return in the fall. With that decision came another dilemma: what would we do that summer? We had planned to work. In fact, a position for singing secular music had already been secured. Yet within, a desire was growing to dedicate our voices solely to praising the Lord. How does one determine God's will?

We sought the counsel of Don DeWelt, one of our professors, who was a Godly man. When we explained to him our quandary, we were surprised that Mr. DeWelt did not weigh our options to give advice. He simply said, "Let's take it to the Lord in prayer." He knelt beside his desk. We joined him in prayer.

"Now let's leave it in God's hands to make the way clear. He has promised, 'Trust in the Lord with all your heart, and lean not on your own understanding; In all your ways acknowledge Him, and He shall direct your paths.'" (Prov. 3:5,6)

This clear lesson made a lasting impression. Don DeWelt's example could be followed in the crossroads to come. Whenever we would wonder which way we should go, the answer would be—go to your knees.

God's direction was not long in coming. The job that had been promised us was mysteriously canceled. At the same time, we began receiving requests to sing for revival meetings and youth camps.

We sought out Don DeWelt to relate the news. Faye and I kept interrupting each other in our eagerness to tell how God had already made the path clear. Don DeWelt smiled.

"The Lord didn't have to sign His name to that one, did He? Let's thank Him." So we bowed our heads there and prayed. This was another important lesson—upon receiving an answer to prayer, give thanks.

The summer's travels were in themselves a lesson in faith as we saw God provide for our needs. Each week we marveled when the amount of money given us was just sufficient to cover the cost of our bus ticket to the next location.

"...He will teach us His ways, and we shall walk in His paths..." (Isa. 2:3b)

6

God Knows Our Needs

∼ by Faye ∼

———————●▭●———————

"We don't have enough money for supper," Janice reminded me as we walked from our late afternoon choir rehearsal. Our second year of college was underway with no visible means of income. She sighed with a look of envy toward those heading for the cafeteria. Just then a car pulled up to the curb.

"Rostvits, can you come sing at a church tonight? The trio that was scheduled can't make it."

"Sure! We're done with classes for the day." We were pleased that the evangelistic service temporarily took our minds off our empty stomachs. Then to our delight, a lady approached us after the meeting.

"Can you girls stay for a while? We have sandwiches and cake downstairs."

Can we stay? Of course we could. That type of provision often seemed to come just when we needed it.

At another time of financial drought we found a bag of groceries outside our dormitory room. We never learned who left it, or how they knew of our need.

One day Janice and I were walking through the park adjacent to the college. I paused in the shade of an oak tree.

"I'm hungry for apples," I said, although we seldom crave apples.

"Me, too," Janice said.

Upon returning to campus we checked our mailbox. There lay a brown paper bag with "Rostvits" scrawled across it. It contained four big apples. Although there was no indication who had given the gift, we knew the Lord was ultimately responsible for placing the thought in someone's mind. We thanked Him.

A similar thing occurred some months later. Janice and I again were in the park when she asked, "Do you remember when we craved apples and the Lord provided them?"

"I sure do." The thought made my mouth water. My conversation turned to prayer. "You know, Lord, I wouldn't mind another juicy apple."

"Mmm," Janice turned her gaze skyward. "I'd like one, too, Lord. Please?"

Minutes later we returned to the dormitory. We shook our heads in amazement when we entered our room. On each of our desks was an apple. As before, we never discovered who placed them there.

> The eyes of all look expectantly to You, and You give them their food in due season. You open Your hand and satisfy the desire of every living thing." (Ps. 145:15,16)

Near the end of the semester we received money from various unexpected sources—more than was needed each week.

"Why is God suddenly supplying so much money?" Janice said.

"Maybe there's a bigger expense coming up in the future."

"That's it," she said excitedly. "Second semester tuition." We had nearly forgotten that the college had established a new financial policy. Tuition had to be paid in full during enrollment. She picked up our bankbook to see how much we had.

"Faye, we lack only $100 of having enough!"

That same day a letter arrived from Uncle Paul. "I have sold a piece of my farm and am sending you some money to help in your schooling." Enclosed was a check for $100. The next day I was still overwhelmed.

"Just think of it, yesterday you said we were short $100, and we received $100!" I said.

"Yes, now all we need is some spending money for Christmas," Janice teased.

That day a letter arrived from another relative, the Stahls. A check was enclosed and a note from Auntie Inger. "Use it for 'spending money for Christmas'." Janice's very words!

"Wow!" I exclaimed, "Yesterday you said we needed $100, and we received $100. Today you asked for spending money for Christmas, and we received spending money for Christmas. We get anything we ask for." Then in a jocular manner I added, "Why don't you ask for $1000 dollars while you're at it?" No, a thousand dollars did not come in the following day's mail, nor did we expect it, for we didn't need it—at least not yet.

It was around this time that I penned the words of a poem that we would later put to music.

GOD SUPPLIES OUR NEEDS

God knows our needs and He always supplies.
If we fail to see proof, it's the fault of our eyes.
Ask and ye receive, seek and ye shall find,
If we don't believe His Word, it's all because we're
  blind.
The Lord's Word is true. We need to realize,
Answered prayer is all around, if we'll open up
  our eyes.

Faith is the answer if our vision is poor.
He will supply our every need. His promise is
      secure.

Second semester arrived. Our store of money was all
spent on our tuition payments. For two months we
again were seeing the Lord's provision on a day-to-day
basis. The prayer "Give us this day our daily bread"
(Mt. 6:11) was very real. Our parents would have helped
us if they had known of the need, but we wanted to
show responsibility and not be a burden to them. The
funds did not continue to increase as they had in the
previous semester.

By February 29, we had only sixty-two cents. It was
on that day that Evangelist Reggie Thomas approached
us and asked if we would go with him during the
summer months to conduct crusades in Africa. We
readily accepted. It was a dream come true. Our interest
in missions had first been kindled at age eleven when
missionary Alfred Cole had shown slides of New Guinea
at our home church.

Less than a year later Woodrow Phillips, missionary
from Jamaica, spoke at our youth camp. Now a decade
later that same Mr. Phillips was the Missions Director of
the Bible college. Through his gentle, Christ-like spirit,
we had been challenged to answer God's call and dedicate our lives to missionary service. About that time, we
wrote this song.

WILL YOU GO?

The people of all lands   ♪   ♪
Are reaching out their hands,
And God's love demands that we go.
No matter what the race,
The color of the face,
How distant the place, Will you go?

The world is in need of a Savior,
And Christ commanded we go.
He's waiting now for the answer.
Must we always answer, "No"?

Do we really care? ♪♪♪   ♪
And are we aware,
That Christ will be there, If we go?
Then hearing His cry,
And knowing He's nigh,
Let's gladly reply, "I will go!"

Within months of that commitment we were being directed overseas. We telephoned home to share the exciting news with our parents. The remainder of the afternoon was spent in writing letters to relatives or bubbling over to friends on campus.

The twins keep a busy singing schedule during college.
They learn to trust God to supply their needs.

That evening in the solitude of our dorm room we took time to pause and contemplate the reality. I dumped the contents of our coin purse into my hand and fingered the change. A smile of amusement came to my lips and I shook my head.

"Africa! We're going to Africa, and we have only sixty-two cents!" There was no doubt in our minds that we would be going, yet we knew that we had less than three months to raise $2600 for the tickets.

Needing encouragement, I reached for my Bible with intentions of locating the verses: "Delight yourself also in the Lord, and He shall give you the desires of your heart. Commit your way to the Lord, Trust also in Him, and He shall bring it to pass." (Ps. 37:4,5) But instead of turning to Psalm 37, I accidentally turned to Psalm 137:4 and read, "How shall we sing the Lord's song in a foreign land?"

"Oh, that's some encouragement!" Janice teased. Admittedly the verse did fit our situation.

As we entered into a prayer time with the sixty-two cents still in hand, the Lord impressed upon our hearts that He had allowed us to get this low on cash for a purpose. Now He could make it clear to us that He would be the one to supply the needed amount for the trip.

The following day one of the professors approached us and offered advice on how to raise funds. He suggested that we write letters to the many churches where we had sung and request their help. We did so, typing each letter personally, yet trying to make our request in such a way that the churches would not feel obligated.

One response stands out in our memory. It was from a church in which we had sung on several occasions, and always had felt welcomed and appreciated. Admittedly we assumed they would respond generously. There was a seed of greed in our expectations. When their letter came, we were surprised that no money was enclosed. The letter stated something to this effect: "We're sorry we will not help you in your endeavor to go to Africa. We personally feel because of your effectiveness here in the United States, your talents would be wasted elsewhere. Nevertheless, if the Lord does supply what you need for the tickets, and you do go, our prayers will be with you."

Although we felt disappointment, we respected and appreciated their honesty. Over the years we have thanked God many times for that letter. One thing was made clear to us—God did not want us to use the 'plea letter' method for gaining support. He would not supply our needs from sources devised by our own cleverness.

"And my God shall supply all your need according to His riches in glory by Christ Jesus." (Phil. 4:19)

Since that time, when in need, we only ask God. Just as our dad has always provided well for our family's needs, we need to daily leave the business of providing in the capable hands of our Heavenly Father. To take the privilege from Him is to miss the blessing ourselves.

Our first gift came from Uncle Paul. We were dumbfounded to read in his letter. "I've had a bond in the bank since World War II. I'm cashing it in to help you girls go to Africa." Enclosed was a check for $1000. That brought to mind the day in December when I had jokingly suggested, "Why don't you ask for a thousand dollars?" Though we had not asked Uncle Paul for anything, God had chosen to supply this first milestone of our needs through him. Uncle Paul was not a wealthy man by the world's standards. His wealth was measured in the inner man, his simple life of faith.

Later in the three months when funds were not coming, we would feel discouraged. We had to remind ourselves of this first large sum. The $1000 gift was as much a sign of God's presence with us as was the crossing of the Red Sea to the Israelites. I had tended to be harsh in my judgment of the Israelites when in the wilderness they would complain. Why couldn't they remember the mighty works of God leading them across the Red Sea? As we were going through the same thing, we were put to shame when we would doubt or worry.

The remainder of the money came from unexpected sources: some anonymously in the mail, others from people who had heard of our opportunity. On our weekend trips to churches, Professor Wartick would suggest that people hand us donations if they wanted to help. We were humbled by that kindness. When the due date arrived for purchasing our tickets, we were grateful to God and to His people that we had the sufficient amount.

7

Learning to Sing
in a Foreign Language
~ by Faye ~

───────────●───────────

It was not our plan to learn songs in other languages. On this our first overseas trip, we had been told that the majority of meetings would be in cities and towns where English was widely used by the Europeans. However, as the schedule in Rhodesia (later Zimbabwe) progressed, we participated in occasional African services. The first one was near the city of Bulawayo. We listened with fascination as the people sang in Sindebele, a language that included clicking sounds.

We had taken ten hours of linguistics under Professor Wallace Wartick. Little had we realized how essential those studies would be in preparation for a cross-cultural ministry. Some assignments had us listening to tapes of various sounds, learning to reproduce them correctly. When we had studied the clicks, we had laughed, doubting that such articulations would actually be consonants in any language.

What a surprise that the first language we would encounter would be one of these. God's timing for these studies had been perfect. Yet in that brief visit with the Sindebele congregation, we had not yet thought to use our linguistic training by learning their songs.

Our schedule took us into another language area among the Shona people. Still we sang in English. With the help of an interpreter, we explained the meaning of the lyrics, yet we felt ill at ease, knowing that only a few could understand.

After one meeting the ladies prepared a fellowship dinner. Cornmeal was added to boiling water in a large caldron. They stirred vigorously the thickening corn-meal mush as they sang *"Mumwoyo ndaka shambwa ne ropa ra Jesu. Ndino rufaro mumwoyo."* (In my heart I am happy because I'm cleansed by the blood of Jesus. I am happy in my heart.) The song was repeated over and over for more than half an hour.

The twins begin to sing songs in the local languages.

When it came time for us to leave, the Christians encircled us, singing yet another chorus. They danced as they sang. The louder the volume, the more vigor-ously they danced. Many of them had babies tied to their backs. The infants, accustomed to being carried in this manner, bounced contentedly. The circle slowly escorted us to the Land Rover. As we drove away, we watched the ladies. They kept singing and dancing, waving with both arms until we had gone from view. We were told their song said, "Good-bye, we'll see you in the new world." We loved the genuine warmth of the African people.

Some days later, a crowd of nearly two hundred assembled beneath the spreading branches of an umbrella tree at the Dewure Mission Station. We took part in the program, but again felt uncomfortable to be singing in English. I doubted our effectiveness. What did we have to offer these people? Perhaps the one who had written the letter suggesting we stay in America, was right. We reflected on the Apostle Paul's words:

> "But in the church I would rather speak five intelligible words to instruct others than ten thousand words in a tongue." (I Cor. 14:19 NIV)

We longed to minister to the Shona people in their own language.

Dusk was settling in when the afternoon meeting ended. Some people encouraged us to follow as they walked to their nearby village. They sang as they walked. *"Famba na Jesu, haleluya, ndinofamba na Jesu."* The song meant, "Hallelujah, I'm walking with Jesus." How appropriate! Over and over the chorus was repeated as we all walked to the rhythm of its beat. I watched as the leather-like callused heels of their bare feet shuffled along the dusty path. Their ragged garments were faded and patched. These people had never known earthly wealth, yet to hear their exuberant singing and see their contented smiles, it was obvious they had a wealth of joy in the Lord.

> "Has God not chosen the poor of this world to be rich in faith and heirs of the kingdom which He promised to those who love Him?" (James 2:5)

Just over a hill we could see the glow of a campfire. The crowd gathered there, still singing the same chorus. A man added flavor to the music by blasting bizarre sounds on a long, corkscrew-like horn of a Kudu. For more than half an hour the people had repeatedly sung *"Famba na Jesu."* By that time we had it memorized. As evening's coolness set in, Janice and I walked back over the hill to the mission house to bed down for the night.

The following morning we were up bright and early. With missionary Lester Cooper, we took several hours to walk from village to village inviting more people to Dewure for the following night's meeting. As we neared each village we would wait while one man ran ahead to gain permission. Lester explained that each village is a family group. To enter a village without permission would be like barging into a home without knocking.

The Rostvits gathered a crowd wherever they went.

For us, the villages never ceased to lose their fascination. Each contained several mud-walled, thatch-roofed huts, an ox cart, and grain stored up on racks to dry in the sun. A bicycle or a homemade plow would be leaning against the wall of a hut. Chickens scurried about, and pigs or mangy dogs scrounged around for bits of food. Adults and scantily clad or naked children would come to meet us. Many followed us to the next place, singing as they went.

While a small crowd was together at each location, a short devotional was presented and we would sing. One time we braved an attempt to sing *"Famba na Jesu,"* and the *"Mumwoyo"* songs. We wondered how the people would react. Would they feel we were making fun of their language? Would our pronunciation be poor?

Our apprehensions were quickly dispelled as surprise and joy swept across their faces. Many even sang along, clapping to the rhythm. Some of the ladies rushed forward to embrace us. Their reaction completely overwhelmed us. It was apparent the mere attempt to communicate in their heart language conveyed a message of love. I recalled the Scripture I had accidentally read to Janice when preparing for this trip.

"How shall we sing the Lord's song in a foreign land."
(Ps. 137:4)

We had discovered the "how"—by phonetically memorizing songs! God had equipped us in advance, as is written in Hebrews 13:20a,21a NIV:

"May the God of peace,...equip you with everything good for doing His will, and may He work in us what is pleasing to Him..."

By mid-afternoon four hundred people were assembled in the shade of the trees at Dewure. During the service Janice and I attempted a longer song in Shona. We were nervous to tackle the endless lines of rote syllables, but we made it. The audience responded with loud cheers. This gave us confidence to learn additional songs. The Shona songbook was written phonetically,

so it was easy to pronounce the words correctly. Some
we learned were translated hymns, but the people especially loved our singing their indigenous tunes. We
were enjoying putting our linguistic studies to use.

For a few days we stayed with Jack and Peggy
Pennington. They labored alone in the Zambezi Valley
among the primitive Batonga tribe who, materially
speaking, had even less than those of the Shona tribe.
Babies were tied to their mothers' backs with crudely-
tanned animal hides. Adults wore but a black cloth
wrapped around them, tied on one shoulder.

Women were missing their front teeth. By tradition
they had them chiseled off when they reached maturity.
Some had a stick through a hole pierced in the center
cartilage of their noses. Others had scars on their faces,
forming various designs on their cheeks or foreheads.
These had been made by cutting themselves, then filling
the wounds with ashes to assure a scarred healing.

These customs, now done for beauty, had origi-
nated a hundred years earlier when their tribe was
falling prey to slave traders. They chiseled teeth, scarred
faces, or pushed sticks through their noses to disfigure
themselves in hopes of making themselves undesirable
to the plundering merchants of humanity.

In our few days among the Batongas, we were able
to learn a couple of songs in their language. Again our
efforts were appreciated.

The final three weeks of the summer were spent in
the country of Zambia. There several young couples
were effectively evangelizing new areas among the
Tonga and the Bemba people.

It could not be said that the gospel had never reached
these areas. David Livingstone had labored there shortly
before his death in 1874. While we participated in village meetings with missionaries Don and Linda Mechem,

we met an aged man, Mwakwengu, who claimed that when he was a small boy he had seen David Livingstone.

When we first saw Mwakwengo, he was seated on the ground by the wall of his hut, legs outstretched, enjoying the warmth of the afternoon sun. He was over one hundred years old. We bowed low in the customary way to show respect when we greeted him, then seated ourselves on a mat beside the withered gentleman. Slowly and deliberately, the old man related his memories of having heard David Livingstone proclaim God's Word.

"I waited for years for another white man to come and again bring God's message to my people." A sad, faraway look in his eyes expressed his deep thoughts. Then he slipped a thin hand onto Don Mechem's arm. A toothless grin eased its way onto his leathery face.

"I'm glad to have lived long enough to have seen the fulfillment of my long-awaited dream."

We reflected upon the words of the old man as we boarded the jet at summer's end. We also visualized each dedicated missionary who takes seriously the importance and urgency of the task. The plane lifted off and the African landscape spread endlessly before our gaze. I caught sight of a village, its golden thatched roofs contrasting against the surrounding trees. As we ascended, the huts diminished in size until they appeared as mere copper coins on a mottled green carpet.

How many people in remote areas are still waiting to hear God's message? Would God allow us the privilege of sharing His good news again, in our small way —through music?

The twins take the local "ferry boat" to cross a river.

Janice and Faye greet an area chief in Zambia.

8

Empty Pockets, Yet Ample Provision
∼ by Janice ∼

———————⬤———————

Jetlag—we didn't know what it meant, but our exhaustion was a clear indication we were feeling its effects. Flights had taken us straight back to Joplin, Missouri for our third year of college. After the relaxed lifestyle of Africa where nothing happened on time, it was difficult to get back to the strict schedule of college life. We were overwhelmed to learn that our father had sent money to cover our tuition costs. Our parents paid each semester's tuition for our remaining years of studies. We know that was a great sacrifice and a true gift of love.

Oh, For a Projector!

On weekends, we presented our slide programs of our African trip to church groups. The first weekend, we were to present a mission program in a church. Since we had no projector, we rented one from the college library. Saturday night we tried to rehearse our program, but the projector kept jamming the slides. The sympathetic preacher saw our dilemma.

"Girls, it will be difficult enough for you to present your first program without having to struggle with that antiquated machine." He generously let us use his automatic projector and advised us to buy ourselves one like it before the next Sunday.

We thanked him, but he didn't know we couldn't afford one. We had about ten dollars and had already determined to give that in Tuesday's chapel offering at college. When Tuesday's chapel time came, Faye dug into the purse to find only $9.75. She hurriedly slipped it all into the offering plate before she'd be tempted to keep some of it.

At such a time, a twinge of anxiety is mingled with hope and expectation that God will indeed supply. Oh to completely trust and be contented like the writer of Hebrews:

> "Keep your lives free from the love of money and be content with what you have, because God has said, 'Never will I leave you; never will I forsake you.'" (Heb. 13:5 NIV)

Since we had determined to give $10, we prayed, "Lord, if You will supply the twenty-five cents, we will give it in Thursday's chapel offering."

According to Ephesians 3:20, God is able to do more abundantly above all that we ask or think. We asked for twenty-five cents by Thursday, but during Wednesday, God was working the exceeding abundant part of the Ephesians promise. Some money came anonymously in the mail, plus we sang for an afternoon program for which we unexpectedly received remuneration. By evening we had $97.

"Perhaps the Lord is providing a projector before next weekend," Faye said.

We agreed to go shopping. On display in the camera shop was a projector like the one loaned to us on Sunday. Pointing to it I asked the clerk, "How much would that slide projector be with tax included?"

When the total came to $96.77, we placed our $97 on the counter. We were delighted with our purchase. On our way back to campus, Faye said, "Oh no, now we have only twenty-three cents for tomorrow's offering." We felt guilty for coming up short for that which we had determined to give. Some might say, "That's silly! What's two cents?" Yet a promise is a promise. God never slights us. Why should we slight Him, even in the smallest matters?

Thursday morning dawned and we attended classes as usual. Just before the chapel service we had a few spare moments to spend in our dorm room. I busied myself cleaning my unusually cluttered desk. To my surprise, a penny lay in one corner.

"Hey, Faye, look what I found!" I flashed my find with an air of pride.

Faye, who was sweeping the floor, glanced up and smiled, then resumed her work. Seconds later she swept a penny from beneath her bed. She held it up, excited that we had a full twenty-five cents for the offering. Our joy was as that of the woman in Luke 15 who swept her house and found her lost coin.

When the Lord supplies, He doesn't come up short
—not even by one cent.

Tom Cary taught the twins songs in Spanish. In 1969 they sang as
a trio on a summer's mission trip to Mexico.
Left to right, Faye, Tom, Janice

Oh, For a Spanish Album!

Why is it that with each financial crisis, faith has to
begin anew? Could God supply $1000 during a busy
college year to record a Spanish record album? Fellow
student Tom Cary had taught us many songs in Spanish. During the following summer we planned to go
with a group to Mexico and sing as a trio with Tom. The
churches requested we make a recording, yet all three of
us were broke.

George and Tasci King and Willis Harrison, heading
the music department of the Bible college, offered to
help. With their technical and musical expertise along
with guitar playing by classmates Dan Neldeberg and
Ed Skidmore, the initial taping was completed.

The actual pressing of the albums, the major financial burden, had to come next. I telephoned a man in
California through whom we had produced a duet

album. I asked him if production could begin on this Spanish album. Knowing that the full cost is usually required in advance, I wasn't surprised when the man quoted a needed payment of $1000. We admitted we didn't have that much. I asked if the work could be started and if he would allow us to pay later.

"Could you send me at least $100?" the man asked.

"One hundred? No, I'm sorry, we don't have that much either."

"Exactly how much can you send?"

I bit my lower lip, then timidly admitted, "Six dollars and thirty one cents." My own words sounded absurd. Why did I make this phone call? For a long moment there was silence.

"I'll tell you what. If you'll send me five dollars along with the tape, I'll take the remainder of the $1000 out of my personal bank account. You can pay me back as you are able," he offered.

When the telephone conversation had ended, I shared the good news with Tom and Faye. Tom suggested we pray, thanking the Lord for the kindness of this Christian brother.

"Cast all your anxiety on Him, because He cares for you." (I Peter 5:7 NIV)

When we had finished praying, Tom, with a confident smile said, "I feel certain that the Lord will provide the $1000 before we receive the albums." Knowing that production usually took three to four months, we each set diligently to work at odd jobs, saving everything we earned.

Payments of varying amounts were sent at irregular intervals. One day just over three months later, we mailed a $115 check, the final amount to pay off the $1000. That very day the test pressing arrived in the mail.

The Lord had honored Tom's faith and ours.

Oh, the Joy of Giving!

During one chapel service, the offering was to go for a particularly worthy mission. With a great desire to help, we gave all that we had at the time—ten dollars. After chapel, while we were talking with Professor Ken Idleman, someone approached him.

"Excuse the interruption. Ken, I've owed you this." He handed Ken some money. When the man was gone, Ken Idleman smiled to see the amount.

"Wow, God is so good!" Then he explained, "The offering need was so compelling today, I put all that I had into the plate. Afterward I recalled I was supposed to buy groceries with that money. Now, even before leaving the chapel, the Lord has replenished the exact amount I gave!"

> "Give, and it will be given to you.... For with the same measure you use, it will be measured back to you." (Luke 6:38a,c)

We didn't want to tell Ken that we, too, had given all we had, lest he feel obligated to help us. Besides, we had willingly given, not expecting anything in return except for the satisfaction that we had done the right thing. We thanked God that the college motivated us in the area of stewardship: giving of time, talent, and money, and that they wanted that surrender to be voluntary and from the heart. We returned to our dorm room only to find two five-dollar bills slipped under our door. Only God knows who gave them. In our excitement, we ran to Professor Idleman's office to tell him that the Lord had replenished our offering gift as well.

> "Oh, that men would give thanks to the Lord for His goodness, and for His wonderful works to the children of men!" (Ps. 107:15)

9

In Stormy Times

∽ by Janice ∽

In a Snowstorm

"I don't like the looks of this." Professor Wallace Wartick brushed snowflakes from the sleeves of his jacket before sliding into the driver's seat. "I'd prefer not to travel this weekend." He sighed, pausing to pray before he put the car in gear. It would be a long drive on snow-packed two-lane highways across Kansas.

Mr. Wartick's apprehensions were not unfounded. The wet snow had begun falling the previous night. With temperatures dropping, ice had formed on the highways. I tried to study to keep my mind off the icy conditions, but concentration was difficult. We had been on the road a couple of hours when a speeding sports car topped a hill some distance ahead.

"That one is driving awfully fast. He's going to end up in trouble." No sooner had Mr. Wartick said the words, then the blue Corvette fishtailed out of control. It spun in a complete circle, slid partially off the shoulder and glided sidewise, spraying snow like a rotary plow. We expected the Corvette to settle into the shallow ditch on the far side, but just as we approached, it shot back up onto the highway and sped directly toward us. The only thing the professor could do to avoid a head-on collision was to steer for the ditch.

With a sickening crunch, the Corvette struck our left front fender. The two vehicles slid off the shoulder, settling into deep snow. Though shaken, we praised the Lord that no one was injured. I glanced at my watch. It was 11 o'clock.

A wrecker towed the professor's vehicle to the nearest town. Mr. Wartick's parents lived there, so they loaned us a car. Eventually we reached our destination. At our first opportunity we telephoned home. Mom, who had been praying at the time the accident occurred, answered the telephone after the first ring.

"Are you both all right?" A tone of urgency tinged her voice.

Her question had taken me by surprise, "Ah...Yes."

"What happened at 11 o'clock?" Mom asked.

After we related the details of the accident, Mom explained that at that moment she felt a strong compulsion to pray.

"Though I knew the cuckoo clock would be sounding off during my prayer, I didn't hesitate. I knelt by the couch in the living room," she said.

We were thankful
that our mother
was attuned to
the urgings of
the Holy Spirit.

In a Thunderstorm

"I believe above a storm the smallest prayer can still be heard...." Those words from a song bring to mind a problem we encountered on another weekend trip. Following a Sunday evening service in Wichita, Kansas, we were riding eastward to return to campus.

The pavement was pitch black on the rainy night. Windshield wipers could not keep up with the heavy downpour. A driving rain mercilessly sent torrential sheets of water across our field of vision.

Our only guide was the blurred red of another vehicle's taillights. How could that driver see where he was going? Just then our "guide" pulled off onto the shoulder. Now with visibility next to nil, our driver, classmate Ron Carter, uttered a prayer of desperation.

"Lord, please stop this rain." Immediately the road came into clear view, as if we had broken through a wall. Not another drop of rain hit the windshield! Roads remained dry all the way back to campus.

When we wrote a letter home to tell our parents about this, we loved our father's insightful response. "I think God delights in doing those little things for us, if they don't interfere with His bigger plans," he said.

In an Ice Storm

We were with a preacher bound for a church in Oklahoma. Roads were slippery from the sleet that had fallen. We rode in silence, tensing each time the car threatened to slide. Many trucks had jackknifed. Cars were in the ditches. We were making our way through Tulsa when we witnessed a strange occurrence. We had topped a hill and were starting down the long descent. We watched with dread as the traffic light at the bottom changed from green to amber. It would soon be red and we feared we wouldn't be able to stop. Several efforts at touching the brakes didn't slow us. The car slid uncontrollably, gaining momentum on the icy slope.

The intersection was a major one with several lanes of cars waiting for the light to change. In the seconds that followed, each of us visualized how much traffic would soon be in our path. Then to our surprise, when the yellow light should have changed to red, it turned instead back to green. We sat transfixed as we glided safely through the intersection. About a block farther on, the preacher broke the silence.

"Did that light really do what I thought it did?"

Yes, it had! Even man-made devices can be God-controlled.

In a Flood

Rain! Rain! One year, spring rains were exceptionally heavy for Colorado Springs. After some time the ground became saturated and water began seeping into our basement. With each storm, our mother and father laid towels along the areas where the water oozed in. Seepage grew worse until it extended along the entire west wall as well as much of the north and south walls.

When we arrived home, Mom and Dad were weary from keeping the "flood" at bay. The constant vigil was taking its toll on their endurance. For days, we joined the fight. We were removing more than 1000 gallons every day or two.

One weekend heavy downpours kept us rotating shifts so that someone was always in the basement. At night we took turns hourly. When we were at church, we would return to find the water inches deep. Dad telephoned the water company, fearing there was a broken water main. He was told that an underground river vein ran beneath our area, and the saturated ground prevented the water from staying in its usual course.

At 4:00 one morning, I was exhausted. I had just finished a turn in the basement and had retreated up-stairs to slip back into bed. Admittedly this trial paled in comparison to what some people endure when floods ruin furniture or even entire homes. Yet this did seem like quite a plague to us. The story of the plagues in Egypt came to mind. During one of them —that of frogs —Moses asked Pharaoh when he wanted the plague to end. I thought, "When will this plague end, Lord?"

The time 10:05 came to mind. 10:05? Strange! Why not 10 o'clock? As much as I tried to shake the idea, 10:05 persisted. Lord, am I making this up, or is it your idea? I didn't want to tell God what to do. Neither did I want to turn a deaf ear if this message was from Him. I prayed and dozed off. At breakfast I shared the strange thought with Mom, Dad, and Faye. Then we prayed that God would move that river vein by 10:05.

The morning progressed as other days, going to the basement about three times an hour to keep the flow under control. At one point I had just finished squeez-ing all the towels when Faye called down the stairs, "Janice, it's 10:05." Usually by the time the last towel was squeezed, the first one was already saturated. I went to the far end of the basement to check. The towel was merely damp. No water was coming in. I pulled each towel away from the wall. NO OOZING! At noon more torrential rains came. Water gushed through the streets. Ordinarily this would have guaranteed more seepage in the basement, but there was none. It all had ended at 10:05.

God may have sent that extra downpour to prove to us that the problem was fixed. The following year when neighbor's basements again flooded, ours stayed dry.

"God is our refuge and strength, a very present help in trouble." (Ps. 46:1)

Janice and Faye call upon God in stormy times.

10

Bus Ministry

∼ by Faye ∼

———————●———————

During college and for a couple of years following, Janice and I had no vehicle so we traveled by commercial bus. Some of those experiences were adventures in faith. We had by now begun to play instruments—the ukulele and later the larger baritone ukulele. These proved to be tools for evangelism on our bus journeys. Often passengers saw our instruments and would ask us to sing.

Seventeen-Cent Journey

Perhaps one of the most memorable bus trips was a two-day trip from Joplin, Missouri, to Roanoke, Virginia. We purchased the tickets well in advance, eagerly anticipating our Friday departure. We prayed that God would open doors of opportunity not only in Virginia, but also during the journey.

On Thursday, the day before we were to leave, the travel agent phoned to inform us that she needed $250 as an advance payment on our upcoming overseas travel. She insisted we pay it before we left town. We had only $90 on hand.

The next day at 11 A.M., the morning's mail brought a letter from home. In it, our parents enclosed a check for $160, a compilation of gifts from friends who wanted to help toward the costs of our summer's mission tour. The Lord had provided the needed $250 just in time! In less than an hour we were to leave for our trip to Virginia. We paid the deposit to the travel agent on our way to the bus station. However, any joy of the Lord's provision seemed clouded by insecurities. Although we had our bus tickets in hand, we were left with only a handful of pennies, seventeen in all, hardly enough to pay for meals during the two-day bus trip. We boarded the Greyhound bus and sat down in the front seat.

"Let's pray, asking the Lord to either supply our food along the way, or to prepare us to be content with a two-day fast," Janice said. I nodded and bowed my head. It felt good to close my eyes. We were exhausted since we had stayed up the previous night to study. I wanted to sleep all the way to Virginia. A pang of guilt struck me at the thought. I was supposed to be praying. With the constant hum of the engine and the gentle motion of the bus, I was unaware of when my prayerful meditations made the transition into the dream world.

"I noticed you gals have some musical instruments." The driver directed a question over his shoulder. "What kind of music do you sing?"

My eyelids were reluctant to open. I heard Janice reply, "Gospel music."

"I love gospel music! How about singing for us? I'll be driving as far as Springfield."

I whispered to Janice, "I had forgotten about having prayed for opportunities to witness. Obviously the Lord didn't forget."

Janice nodded with a knowing smile. Instruments in hand, we sang as miles of Interstate 44 passed beneath us. An hour later we reached Springfield. Knowing we were to change to Continental Trailways bus line and proceed toward Memphis, we stowed our instruments back in their cases and gathered our things.

"Hey gals, don't get off the bus yet. We don't want to lose you to that other bus company. That's brand X, after all," the driver teased with a wink. "Besides, the other bus depot is four blocks away. That would be a long way for you to carry your luggage. I could reroute your tickets and have you make a change in St. Louis instead."

As tired as we felt, his suggestion sounded marvelous. We settled back into our seats and soon were rolling down the highway. Only minutes out of Springfield, the new driver spoke.

"I hear you girls can carry a tune. Would you mind singing some more?" He was already passing us the microphone.

Standing and facing the passengers, our on-the-road concert continued. At Springfield we had seen two Mexicans board the bus, so we included some Spanish songs for them. They grinned with obvious delight.

Late in the afternoon we reached Rolla, Missouri, the supper stop. We entered the station to see if our seventeen cents could buy anything. One glance at the menu on the wall revealed that the cheapest item, a cup of coffee, cost twenty cents. We found a drinking fountain to satisfy our thirst, then returned to the bus.

The Mexicans were nearly the last ones to board. When they passed our seats, they handed us two small packs of potato chips.

"*Muchas Gracias....*" Though we didn't understand all they said, we knew their expression of gratitude was for our songs. We felt badly that we couldn't make any reply beyond a simple "*Gracias.*" Our Spanish at the time had been limited to a repertoire of songs.

I savored every bite, making the chips last.

"It was nice of the Lord to provide potatoes for our supper, but these chips are salty. They'll make me thirsty," Janice said.

"Don't complain. Be thankful for what you get."

Moments down the road the bus pulled into a small town. No passengers were getting off, but the driver disembarked to unload some freight. When he returned, he held a cup of Sprite in each hand.

"Here's to wet your whistles for singing for us." We thanked him and eagerly sipped the soft drinks.

"I guess the Lord heard your complaint about being thirsty," I whispered to Janice. "I suppose next you'll be begging for a full meal!"

St. Louis. 10:30 P.M. Two weary travelers enter the spacious bus depot.

"Say, Twins!"

We turned to see the driver who had just brought us from Springfield.

"Don't forget you're changing to the Continental Trailways' Depot here. It is several blocks away and in a rough part of town. It's dangerous at this time of night. You had better take a taxi." Not willing to admit we didn't have enough money for taxi fare, we made no immediate comment.

"On second thought, even that isn't necessarily safe. Let me see what I can do for you. Give me your tickets." He headed toward the ticket office and returned with a smile. "Here, this will be better. I've rerouted you through Cincinnati. Now you can stay with Greyhound. You'll be leaving from this gate at 11 o'clock." He pointed to the long line already forming by gate 10. We took our places at the end of the line. Glancing to one side I saw three drivers standing near gate 9. One of them was signaling for us to come there. We picked up our things and joined them.

"Hi," the driver who had summoned us said.

"There's no sense in waiting at the end of that long line. That bus will fill up. A second bus will load here at gate 9. With only a few passengers on it, you'll get your choice of seats." Janice thanked him for his kindness.

"By the way, I'll be your driver. My name is George."

The journey found us once again in the front seats. Since a rule had only recently been made that cigarette smoking be limited to the back of the bus, we had preferred to sit as near to the front as possible. The bus wound its way through the darkened city streets. I was drifting off to sleep even before we reached the freeway that would take us eastward into Illinois.

What peaceful slumber! But then, like before, there were voices. I awoke. The driver was speaking, "...and I heard through the grapevine that you two sing. I'd be pleased if you'd sing for the passengers now."

Now? No! My exhausted body rebelled. All I wanted to do was sleep. Yet, not wanting to refuse the request, we stood and took the microphone George handed us. As we praised the Lord, the unwilling fibers of my weary being gave way to humble submission and ultimately to joy of service. Song after song we continued. As it neared midnight we chose slower, quieter songs for the sake of those who desired to sleep. Each time we thought of putting an end to our late night concert, George would urge us to sing another one.

"I'm afraid we're keeping the passengers awake," I finally admitted.

"Isn't it more important to keep me awake?"

So, as the night wore on, we continued to comply with the driver's wishes. Eventually we relinquished the microphone and returned to our seats. The driver then struck up a conversation, asking us questions about our faith. We asked the Lord to help us give the best responses.

Once, in the dead of the night, the headlights of a car

glared directly at us. Someone was on the wrong side of the road. George blinked his lights repeatedly, but nothing altered the course of the oncoming car. We sat wide-eyed in terror, bracing ourselves. At the last moment George swerved the bus violently onto the shoulder of the road to avoid a head-on collision.

"Well, looks like your God was with us that time." George eased the bus back onto the highway. "It could have been someone asleep at the wheel."

The night hours passed with more discussion and an occasional song. When the lights of Indianapolis came into view at 4:30 A.M., George said, "This will be the end of the line for me. Indianapolis is my home. I want to thank you girls for singing and talking with me all night. I couldn't have made it without you."

It was God who had revived our spirits, keeping us awake when we were needed, and hopefully George's soul was awakening to the reality and presence of God. Once inside the depot, fatigue set in again. Our bloodshot eyes burned. With our backs toward the snack bar, we failed to see George approaching with two cups of soft drinks for us. When he came into view, we smiled and gratefully accepted his gifts.

"We thought you'd be on your way home by now," Janice commented.

"Well, I should have been, but I've been doing some thinking. I have never met anyone like you two. I mean, ones with the conviction you have about God. Anyway, I'd like to see if I can drive the bus on to Cincinnati, so I can talk with you some more." With that he excused himself and was gone. Moments later he returned.

"There are already two buses scheduled to go to Cincinnati, but neither of the drivers want to exchange with me." He glanced at the long line of passengers already forming by the door. "Wait a minute. Maybe there will be enough passengers to need a third bus."

George motioned for us to stay seated. "I'll be right back." He dashed away. When he returned, it was with a look of disappointment. "They don't expect to need a third bus," he said, slumping into a chair across from us. After a moment's contemplation, he leaped back to his feet with renewed determination. "I'll count them myself."

We watched incredulously as he went first to the long line of people. We could hear him asking each one if they were going to Cincinnati. George's countenance would fall when anyone would give a negative nod or would explain they were only seeing a friend off. Next he went around to those seated in the waiting area.

"Are you going to Cincinnati?" If their reply was, "No," he would then say with a smile, "Are you sure you don't want to change your plans? Cincinnati's a lovely place this time of year."

I could hardly believe what I was hearing. The expression on Janice's face displayed equal disbelief and amusement. When George finally finished his tally, he came to us.

"I'm going to the dispatch office to try again to get a third bus." Just after he had exited the building, an announcement came over the speaker system that buses for Cincinnati were ready for boarding. We gathered our things and joined the slow-moving line. The first bus filled to capacity. The second had begun to load when George came running, breathless.

"Don't get on. I got the okay. I'm going to the garage for a third bus. Wait right here." He was off again at a run.

The last passengers boarded and both buses pulled out of the station. As we stood alone, minutes ticked by. Would the illusive third bus ever come? Finally it did. George emerged with a triumphant grin. One other passenger, a man who had come late, boarded with us.

He seated himself toward the rear, reclined, and fell asleep.

"Well, here we are on our way to Cincinnati at last. You know, this bus wasn't needed."

"It wasn't? Weren't the other ones full?" I asked.

"Nope," he admitted, "There were six empty seats on the second bus."

God was entrusting us with great responsibility. George's whole desperate effort to obtain this bus had been for the purpose of discussing the things of God.

> "...Always be prepared to give an answer to everyone who asks you to give the reason for the hope that you have. But do this with gentleness and respect." (I Pet. 3:15 NIV)

With no one else near to overhear the conversation, George wasted no time in freely opening his heart to topics of serious discussion: the love of God, forgiveness, freedom from guilt and sin, eternal life. At one point he said, "You know, I had never heard anything about life after death. I always presumed that this life was all there was—seventy, eighty years if you're lucky. I thought it was man's duty to raise a family, teach the kids to be good citizens, enjoy grandchildren, and when you die - well - pfff, you're gone. Buried! Forgotten!"

Janice and I impressed upon George what joy, peace, and hope accompany those who surrender their lives to the Lordship of Jesus Christ.

The journey passed quickly. Our conversation came to an end when Cincinnati loomed before us. George turned the bus off the freeway into the downtown area. Once among the city's tall buildings, he made a surprising admission.

"Girls, I don't know how to find the bus depot. I have enough seniority to have a regular run, so I haven't been to Cincinnati in probably eleven years."

Amused by this unusual turn of events, we obeyed

George's request to station ourselves at opposite windows and search for the depot down each side street.

We wondered if he were only teasing, as he was the one to ultimately locate it. At the depot we went separate ways. When George had finished his duties, he found us and asking if he could take us out for breakfast. Although our stomachs were growling, we tried to politely refuse.

"Please don't turn me down," he insisted. "I've checked your schedule and your next bus doesn't leave until 10 A.M. That's two hours from now. I can't catch a ride back to Indianapolis before then either. So, let's go." We didn't protest any further.

We slipped into a booth at the Pancake House near the depot. George teased us when our order came.

"I can't believe you ordered chocolate pancakes."

"Chocolate is good in anything." I met his gaze and marveled. The Lord had faithfully answered our prayers to have opportunities to share a message about God's love with others. Now He was also answering our prayer to provide our meals along the way. I eased the first forkful into my mouth. My eyes closed as I savored the moment of ecstasy. "Mmm! Chocolate pancakes never tasted so good."

"You've had them before?" George asked, bewildered.

"No." I admitted. I had to hold my hand over my mouth to prevent a messy disaster as it set us all to laughing.

George walked us back to the depot where we said our good-byes. Janice was thanking him for the breakfast when she added, "Thank you for being an instrument used by God."

"Huh? How's that?" George's eyebrows raised in puzzled wonder.

"We started on this trip with very little money,"

Janice explained. "We prayed, asking God to supply our needs along the way. He must have put it in your heart to buy our breakfast. Thanks so much for being attuned to Him."

A slight smile tempered his thoughtful expression. "You certainly make me think in a whole new way," he admitted. Then it was time to part.

We boarded a southbound bus and sat in quiet contemplation. I wanted to meditate on the Lord's goodness until I would drift off into a peaceful sleep. But I wasn't surprised when the pleasant driver said: "I'm told you sing. Would you give us a sample?" Off and on for the remainder of that day we sang.

At one point, the driver struck up a conversation with us and with the men across the aisle. For more than two hours we all discussed various Scriptures and shared personal experiences of God's direction in our lives. We sensed Jesus' presence in a faith-building fellowship that uplifts and strengthens.

Throughout the time, none of us had disclosed our denominational background. We were surprised when we eventually learned what a wide spectrum of Christianity was represented among us. We praised the Lord that our conversation had not begun with the question "What church are you with?" That only tends to divide, focusing on differences, as each has a judgmental attitude concerning the teachings of the other. It often ends in debates, arguments, or defensive mistrust rather than establishing unity of faith in Christ Jesus.

In mid-afternoon a lady across the aisle talked with us. We explained that we were in Bible college. When she neared her destination, she said, "My son is dating a girl in a Bible college. I know students don't always have a lot of money. Maybe you can use this." With a tender smile, she slipped us two dollars, then exited the bus.

Janice and I enjoyed a juicy hamburger for supper. The Lord sustained us on our long journey without having asked anyone for help. In fact, we arrived in Virginia with 22 cents.

The Night in Jail

We had arrived in a small town in New Mexico at midnight and discovered that the bus depot was closed for the night. A police station a couple of blocks away seemed to be our only source of refuge. One of the officers gave us permission to stay in a hallway near the entrance. There were no chairs there, so we sat on our suitcases. For a while I was entertained by watching squad cars come and go. It was a busy night—the fourth of July. Several inebriated men were brought in. As the night wore on, we dozed off against the wall.

I jerked awake when someone leaned over against me. It startled me to see a whiskered old man with greasy pants sitting on one of our record boxes. He slept soundly against my arm. For an instant I sat motionless, not knowing what to do. Gingerly I placed my hand against the shoulder of the man's ragged brown jacket and gently eased him away. At my touch the man awoke.

"Oh, hallo there," he said with slurred speech, his foul breath reeking of alcohol. "Who are you?" He leaned farther away as if to try to focus his blurred vision and nearly fell off the box of record albums. Shifting the box more squarely beneath himself, he stared again toward us while running his fingers through his disheveled hair. He tried in vain to focus the two of us into one image. Finally concluding that in more ways than one he was "seeing double," he continued the one-sided conversation. "I betsha I know why you're here." Then slowly, obviously trying to avoid extra movement that could once again set him off balance, he raised his right arm and pointed at us. "Yesh shir, you mushta wrecked your car jusht like I did." Then, as if great effort had been expended, he allowed his arm to flop limply to his side, his head leaned back against the wall. Seconds later he was snoring loudly.

An officer then came to escort him away. We pitied the man. His soul was perhaps in a more wrecked condition than was his car.

When morning dawned, a policeman offered to drive us to the bus depot. The young officer said it was a welcome break to perform a good deed after all their unpleasant tasks throughout the night. When we arrived at the station, he helped carry our luggage inside. With curiosity people watched us being escorted from the squad car. Before exiting the depot, the officer turned back toward us.

"And this time—stay out of town!" he said, a teasing smile on his face.

Encounter With an Angry Man

Seated in the fourth row from the front, we enjoyed the ride northward from New Mexico, dozing off from time to time. About midday the bus stopped at a station and we noticed that the man across the aisle got up to go to the back of the bus. Just then new passengers boarded. A tall, broad-shouldered man came and sat in the place that had just been vacated, flopping his belongings into the adjacent seat.

Expecting the other passenger to return, Janice thought she would be helpful by warning the newcomer. "Excuse me, but a man was sitting there."

"I don't give a blankety blank who was sitting here," the man swore loudly. "I don't see anyone's name on this place, so it's mine now!"

Shocked by the angry outburst, we thought it best to leave the man alone. Just then he pulled out a cigarette and proceeded to light it. Although smoking was supposed to be limited to the backseats of the bus, we didn't dare raise another objection. As though the man could read our thoughts, he leaned halfway across the aisle and exploded into another tirade.

"And I suppose next you'll be objecting to my having a smoke? Well, don't you believe you're going to chase me out of here. All my life it's been, 'Blacks to the back of the line,' 'blacks defile the ground they walk on,' 'blacks aren't worth anything.' Well, don't think for a minute you can send me to the back of this bus, no sir!"

By this time other passengers on all sides were turning to see what all the commotion was. We felt warm with embarrassment as others looked accusingly in our direction. How could we convince the man that our remark had not been racially motivated? The man's angry outburst wasn't finished yet. With volume intensified, he continued.

"I came all the way from Louisiana and haven't had anything but trouble all the way. I haven't slept a wink in two days," he said. We felt sympathy for the man. It's often when we are tired and when things have gone wrong that we are likely to snap at others or misjudge someone else's motives or intentions. We felt badly that we had unintentionally added to his frustration.

Wondering what could curb this man's anger, the Scripture came to mind. "A soft answer turns away wrath." (Prov. 15:1a)

Janice, evidently thinking along the same lines, gave a quick glance down at the candy bar between us. Looking then at me as if for approval, I gave a nod. Bravely, she interrupted the man in mid-sentence.

"Would you like to have a candy bar?" she asked softly.

"Well, ah," he sputtered, not knowing quite how to react. "Yes, Ma'am, I'd like that. I'll tell you what, I'll take it home and let my kids share it." He named the town in Wyoming where he was headed. Having calmed down, the man reclined his seat and closed his eyes.

Soon afterward, someone asked us to sing. The driver urged us to stand at the front and use the microphone. Being the day after Independence Day, we included some patriotic songs. Many joined in on "God Bless America," "America the Beautiful," and "My Country 'Tis of Thee," but the black man slept on. I half wished the man would be awake to hear the messages of the gospel songs, yet the other half of me felt relief to see him in the harmless state of sleep.

Off and on for hours we sang, and still the man slept. Just after we had quit singing and had returned to our seats, a tall, slim Montana cowboy made his way to the front of the bus. Removing his cowboy hat, he made a speech.

"Folks, these young ladies have been entertaining us for a long while, and it has sure made the otherwise boring miles pass pleasantly. I think we all owe them a debt of thanks, so I'd like to suggest we take up a collection." With that he sauntered down the aisle with the sweat-stained hat extended. When he had finished, he tipped a pile of coins totaling $10 onto my lap.

Just then the driver announced the next stop. Janice and I recognized it to be the hometown of the man across the aisle. I glanced over at the imposing figure still fast asleep. We feared the consequences of disturbing him, yet dreaded more the anger we might arouse if we failed to do so. Hesitantly Janice reached over and gently tapped the man on the shoulder.

"I hate to have to disturb you, but we've reached your destination," she said.

No signs of anger followed. In fact, the man thanked us, then busied himself to gather his things. Before getting off the bus he turned toward us and said, "I want to thank you for all that nice singing." Looks of astonishment must have shown on our faces as we had presumed he had heard none of it.

"I know I was asleep for a lot of it, but what I did hear was mighty pretty. It just lulled me off to sleep. That's the most peaceful sleep I've had on the whole trip. I sure thank you. One more thing. I want to ask a favor of you," he said, glancing toward the driver who was showing signs of impatience. He handed me a small piece of paper. "Here's my address. Please pray for me. I've not always been a good man and I need God's help. Write to me and my family." He walked up the aisle but called back, "Thanks again for your singing." Then he exited the bus.

We praised God who had taken a frustrating incident and transformed it into something good. We did write to the man's family but never received a reply. We are reminded that one plants the seed and another waters. So we prayed that God would direct others into their path.

We can't get off the subject of bus adventures without also sharing about our college choir tours when a driver's heart was touched.

Faye and Janice often gave concerts
to the passengers on commercial buses.

Ozark Bible College
Concert Choir

11

The Driver With
the Open Heart
~ by Janice ~

A late March blizzard raged, already spreading its blinding white blanket over Missouri's landscape as two commercial buses forged southward. The ten-day choice tour had gone quickly. Too quickly. I glanced up and saw the driver's face reflected in the rear view mirror. Robert Rayl's expression mirrored intense concentration as he maneuvered the bus through the mesmerizing swirl of flakes. The increasing accumulation on the highway made driving treacherous.

I closed my eyes to pray. Admittedly my thoughts were not only on the road conditions. I was thinking of Robert's spiritual condition. He was congenial and had a keen sense of humor, yet he also had a serious side. I could still visualize his expression during the final concert. At one point we ladies had descended the platform's steps, leaving the men to sing "Wherever He Leads, I'll Go."

Faye and I paused in the doorway where Robert stood tall in his blue uniform. He was silent for some time, listening. Then he whispered, whether to himself or for us to hear, "I guess a man is never too old to cry."

Tears were welling up in his eyes. He sighed, reached for his handkerchief and turned to leave.

We wished for the tour to be prolonged, but not even the snowstorm delayed the inevitable return to campus.

After equipment and luggage were unloaded, both the drivers were eager to push on to their homes in Wichita, Kansas. There were hurried good-byes. A sadness enveloped us as the buses pulled away.

About six weeks later as the choir was rehearsing some new songs for the final spring concert, I spotted a Continental Trailways bus pulling onto campus. I mentioned it to our director. By the time Mr. Rayl stepped off the bus, he could hear the familiar refrains of our choir tour repertoire. When he slipped into the rehearsal room, an enthusiastic cheer broke forth from the choir members, making him feel welcome.

I've really missed you kids," Robert commented, a warm expression in his pale blue eyes. "Don't let me stop your singing. I'd love to hear more." He sat thoughtful through the remainder of the rehearsal. At the sound of the bell, students gathered their things.

"Good to see you again, Robert," they said, before hurrying out the door.

With the classroom nearly empty, Robert approached us. "Do you twins need to go somewhere, too, or can we find some place to talk?"

"We're free. This was our last class for the day." We led him to the administration building where there was a reception area with comfortable chairs.

"I had to come back. You kids got something I don't have, and I want it. When you choir kids sang, there was such joy on your faces. It was like light shining in your eyes," Robert said.

"The eyes are the windows to the soul," Faye said.

Robert leaned forward, looking puzzled as he rested

his elbows on his knees.

"We are body, soul, and spirit. We humans tend to spend our time and energy on physical needs and desires, but the body won't last. The spirit will. It is eternal. God who made us wants us to have peace and joy in life," I said.

Robert gazed at his folded hands. "Yeh, I've been thinking life should be more than just getting a job, raising a family, and growing old. That tour with the choir gave me a lot to think about. You kids have purpose in life." Kids! It amused us that he'd call us that. Robert was in his early thirties.

"You know, Robert, God is getting your attention. He loves you," I said.

Robert looked up, his expression warm, serious. "You're right you know. I guess I knew it all along." Then with a grin and a glint in his eye, he said, "But you kids got a head start on me." We laughed.

"God doesn't measure spiritual growth in years." Inwardly we prayed that the Holy Spirit would implant the truths in his heart, causing God's seed of love to take root and grow.

Time passed quickly. Soon Robert had to leave. As the familiar bus pulled away, our thoughts turned to prayer, "Lord, whether or not we will see him again, please continue to convict Robert, using other people and circumstances."

Months passed. By the following spring, we would have one more choir tour before graduating. Did we dare hope that Robert would again be one of the drivers? It was a warm but windy day in March as we stood outside the chapel with bags packed, eagerly awaiting the arrival of the buses. Teresa Peterson said to me, "I hope we'll have the same drivers again."

"Me, too. We'll probably have Joe for sure. He's a regular," I said. Joe Thomson, a Christian who had attended the college, usually volunteered for the choir tours. "But whether or not Robert will come, only God knows."

"I could tell Mr. Rayl was seeking God, so I've been praying for him all year," Teresa said.

As the first bus pulled to a stop, we recognized Joe. He grinned and waved at us. Then he leaped out to give us a joint hug. "Hey Rostvits, you still around here?"

Drivers Joe Thomson and Robert Rayl

"Did you think you could have a nice quiet tour without us?" Faye teased.

"It is our final semester." I said. As we chatted, we could hear the second bus parking, but Joe's bus obscured our view. We didn't want to be rude and break away from Joe to see who the other driver was. Suddenly large hands fell on our shoulders. Robert's familiar voice greeted us.

"Hey Double Trouble." That was the nickname Joe gave us when he had first introduced us to Robert the previous year. "You're not going to ride on Joe's bus, are you? You belong on mine." He greeted Teresa, too, and before long he was helping carry our luggage to his bus.

By the third evening's concert, it was evident that Robert was under conviction. Following the concert, choir members would be taken to various homes. As Faye and I approached the bus, Robert retrieved our suitcases from the luggage compartment.

"Now you kids have a good night," he said.

"Thank you. We'll be praying for you, Robert," I said as I met his gaze.

"Thanks, you know I need that." His serious eyes took on a tender expression.

That night we prayed that God would continue to burden Robert, not allowing him to be content until he would surrender his heart to Jesus.

The following day while traveling, we were in the middle of the bus talking with other friends. At one point while making my way up the aisle, I spotted Robert's face in the mirror. He was motioning me to come. We didn't make it a habit of talking with the driver while on the road, but assuming he needed something, I stepped down beside him.

"Yes?"

"I need to talk to you twins. I know I can open up and share my thoughts without you laughing at me. I've got to tell you what happened last night. It all started at 11:20." His voice took on a tone of urgency, yet he paused, struggling in thought. "Oh, I can't tell you now —not while I'm driving." He cast a troubled glance in my direction. "Maybe we can get together later today." I nodded, then made my way back down the aisle to join my twin.

"Faye, did you happen to notice what time it was when we began to pray last night?" I asked.

"Yes, I did. It was 11:20. Why?"

"Hmm, that's interesting." Then I related what the driver had just told me.

The daily routine of the choir's devotions, rehearsals, travel, and concerts generally left little time to talk with the drivers. So we prayed specifically that God would provide the opportunity.

Later that afternoon, the buses pulled into the parking lot of the church where we were to have the evening concert. The choir gathered in the sanctuary for instructions.

"Since today's travel was short, you'll go to your separate homes now. Your host families will bring you back here in time for the fellowship dinner," George King explained.

A wave of disappointment swept over me. I wished we could stay that extra time at the church so Robert could talk with us. Housing was immediately being arranged. To dispel our feelings of deferred hope, I whispered to Faye, "Let's see if we can stay with some other choir members. That would be fun." We then put in our bid for one of the host families who wanted four girls. We were disappointed they allotted those homes to others.

"You twins will be staying with a widow named Thelma Friddle," we were told. Thelma Friddle! Thelma Friddle! My mind chewed on the name like a pouting child who didn't get her way. We had been the first to ask for a house for four. Why did others get them? It wasn't fair! Whenever we face disappointment, it's easy to recall the first half of Proverbs 13:12, "Hope deferred makes the heart sick...." In this case, God was preparing to turn our attention to the positive aspect in the latter part of the verse, "...but a longing fulfilled is a tree of life." The lady with the housing list turned to us.

"By the way, Twins, I'm sorry, but Thelma could not come early. You'll have to stay here at the church for the afternoon."

Stay at the church! We'd be the only ones staying

and would have that opportunity to talk with the bus driver. Shame swept over me as I considered that I had wallowed in self-pity, while God was answering our specific prayer. Our disappointment turned to elation.

Robert was overjoyed when he learned we were staying. As we were pulling up chairs to talk, I spotted Joe Thomson entering the doorway. He smiled and gave a nod in our direction.

"Hey, Robert, if you should need me for anything, I'll be out in my bus," Joe said.

"Okay, thanks." Then Robert turned his attention back to us, his expression serious. "I've wanted to tell you about last night. I was in my motel room. At 11:20 I wanted to go to sleep, but I dreaded shutting off the light. I was afraid of the darkness. So I tried reading a magazine, but I couldn't concentrate. It was like I was hearing you kids saying, 'What are you waiting for, Robert? What are you waiting for?' Eventually I shut off the lights, but still felt uneasy. There was a presence in the room. A Godly presence, yet I was afraid."

"The fear of the Lord is the beginning of wisdom," (Prov. 9:10a) I commented. "God is trying to speak to you, Robert."

Meeting my gaze, his eyes brimming with tears, he blurted with frustration, "I know. But what's He trying to tell me?"

"God loves you and wants you to know Him." We opened the Scriptures to let God speak for Himself.

Time flew. All too soon fellow students were returning for the fellowship dinner. During the concert Robert
again was visibly moved, but as an invitation was extended, he slipped out, weeping.

Afterward, choir members scattered with their host
families. We set out to locate our hostess. We were
informed that Thelma had gone to the kitchen. Mrs.
Friddle was an elderly lady with a gentle nature and a
warm smile that radiated from her good heart.

"You girls got a real dud for a hostess when you got
me," she said. "I couldn't come this afternoon, and now
I have to stay to clean up the kitchen."

Just then Robert entered the fellowship hall. He
asked if he could talk with us some more. We were glad
for the additional time with him.

At one point Thelma came out of the kitchen, apparently ready to go home. But when she saw that we were
having a serious talk with a teary driver, she gave an
understanding nod and tiptoed back into the kitchen
under the pretext she still had more work to do.

Knowing we needed to leave shortly, Faye suggested, "Robert, will you try praying tonight?"

"Yes," he said with some hesitation. "I'll try, but I
don't know how. I tried last night, but I was too emotionally shaken."

"Prayer isn't just a use of fancy religious jargon. It is
communication with your best friend. Just try opening
up and being honest with God. Would it help if we pray
at the same time?"

"I'd like that," he said. With that we established
11:30 to be our joint prayer time.

That night in Mrs. Friddle's home, Faye and I knelt
by our bed from 11:30 to 1:00 A.M. The hour and a half on
our knees seemed like mere minutes. We thought to
pray longer, but sensing the urgency had passed, we
slipped beneath the covers to get some sleep.

The following day when we saw Robert, I asked, "How was your night?"

"That's the first time I've spent an hour and a half on my knees." He was overwhelmed to learn that we had prayed for the exact amount of time.

That day we were to sing in a Chicago suburb. Our cousins Bud and Jody Hornburg came. After the concert, housing was being arranged.

"Let's not interfere tonight. If God has a specific place for us, let Him arrange it," Faye suggested. "Let's go talk to Bud and Jody." When we were halfway down the aisle, Robert met us.

"Can you stay around and talk?" he asked.

"I doubt it. We'll be going to our home soon," I said.

He nodded understanding.

While we were seated in a pew talking with our cousins, Teresa Peterson approached us. "Twins, I hope you don't mind, but I got housing for the three of us."

"That's great," Faye answered. Then our hostess came and introduced herself.

"My home is right across the street. Feel free to visit with your relatives as long as you want before coming over," she said.

Only moments later Bud and Judy stood to leave, "We have a long way to drive and it's late." We were grateful they had come. After they left, we wished we could linger to talk with Robert, but we assumed our hostess was waiting. We crossed the street to our home. To our surprise, it was Teresa who let us in. Our hostess was not there. A note on the coffee table read, "Girls, make yourselves at home. I'm staying the night with a friend. You'll find all you need for breakfast in the refrigerator. God bless."

What a shock! When are we guests without hosts? We could have stayed and talked with Robert. I looked out the window. The buses were already gone. I turned from the window with disappointment, explaining to Teresa about the foiled opportunity to talk with the driver. Then a thought struck me.

"Hey, maybe it's no coincidence that I know where the drivers are staying tonight."

"What do you mean?" Teresa looked puzzled.

"Before the concert when we were assembled in the basement, I overheard Joe making a reservation by phone for a room at the Holiday Inn. I don't want the drivers to get the wrong idea, but we could ask if they know when the church building will be open in the morning. If Robert wants to talk, he can get the hint to come early." I found the number and dialed.

At that moment, Robert and Joe were busy writing the day's statistics in their logbooks. When the phone rang, Robert jumped up, nearly tipping his chair over. I asked if he knew when the church building would be open in the morning. His response took me by surprise.

"Would there be any possibility I could come tonight, so we could talk?" Robert asked. Then he turned to Joe, "Hey, there's nothing going on here, you understand, but I'm going back over to the church so I can talk with the twins." Joe later told us he had a hard time to keep from grinning as he knew Robert was under conviction.

Faye and Teresa looked surprised when I told them that Robert was coming. Teresa promised she would pray for us while we talked with him.

That evening we sat with Robert in the bus. God's Word was laid open to answer more of his questions. After a couple of hours he said, "Now I'm ready to surrender to Jesus." We prayed with him before he left.

The following night in St. Joseph, Illinois, one of the directors, Willis Harrison, who had also developed a special friendship with this driver, stood at the front of the sanctuary at the close of the concert. An invitation was given for people to publicly proclaim their faith in Christ. Robert walked forward with tears in his eyes. There wasn't a dry eye in the choir. Afterward he took the time to hug each of the sixty-some members in the choir. When he jointly hugged the two of us, he whispered repeatedly, "Thank you, thank you, thank you." Could there be any greater joy on this earth? We also knew that angels in Heaven were rejoicing with us as John 15:10 states: "There is joy in the presence of the angels of God over one sinner who repents."

Some weeks later we learned that Robert Rayl was going to be baptized in a church in Wichita. On that particular weekend, we were scheduled to travel with a professor and some other students to a church in Hays, Kansas. To our surprise, when we arrived, the pastor informed us that they wanted singing and preaching on Friday and Saturday only. They had no plans for us to take part in the Sunday services. That was extremely unusual!

We then headed back toward Missouri Saturday night. At our request, the professor left us in Wichita so we could sing for Robert's baptism. We knew the Lord had worked out those details.

After graduating from college in 1971, Janice and Faye
traveled with an evangelistic team on a
three-month around-the-world tour.
For the first time they flew on a 747.

PART III

Reflecting on God's PROVIDENTIAL Care

With college years behind us, travel takes us all over the globe. Facing the daily responsibilities in God's work is not always easy. We are not spared the physical, emotional and spiritual trials of a life of travel. Yet we stand in awe as we reflect on God's providential care in various situations.

> "…Make known among the nations what He has done, and proclaim that His name is exalted. Sing to the Lord, for He has done glorious things; let this be known to all the world." (Isa. 12:4b,5 NIV)

Lord, hear my voice, ♪ ♪ ♪
As now I rejoice,
I do not deserve the favor You have shown to me.
Lord, take my days,
To sing forth Your praise, ♪ ♪
For Your ways are higher than our ways.

(Portion of the song "Your Ways are Higher" by the Rostvit Twins)

Music Around the World

1971: When in India, Faye and Janice dressed
in saris to be culturally accepted.

12

Music Around
the World
～ by Faye ～

I glanced out the window of the airplane as we taxied away from the terminal. To one side I could see a crowd of people. A senator was giving a speech. It mattered little to us that it was the dedication day of the expansion of that airport. We were eagerly anticipating a trip around the world. Only two days earlier we had graduated from Bible college. How fitting that the final song of the commencement service had been "Wherever He Leads I'll Go."

My reverie was interrupted as the plane slowed to a stop, then shut down the engines. We wondered what the problem could be. Just then a stewardess leaned in front of us.

"Excuse me, I noticed you two are dressed alike and I was wondering if . . . Oh!" She stepped back with a look of surprise. "You're TWINS! I had hoped you were a music group."

"We are that, too, we are gospel singers," Janice said.

"Oh, really?" She brightened. "Could I ask a favor of you? The control tower just informed us that we can't

take off yet. The Blue Angels are arriving to give an air show for the airport dedication. We'll have to wait here until the show is over. I'm afraid some of the passengers will become impatient. Would you mind entertaining them until we get clearance for take off?" And so, our three-month journey began with a 45-minute concert in the airplane.

In Chicago we were thrilled to learn that our flight across the Atlantic would be on a 747. Our first experience aboard a jumbo jet did not disappoint us, especially when we were invited to the cockpit to sing for the pilots. Fascinated by the myriad of instrument panels, it was surprising we didn't forget the lyrics as we sang "I'm Going Higher Someday."

Our sister Sharon and her husband Tom, a sergeant in the Air Force, met us in Frankfurt, Germany. The few days' visit with them were filled with excitement: viewing quaint hamlets and exploring ancient castles along the Rhein River, savoring local cuisine, and taking walks through dense forests. To this point, the trip had exceeded our highest expectations.

On the next leg of the journey we were still on an emotional high. Again we were escorted to the cockpit to sing for the crew. As we gave our mini-concert, Istanbul, Turkey, and the Black Sea were in view far below. Once back at our seats we drifted off to sleep with dreams of the mission opportunities that lay ahead in India.

We were not prepared for the shocking sights and foul odors that bombarded our senses as we passed by bus through the squalor of Bombay's slum districts. Makeshift shelters were crowded together. Hovels served as homes for entire families. Others took refuge in large cement culverts intended for road repairs.

To worsen the already deplorable conditions, heavy monsoon rains had been ravaging the region. Some shanties had collapsed; others stood in deep water. People looked thin and sickly. Many waded aimlessly through mud and water. Some survived the nights only by sleeping on chairs with their small children on their shoulders. As we viewed the destitute masses of humanity, we felt helpless. We could do nothing to alleviate their suffering.

For the next two months we saw another side of India. We saw the cities where people were well dressed and the countryside where there were hard working farmers. Villages were tidy. Children seemed relatively healthy. It is not to say the people were not poor, yet those who knew Jesus as Lord reflected an obvious contentment in their lives. We grew to love these humble people who gladly provided us hospitality.

The months for us were not without hardship. The schedule of three or four meetings each day took the discipline of rising by 4:30 or 5 A.M. Naps had to be snatched in the car between villages. The summer's oppressive temperatures also took their toll. One time we had made a rough four-hour journey from the missionary's home. As there were no Christians to house us in the town, rooms were booked in a modest Indian hotel. Many village services were scheduled. However, several of the team, including the missionary and the Indian who cooked our meals, became ill.

Only our interpreter Sathya, our driver Kandasami, and the two of us remained in good health to fulfill the commitments in the villages. The four of us headed out alone. Later in the afternoon we reached the village of Kalathur for the fourth meeting of the day. An elaborate welcome awaited us. Crowds hovered around us. Garlands of flowers were placed around our necks, and we were paraded through the entire village while people sang, clapped, beat on drums, and clashed cymbals.

I didn't mean to be ungrateful for this gesture of honor, but I wasn't enjoying the parade. That day the temperature was over 110 degrees; I felt faint. I was relieved when we reached the *pundal,* a temporary platform with a leafy overhead shade. We were escorted to some chairs. Despite the leafy ceiling, the heat was still unbearable. The throngs crowded around, eager to view the Americans. The atmosphere was stifling. I didn't tell Janice that I was feeling faint. I assumed it was only from the long walk in the scorching sun. I hoped I wasn't getting sick.

A glass of coconut milk was offered to us. Usually nothing was more refreshing, but this time the smell made me queasy. Slowly I sipped the liquid, hoping my stomach would accept it. The longer we sat there, the better I began to feel.

Eventually the meeting began. Sathya spoke to the audience, offered a prayer, then introduced us. As I stood, I felt a wave of nausea. I ignored it, certain that the feeling would pass. Our Telugu songs were appreciated, but the nausea persisted. After the third song, I whispered to Janice, "I'm turning green." I steeled myself, determined to complete our portion of the singing.

My mental pep talk didn't help. Soon I was swallowing hard. By the time the next song had ended, I couldn't even say a word to Janice. With hand held over my mouth, I dashed from the platform and pushed my way through the packed crowd.

Kindhearted Kandasami saw me leave and followed closely behind. He was there to offer a handkerchief after I had vomited, then led me to the shade of a tree. A concerned villager brought a rope-woven bed and Kandasami sat and fanned me as I rested. I could hear Janice singing alone, then Sathya preached. The same man who had brought the bed came with a bowl of liquid and gestured that I should drink it. Although I preferred to let my stomach have a rest, reluctantly I leaned on one elbow, cradled the bowl in my hand and took a swallow.

"Ai-yo," I cried out as my throat burned and tears welled up in my eyes. It was pure liquid from chili peppers, hotter than anything we had ever eaten, even in Mexico. I looked at Kandasami hoping he would rescue me from having to drink any more of it. With kind eyes he urged me to continue.

"It's good for you. It will settle your stomach."

Like an obedient patient, I swallowed the remainder of the "fire water" and thanked the man who gave it. Kandasami was right; the medicine stayed down. However, for the next few days a high fever raged and nothing I ate or drank would stay down. I lay in bed at the little hotel too sick to move. I slept a lot. When I was awake, my only entertainment was to watch monkeys. The little would-be thieves stretched their long arms through the barred window. They chattered with annoyance as if to scold me because nothing was in reach.

Janice, Sathya, and the driver, continued to fulfill village commitments. One day they had six services. They still found time to come to the hotel between meetings. What a welcome sight each time Janice entered the room. With a wet cloth, she swabbed my face and arms in an attempt to reduce my fever. Then she would go down the hall to do the same for the rest of the team. We were all too weak to check on each other.

Our situation was grave. With little success Janice would urge us to eat or drink. Our systems violently rejected any nourishment. Dehydration caused much weight loss. Previously Janice and I had weighed the same, but now I had dropped to ninety-eight pounds, seventeen pounds less than Janice. Sathya started calling me "the lean one."

After several days we made the rough journey back to the missionaries' home. Gradually strength returned, and so did my weight. The busy schedule continued in south and central India. Before we knew it, the two months were over. Despite the heat and sickness, we were not eager to leave. We had come to love the people.

Our last view of India was Calcutta. Its streets were packed. Such traffic and noise! Large trucks and buses impatiently blared their ear-splitting air horns while belching clouds of black diesel fumes into the already stifling air. Cars, motorcycles, and bicycle rickshaws squeezed between the larger vehicles. Wagons with wooden wheels squeaked and groaned to the rhythm of the steady plodding bullocks. Men strained every muscle to inch along with heavily loaded hand-drawn carts. Street vendors with high-pitched nasal tones repetitiously announced their wares, adding to the din of the city. And people, they were everywhere!

As in Bombay, we witnessed devastating living conditions. Like ants, hordes of people filtered through every garbage heap, scavenging any edible morsels. Homeless families huddled together, living on the sidewalks. We were helpless observers of a hopeless situation. Then we reached the airport and boarded our flight bound for Burma.

As on other flights, we were pleased to be invited to the cockpit. The crew members were all Burmese. Jesse Yangmi, a Burmese student at our Bible college, had taught us some songs and phrases in his language. So, we sang in Burmese.

We didn't realize how much we should have appreciated our opportunities to sing for airline crew members. Within the year, terrorist activities began. Hijackings became frequent and occasional airport massacres took place, forcing airlines to increase security. The invitations to the cockpit became a thing of the past.

After singing to the Burmese crew, we returned to our seats and quietly reflected upon the months in India. A stewardess handed us a current newspaper. August 1, 1971. The headlines read, "Doomsday for 300,000 children." With East and West Pakistan at war, seven or eight million refugees had poured into India, escaping the birth pangs of Bangladesh. The article described the deplorable conditions of refugee camps.

"The problem of malnutrition has assumed tragic dimensions. Three hundred thousand children (a conservative number, probably a million) will begin to die this week. With their stick-like limbs and ribs almost bursting through the skin, they hover on the verge of death." Scenes of the overcrowded city of Calcutta haunted our memories. Our hearts ached for the unimaginable suffering.

Another month of ministry followed in various oriental locations. It was a challenge to shift mental gears and sing in other languages. The trip around the world proved to be more than mere adventure. Our hearts had been touched. In Burma where Christians are oppressed by the Communist government, our fellowship was greatly appreciated. We could not forget those we met in Japan, in Taiwan, or in tiny apartments in Hong Kong where Christians are few in number. Most of all, our hearts would return often to the memories of India.

"For You have been a strength to the poor, a strength to the needy in his distress..." (Isa. 25:4a)

There is more than one way
to cross a body of water!

When needing to cross a stream,
Janice and Faye caught a
ride on a bullock cart in India.

To complete the trip around the world,
the twins would be taking a portion of their return
by ship. They looked forward to the relaxation.
Little did they know the Lord would
have a purpose for their being on board.

After the 1971 trip around the world, the evangelistic team had booked passage by ship to sail from Hawaii to the mainland. However, circumstances led some of the team to fly home. The Rostvit Twins and Patty Briggs were the only team members to travel by ship—the *S.S. Monterey.*

13

On the High Seas

⌒ by Janice ⌒

———————————⬤———————————

The soft tropical breeze of the Hawaiian Islands whipped our hair as we stood at the railing of the ocean liner's upper deck. We watched with fascination as other passengers threw colorful streamers to their friends and relatives on the dock. The well-wishers clung to the ends of the streamers, like a final extended touch and farewell. As the ship edged away from the dock, the streamers stretched and finally broke the ties, trailing their colors into the churning waters of the Pacific. The ship nosed its way into the aqua blue waters. We remained by the rail until the volcanic cone of Oahu's Diamond Head disappeared beneath the horizon.

Our trip around the world was coming to an end. Patty Briggs was the only one from the evangelistic team who was still with us. A relaxing sea voyage from Honolulu to Los Angeles lay ahead. Fascinated to be on a ship for the first time, we three eagerly set out to explore each deck. We located the dining room, souvenir shop, entertainment hall, the swimming pool, and a place to play table tennis.

There were also bars, cocktail rooms, and dance floors. We walked past a glass-walled room where people sat at gambling tables. We were taken aback to see that one man who had a drink in hand and was placing a bet, wore a clerical collar!

A truth pricked our conscience. Our Christian duty hadn't ended with the summer's singing schedule. Our lives needed to set an example even while enjoying this voyage. "Be ready in season, and out of season..." (II Tim. 4:2) Our witness for Christ was as important on this ship as it had been during the months of crusades.

When at last we returned to our cabin, we entered into a time of prayer, aware that the Lord may have some particular purpose for our being on board. Following the prayer time, Faye picked up a leaflet from the dresser. It was a schedule of activities on the ship.

"Look, a church service is scheduled for Sunday. Let's volunteer to sing for it," she said.

The two of us made our way to the purser's office. The gentleman thanked us but refused our offer. He explained that hired singers would be presenting the special music. We had puppets and Bible teaching materials in our luggage, so we suggested we could gather children for an hour each afternoon. Again he informed us that the ship's schedule was also filled with children's activities.

Often when we think of serving the Lord, we think only in terms of what we can do. Perhaps more important is who we *are* and, in particular, *whose* we are as evidenced through our attitudes, actions, and reactions. We were young at the time, in our mid-twenties, and though certainly not spiritually mature, we knew we were called to set an example.

> "Let no one despise your youth, but be an example to the believers in word, in conduct, in love, in spirit, in faith, in purity." (I Tim. 4:12)

After leaving the purser's office, we went out on the deck and prayed. "Lord, we offered what we can do. If you want us to be of witness in some way during these days on the Pacific, please open our eyes to the opportunities."

The first day passed without incident. We three relaxed, read, and took time to write in our diaries. We located a theater on a lower deck and watched *Song of Norway,* the life story of composer Edvard Grieg. Of Norwegian descent ourselves, we longed to see Norway, so we enjoyed the beautiful scenic photography of the movie. As there was no charge, we went to see another film the following day. Movies had not long been given ratings, so we didn't know what to expect. This one was rated PG. In our ignorance, we assumed G stood for "good," and PG meant "pretty good." I did wonder what the "pretty good" meant and by whose standards.

Five minutes into the movie, my conscience bothered me. Bad language was prevalent, and there were inferences that immorality might take place. I knew I should leave. The progression of acceptance always leads downward. As we once heard, "First one hates, then tolerates, then assimilates." A verse came to mind, "... if there is anything praiseworthy, meditate on these things." (Phil. 4:8) The movie was not filling my mind with good things. Satan tried the procrastination ploy: the movie might get better. If you leave, everyone will notice.

"Let's go," Faye whispered. It was all the encouragement I needed. Later when we were relaxing on the deck, a woman stopped to talk.

"Girls, you were smart to have left the theater early. You set a good example. The movie only got worse. I wish I had exited when you did."

Sunday's church service was worshipful and uplifting. The captain was in charge. He read a lengthy passage of Scripture. His reading was done in such a meaningful way that we felt God's presence in the reverent atmosphere.

That evening the opera singers who had sung beautifully during the worship service were to present a concert. Musicians were tuning their instruments when we entered the entertainment hall and found seats. We enjoyed the performance. As it drew to a close, the lights dimmed, the band struck up a lively tune, and people began dancing. Patty and the two of us exited by a side door.

Early the following morning we strolled along the decks. Sunlight brilliantly reflected off the calm waters of the sea. We dared not stay outside for long, however. Faye had developed some sort of sun poison, giving her skin stinging pains with the sun's rays. We retreated indoors. Faye was already rubbing an irritated forearm. As we passed by the sick bay, Faye paused. Her pensive gaze indicated her longing for something to relieve the itching and painful condition. Letting out a sigh of resignation, she moved on. She knew we couldn't afford to see the doctor since we had only $5 remaining. Later when we learned that there was no charge at the ship's medical facility, Faye secured an ointment that alleviated the symptoms.

Near the purser's office our attention was drawn to a large board on which were posted some pictures. A notice indicated that the ship's photographer was charging $5 per print. We scanned the photos with interest, yet with no intention of buying. We thought it best to save our last $5 in case of some unknown expense.

While we were standing there, the waiter who manned the nearby buffet table said, "Say, twins, there's a crew member looking for you. I don't know where he is now, but he was here just a little while ago asking if I'd seen the twins."

We thanked the man and went on our way. As we passed the laundry room, a lady stepped into the hall and called to us, "Excuse me, there's a crew man looking for you twins."

"Yes, thank you, someone else just told us. Do you know his name, or where he is?"

"No, sorry," she shrugged her shoulders.

We decided we had better not retreat to our cabin. As we neared the entertainment hall, one of the band members confronted us.

"Hey, girls, I've been meaning to talk with you." Naturally, we assumed him to be the crew member of whom others had spoken. "I noticed that you attended the concert here but then didn't stay for the dancing. There aren't many single girls on board. Why didn't you stick around?" He tried to persuade us not to miss the next evening's dance.

We explained that we choose not to dance because of our own Christian convictions. The man respected our stand rather than scoffing at us.

We moved on. Waves of the Pacific had become choppy, and we, not having "sea legs," staggered through the inner corridors of the ship. So intent were we on watching our footing and trying to avoid bumping into walls that we were taken completely by surprise when a man hurried around a corner. I tried to jump to one side but nearly lost my balance as the ship was rolling in the opposite direction. The gentleman quickly reached for my arm to steady me.

"It's not easy to walk when everything is rocking, is it?" We found ourselves looking up into the face of one of the ship's officers. He went on to say that he had once been in a storm where the ship listed at such steep angles that it was just as easy to walk on the wall as on the floor. Gold bands on the sleeves of the officer's black uniform accentuated his broad shoulders and impressive six-foot-five-inch frame.

"Actually, I'm glad I ran into you girls—no pun intended." The man grinned, introducing himself as Gene. "I've been asking all over the ship if anyone has seen you. I have wanted to talk with you. I'm on duty now, but would you join me in the snack shop at four o'clock for a cup of tea?" We each nodded. Then he hurried off down the corridor.

At the appointed time we met not only with one officer, but with four. Two were radio operators. Another, Ralph, was the first mate. Gene explained why they wanted to talk with us.

"Word has reached us that you three have not been taking part in some of the ship's activities. This is a pleasure cruise, so we find it unusual to have passengers who take no interest in the cocktail parties, the gambling, the drinking, or the dancing. We are curious to know why you are on board."

"To get across the ocean," Faye said with a grin, but then went on to explain how we were returning from India and the Orient. Since the cost by sea was about equal to that of flying, we were having a relaxing trip back to the mainland. Being assured that we were enjoying the voyage, the men turned the conversation toward getting acquainted. They asked about our mission travels, and we inquired concerning their families and work. Time passed quickly, and soon the officers had to get back on duty. We were pleased that before the men left, Ralph suggested we meet again.

Over the course of the final days, we met with the men several times, usually over a cup of tea. Each time, they had more questions and a progressively deeper interest in spiritual matters. The three of us tried to respond with sensitivity to each inquiry, hoping to draw them to Jesus, the only One who gives true purpose to life and satisfies the longings of the inner man.

After each discussion, we would often chide ourselves for not having answered the questions as well as we should have, or we would wish a particular passage from scripture had come to mind. Keenly aware of our inadequacies, we prayed all the more fervently, hoping that our efforts might help rather than hinder the workings of the Holy Spirit. At the same time, a deep sense of gratitude overwhelmed us for the privilege of seeing God at work.

> "They shall lift up their voice, they shall sing; For the majesty of the Lord they shall cry aloud from the sea." (Isa. 24:14)

On one rendezvous with the officers, Ralph pulled up a chair at one end of the table and reached for an ashtray. Striking a match, he lit a cigar. Even while exhaling the smoke, Ralph spoke, giving the impression of determination to direct the flow of conversation. His questions confirmed that he had been thinking about our previous discussions. At times I wondered if certain questions masked his feelings as his expression conveyed obvious inner conflict.

At long length the struggle surfaced, the Lord triumphing in a spiritual battle. Ralph, eyes brimming with tears, muttered as if thinking aloud, "I should keep my promise." Then he turned to look me in the eye and proceeded to explain. "I was a born-again believer, and I had planned to enroll in a seminary to train for a preaching ministry." He paused, taking a deep breath to curb the tears and to steady his voice. "I went back on my word and went to sailing instead."

Ralph turned a disgusted gaze toward the cigar and gestured with that hand as he remarked, "Now who across the table would even know I'm a Christian?" With a determined firm twist, he snuffed out the cigar in the ashtray, then looked at us to relate his new resolve.

"Girls, I have seen through you that serving the Lord is a great privilege and that it's a life to be lived at all times. I want you to know that as soon as I've finished this term of sailing, I intend to keep my promise and train for the ministry. I want to be God's man, doing His will."

I felt certain that God would use whatever Ralph had been through in this interim to make him a better minister. An expression of peace had settled on Ralph's countenance since he was no longer struggling with indecision. A glance at Gene revealed that Ralph's stand had made a profound impact on him.

"I would like the captain to meet you girls," Ralph said. "How about it?"

Our eager expressions were a sufficient response. Soon Patty, Faye, and I were following the officers past the "crew only" signs to the bridge. Though we had met the captain at the ship's church service, now we were formally introduced. We were pleased when he asked us to sing a song for those of the crew who were on duty. An official photograph was taken of us with the captain, which he later autographed and gave to us.

The officers invited us to return to the bridge again that evening so they could demonstrate how the ship's navigational system operates at night. When we arrived, Ralph was bent over a map. He looked up with a smile of acknowledgment and motioned us to join him. He proceeded to point out exactly where the ship was located.

I overheard Gene commenting, "Ralph is a very conscientious worker." Ralph, too, had heard the remark.

"I wonder how I'll do with a flock," he whispered under his breath.

After explaining some of the other equipment, Ralph opened a side door and urged us to step onto a walkway on the starboard side of the bridge. We pulled our sweaters around our shoulders as the cool night air hit us, carrying its moist scent of the salt spray. We stood silently at the rail, enthralled by the fluorescent glow of the waves and their roar as they struck the ship's hull. I thought of God's Spirit at creation moving over the face of the waters. Ralph broke the silence.

"Whenever I watch the ocean, I'm reminded of God's mighty power and majesty. This is where I come to talk with Him." We all sensed the Lord's presence.

"The voice of the Lord is over the waters; the God of Glory thunders, the Lord is over many waters." (Ps. 29:3)

Our final day on board found passengers busy packing and the crew occupied with their tasks of preparations for mooring the ship at the docks of Los Angeles. As a result we had no further opportunity to speak with the officers. In time we were lost among the hundreds of others who edged their way toward the exit ramp. It wasn't until we were on the gangplank that I thought to glance back over my shoulder to the decks above.

"Faye, Patty, look!" I exclaimed. There again on the wing of the bridge stood the officers with whom we had shared a spiritual experience. It seemed fitting that our final memory should hold them in the very place where the previous evening we had all sensed the powerful presence of God. In our hearts we thanked the Lord for His hand, which directed this encounter on the high seas. We whispered a prayer for those whom the Lord was now drawing to Himself.

At that moment, the officers spotted us in the crowd. It warmed our hearts to see each of them waving enthusiastically with both arms. Quickly dropping our hand luggage, we returned the fervent farewell. What an incredible voyage God had provided, including this final moment. Very likely we would never pass this way again, yet we sensed we had been granted a touch of eternity.

Other passengers then pressed, so we felt compelled to move on. We picked up our flight bags and instruments and proceeded with the flow until the officers were hidden from view.

Now we needed to direct our attentions toward reaching the Los Angeles airport to catch our flight home. We had no idea how far it was to the airport, and we had never given it thought that our meager $5 would fall far short of covering taxi fare. As they say, "Ignorance is bliss." Just then, from the noise of the hustle and bustle around us came a voice.

"Are you the Rostvit Twins?"

We turned and hesitantly nodded assent, but remained perplexed, wondering who this stranger was. His broad smile, the warmth of his expressive eyes, and his relaxed nature immediately set us at ease.

"My name is Charles Richards." He explained that he was the minister of a nearby church that supported the Johnstons, one of the missionary families with whom we had worked in Taiwan. "I heard through them of your plans to arrive by ship, so I thought I'd come down and offer the three of you a ride to the airport."

We readily accepted his offer and had precious fellowship as we rode. We told him about the opportunities on the ship, as well as our unforgettable experiences in Taiwan, India, and other stops. We felt all the more humbled and grateful to this kind servant of the Lord after we had reached the airport. The more than sixty miles we had traveled was proof that the Lord by His providence had again supplied our need.

14

Believe It or Not

~ by Faye ~

———————————————◘———————————————

How often does God meet our needs, but we fail to recognize His provision? Janice and I have had several experiences that have made us more aware of God's presence in everyday circumstances.

Three Dollars and Thirty-One Cents

We were in the midst of a busy spring tour through the central states. One week had remained unscheduled, so we decided to attend a Bill Gothard's Basic Youth Conflicts Seminar in Minneapolis. This would be a few hundred miles out of the way as our bookings before and after that week were to be in southern Missouri.

We budgeted for expenses and went to Minneapolis. We were spared the cost of a hotel room since relatives David and Judy Stahl invited us to stay with them.

On Sunday following the seminar, David asked us to present a concert at their church. To our surprise the congregation gave us a love offering.

The next morning we traveled southward toward Missouri. We discussed the insights we had gained from the seminar. Part of the studies dealt with recognizing the Lord's provision and praising Him for it.

"It would be interesting to add up all our expenses for this week and see if that offering covered it," Janice said.

We listed every expense: notebooks for the seminar, lunches and snacks, and gasoline. We were within a hundred miles of returning to southern Missouri, so we had filled the gas tank for the last time. Janice announced that the offering nearly covered our expenses. It was only $3.31 short. We rejoiced and thanked the Lord for His obvious provision.

In a few miles, we stopped briefly to see a friend who had asked us to visit her if we were ever in the area. When time came for us to leave, our friend handed us three dollars, for what reason we cannot recall. When we were on our way again, a thought occurred to me.

"If we add these three dollars to the amount of the offering, the Lord's provision is even more spectacular. Now we lack only thirty-one cents of having been reimbursed for the entire amount," I said.

A short time later we reached the end of the journey. I opened the car door and stepped out. You can imagine my astonishment when I saw three dimes and a penny lying on the pavement.

First Class Transportation

Returning from a trip to South America, our flight arrived late into New Orleans. A port for frequent drug traffic, security was tight, and clearing customs was a slow ordeal. Everyone's luggage was being thoroughly hand searched. Anxiously we checked our watches, fearing we would miss our connecting flight to Oklahoma City.

The evangelist with whom we were traveling did catch the flight, but we missed it. We boarded another one within the hour. While in flight, a well-dressed gentleman seated across the aisle from us struck up a conversation. Before landing he offered to take us where we needed to go. Remembering our parents' warnings about not riding with strangers, we thanked him for his kind offer but refused. As we deplaned we lost sight of the man, but when we all assembled in the baggage claim area he once again approached us.

"I can take you right to your destination," he offered. When we politely refused again, he asked, "How do you plan to get there?"

"By taxi," we admitted.

"Please let me save you the expense. Your location is right en route for me, and it would be absolutely no trouble."

Finally we consented and followed him to the parking lot. When the man set down his suitcase beside a sleek, black Rolls Royce and reached into his pocket for the keys, our mouths dropped open. We echoed in unison, "Is this your car?"

Already placing the key in the slot, the gentleman glanced in our direction. With a glint in his eye, obviously amused by our wonderment, he said, "I wouldn't be unlocking it if it weren't mine." Soon we were nestled in the plush seats and feeling like we were VIPs. As we rode, our eyes were busy examining every inch of our luxurious surroundings: the soft leather upholstery, the reading lights beside our heads, the tray table that could fold out in front of us, the lighted mirror.

Suddenly it dawned on us that we had been riding for quite a while. Realizing that the man was obviously doing us a great favor, I whispered to Janice, "Shouldn't we offer to give him some money for gasoline?"

"He's already wealthy."

"That's true, but that doesn't give us the right to take advantage of him." Feeling somewhat timid, I leaned forward and offered to help share expenses. The man laughed.

"Don't even consider it. Like I said, it is right on my way. Besides, I'm a Christian and the Bible tells us that it is more blessed to give than to receive. So, I'm the one receiving the blessing."

Just as he finished speaking, we reached our destination. With words of gratitude to our kind benefactor, we stood by our suitcases and watched our royal transport pull away. We had actually ridden in a Rolls Royce!

Later that evening as we were unpacking, Janice reached into the flight bag to find our money. Two dollars was all we had! Since an evangelistic association was covering added travel expenses for that trip, we hadn't needed to worry about how much money we had. I blushed as I realized what a mere pittance we would have given the wealthy man if he had accepted our offer.

"Guess what, Faye," Janice broke the silence. "I doubt if two dollars would have been enough for taxi fare." Out of curiosity, she called a cab company to inquire concerning the price from the airport. The answer was $5.50!

"Before they call I will answer..." (Isa. 65:24a) Truly the Lord had met our need even before we knew we had one, and He had provided it FIRST CLASS.

Strangers Help Us

"Hey, we've got troubles! Our headlights are growing dim." It was a dark night on the prairie of eastern Colorado. We had chosen the back road to Lamar to enjoy the solitude of a less traveled highway. Now with the alternator going out, we questioned the wisdom of that choice.

"There's a car up ahead. Why don't we catch up to it and make use of their headlights?" Janice pressed harder on the accelerator. "How far do we have to go?"

"I'm not sure, maybe thirty or forty miles."

When we neared the compact car, Janice switched off the headlights. For more than twenty miles we trailed the car in our ghostlike fashion, hoping that nothing else would be draining on the battery.

Meanwhile in the compact car, a husband and wife were oblivious to the fact that another vehicle was trailing them. They were headed for their home in Lamar.

"Now what?" Janice pointed to the red warning light on the instrument panel. "Are we causing damage to the engine if we push on farther? I wish that car would stop, so we could tell them our dilemma."

At that precise moment, the man in the car ahead of us reached for something and accidentally tripped a lever, which unlatched the hatchback of his car. He decided he'd better stop and shut it. He flipped on his right turn signal and steered the car onto the shoulder. When he got out of his car, he was surprised to find us coasting to a stop behind him. Janice switched off the ignition and slipped out of the driver's seat. The man made a you-needn't-bother gesture with one hand.

"Thanks for stopping, but I don't need any help. I just need to shut the back."

"But we need help." Janice explained our predicament. Moments later with a small suitcase in hand, we climbed into the backseat of their car to ride to Lamar twelve miles away. The lady turned to talk with us.

"To think, my husband and I were just discussing how the Lord works in marvelous ways!"

"Yes, my sister had just said she wished that car would pull over, and then you flicked on your blinker."

"It probably was no accident that I tripped that

hatch lever when I did," the man said. We drove past the church in Lamar. All was dark, so we asked our "good Samaritan" couple to leave us wherever there was a public telephone. They drove us to the local Loaf 'N Jug. We thanked them, and they went on their way.

The convenience store had a take-away food section with some booths. I sat down at one of them while Janice stood by the phone.

"This is the Rostvit Twins. Our car broke down twelve miles out of town and now we're waiting at the Loaf 'N Jug…" She let out a low discouraged sigh when she hung up the receiver. Slipping into the other side of the booth, she muttered, "I got an answering machine. I hope the preacher checks it when he gets home. We may have a long wait."

We had no options. My thoughts whirled. It seemed strange that God so obviously helped us to get into town, and now we were stranded again. It made me wonder if He had a purpose in our being at this convenience store. A young lady sat alone at a booth opposite ours, her expression downcast. Could God have put us here at this time so that we could help her? I was about to get up and go strike up a conversation with her, when she slipped out of her booth and approached us.

"Excuse me. My name is Pauline Atkinson. I couldn't help overhearing your phone call. You're in quite a predicament. Will you two come home with me? If your friends don't call you back tonight, you'll at least have a place to sleep."

About then Pauline's pizza was ready, so we picked up our bag and followed her to her car. As we rode through a residential district Janice said, "You looked sad when you were sitting at the Loaf 'N Jug. Is there anything wrong that you care to share?"

"Oh, no, to tell you the truth I was just disgruntled because the pizza I had ordered wasn't ready when I arrived. But now as I think about it, maybe God delayed the pizza on purpose so that I'd be there to help you."

At the Atkinsons' home we called and added another message on the preacher's answering machine. Before his arrival we had opportunity to get to know the Atkinson family. They admitted that because of some personality conflict they had quit attending their church. They longed to get involved again. We invited them to the church where we were to sing for a week's revival.

During the days that followed, we saw them several times. Shortly afterward their son gave his heart to Jesus. Later we received a letter from Pauline in which she said, "I thought the Lord had me at the Loaf 'N Jug so that I could help you, but now I realize that He also had you there to help me." Pauline had a thought-provoking comment at the close of her letter. "I felt God was urging me to ask you to go home with me that night. I hesitated while making the decision. Now I wonder how many great things we have missed out on when we don't listen to the Lord."

Oops! There She Blows!

It was a hot summer afternoon. We were traveling with our parents in their mini-motor home returning to Colorado after visiting relatives in Minnesota. I took a turn behind the wheel. The air conditioner was on, but I hadn't thought to check the heat gauge. We pulled into a rest area to fix something to eat, taking a space at the far end of the parking lot.

I had just climbed out of the driver's seat when POW! Steam rolled out from under the hood. The radiator cap had blown, and we discovered that the plastic cap's flanged edge had broken. Nobody carries a spare radiator cap. To top it off, this was a Sunday afternoon. If we could get to a town, there would be no stores open.

The radiator had quit steaming, but we left the hood

propped open. Just then a rusted-out van pulled into the slot next to us. We wondered why they had stopped so far from the facilities. There were plenty of parking spaces closer. Two men got out.

"What's your trouble?" one of them asked. When we explained, the older man went to the back of his van. He returned with a brass radiator cap and handed it to Dad. Screwing it on and finding it to be a perfect fit, Dad reached for his wallet.

"What do we owe you?" he asked. When the two men refused payment, we thanked them.

"What area of Heaven do you come from?" Dad asked. The younger man laughed.

"Angels in disguise, hey? Well, your angel's name is Gary," he said, with a glance toward the older gentleman. The two men immediately got back into their van and started it up. Without stopping to use the facilities, they drove straight back onto the highway. That seemed strange. Angels? Admittedly we had to wonder.

15

We Pray, Yet Worries Prey

∼ by Janice ∼

———————————◁▷———————————

By 1973 we were no longer traveling with an evangelistic team. Missionaries in various countries were inviting us to come alone. We could sing in the language and the missionary could do the preaching without need of an interpreter. But traveling alone added stress. We would need to attend to details that previously had been arranged for us. The following stories involve a return trip to India—incidents that reminded us that God attends to details.

We Need $519

"You'll have to pick up your tickets and pay for them on Thursday." The travel agent's statement came as a shock. The smiles melted from our faces.

"And…pay for them then?" Faye hesitantly repeated.

"Can't we send you our final payment from the East Coast?" We still had a month of travels before flying out from New York. We had been counting on the money we would make during that month of concerts.

"I'm sorry, it is not our policy to accept payment by

mail. I'm afraid you'll have to pay for them next week," the travel agent said.

"But we are more than $500 short," we protested.

"The Lord will probably lay it on your shoulder the last day." Her remark was not intended to be sarcastic. She had seen how the Lord had supplied our funds the last minute on other trips. She was now demonstrating more faith than we felt.

We, too, knew the Lord had provided before, yet doubts crept in. Would He provide again? I berated myself for negative thoughts. I prayed, "Lord, I want to believe. Help my unbelief." We timidly asked the agent the exact costs and found we still lacked $519. We pulled open the door of the office to leave. On the one hand, the overwhelming obstacle implanted a seed of worry. On the other hand, it ignited a spark of faith in our all-powerful God who specializes in the impossible.

As we walked down the sidewalk, we determined to tell no one, assuming that even the slightest mention of it might make someone feel obligated to give. Jesus said, "Ask, and it will be given to you..." (Mt. 7:7) Yes, we would ask no one but God. He could lay the need on the hearts of the persons through whom He wished to supply.

During the following days, we prayed and waited. Nothing came. When worries surfaced, we would remind ourselves of Philippians 4:6:

> "Be anxious for nothing, but in everything, by prayer and supplication, with thanksgiving, let your requests be made known to God."

When Thursday came, we still lacked the full $519. We hoped for something in the mail. Two letters came. One held a check for $50. Now we lacked $469. The other letter was from the Mission's Director of Ozark Bible College, Harvey Bacus. It read, "Please come to my office." When we entered his office, Harvey greeted us warmly and then reached into a desk drawer.

"I have something for you girls." Pulling out a check, he handed it to us. It was $469. We both looked up at Harvey, our eyes brimming with tears.

"Did you know we needed this exact amount today?"

"No," he smiled. "It was determined a month ago that today's chapel offering would be for your India trip."

God knew that was the very day we would need the funds. Why does He often wait until the last day? Probably because then we'll notice and give Him the credit and the praise.

The Taxi, the Hotel, and the Train

As time neared for us to catch our flight, our thoughts became preoccupied with all we would be facing upon reaching Delhi. Three things troubled us. First we dreaded going by taxi from the airport because the drivers often take advantage of foreigners, charging extra. Secondly we worried about a place to stay, knowing we didn't have enough money for a tourist hotel. Our third concern was whether or not we'd be able to secure reservations for the express train to central India. Many times the reservation list gets filled and no more passengers are allowed on board. The particular express train we needed goes only twice a week.

These three worries were a matter for prayer. Yet even after praying, we continued to fret. We had to keep reminding ourselves, "Do not fret, it only causes harm." (Ps. 37:8b) Before leaving New York, mail was forwarded to us. Faye came to me, waving the aerogramme.

"Janice, we have a letter from the Dass family." We had known Kandasami and Shanti Dass when we had sung in southern India four years earlier. We had informed them of our return to India, though we did not expect to get to the south. Now their news came as a surprise.

"We've moved to Delhi. I am the chauffeur for the British Ambassador, so I have a car at my disposal. I will meet you at the airport and take you wherever you need to go." We knew then that we would not have to deal with the taxi drivers. For that we thanked the Lord.

After more than a day of long flights, we descended the stairs of the airplane and set foot again on Indian soil. Despite travel fatigue, it felt good to be back in India, the country whose people had won our hearts.

We passed through customs, then scanned the waiting crowd. There we spotted Mr. Dass looking taller than his actual stature in his chauffeur's uniform. His lips curved into a humble smile and his gentle eyes met our searching gaze with a glint of joy.

In his quiet way, he greeted us and reached to take our luggage in hand, motioning us to follow.

While we made our way through the crowd, a young Indian lady caught our attention. She looked familiar, her face pockmarked from an earlier bout with small-pox.

"Sukmani, is that you?" I asked. We had met her in Madhya Pradesh on a previous tour. She nodded with a smile, obviously pleased that we had recognized her.

"What brings you here?" Faye asked.

"I live in Delhi now. I'm a maid in a rich family's home. I came to the airport specifically to see you and to ask if you would consider staying with me tonight."

That meant we would not have to search for a hotel. We gratefully accepted her offer, anticipating the fellowship with this sister in the Lord.

We three turned to follow Kandasami Dass. Before reaching the car I caught sight of another familiar face. An elderly gentleman was striding toward us.

"Mr. Zamans, what a surprise! We didn't expect to see you here!" We recalled having met this Christian brother when at the Kulpahar Mission.

"I heard through some friends that you were returning to India. Today while I was in Delhi on business, you came to mind. I assumed you would be traveling by the Utkal Express across to Madhya Pradesh. So I hope you don't mind, but I bought your train reservations for you." He was reaching into his pocket to retrieve the tickets. We only needed to reimburse him.

As we all rode together into Delhi, we rejoiced. It was of mutual encouragement for us to share how God had providentially answered our taxi-hotel-train prayer through each of them.

One Hundred Dollars

After the two-day train trip to Madhya Pradesh, we crammed into a rickety bus with twice its load limit for the final leg of our journey. I tucked the flight bag beneath my seat. We were eager to reach the missionaries' place near a village called Sitapur.

Sometime after dark during the ten-hour ride, I reached for something in the flight bag and was alarmed to find that the main pocket was unzipped. Frantically I felt around for the pouch of money. It was gone. Stolen!

People had been getting on or off at every village. There was no way of knowing who had taken it. A feeling of despair swept over us. We had failed to carefully guard the funds that God's people had entrusted to us. We had just cashed $100 that we would need for train travel later. That's what was missing. Now we wondered if we would be short of funds.

The bus took us to the tribal area where Bernel and Joan Getter have been laboring since 1947. Only one week later, we received a letter from a church in the United States. It included a check for $100. Never in all our years of travels had money been sent directly to us in a foreign country—and never had we needed it more! God had a hand in it.

The Silk Saris

While at the Getter's home, a letter came from Eldon and Dorothy Weesner, missionaries with whom we would be serving in south India. In the letter they explained that one of our obligations in Madras would be to sing in a concert hall. They were inquiring if we had a sari that would be dressy enough for the occasion.

We had comfortable cotton saris for village use and nicer ones of nylon or chiffon for use in the towns. Some of them draped beautifully, but Mrs. Getter knew that none of ours were good enough. A concert among higher caste Indians would require a silk sari with interwoven threads of real gold. Joan took us shopping.

Thanks to Mrs. Getter's bargaining abilities, we got the saris for 200 rupees each. The 400 rupees out of our meager funds seemed a monumental expense.

1974: On this trip to India, Janice and Faye saw
the Lord's hand providing their various needs,
including these silk with gold trim saris.

Later we were in Madras to participate in that concert. The Weesners were relieved to see us dressed appropriately for the occasion. Following the concert, a gentleman approached us.

"Would you two mind coming to the All-India Radio Station? I would like to record an hour's program of your songs in various Indian languages." We agreed.

The following day after we had finished the taping, one of the men of the radio studio told us to come with him to the office so he could work out the finances.

As we walked with him, my thoughts clouded again with worry. I assumed we were having to pay for radio time—another unexpected expense!

When we reached the office, the man handed us a check.

"You're paying us?" Faye asked.

"Of course. We pay our performers." The man appeared amused by our exuberant thanks. We were overcome with emotion to see the amount, 400 rupees—the very price of our silk saris! God had again supplied our needs.

The Midnight Stranger

We fidgeted, impatient, in the baggage claim area of the Nagpur airport. Suddenly a man's voice with the distinct Indian accent broke the silence.

"Are you waiting for somebody?" What a loaded question to ask ladies at midnight! We were hesitant to admit we were merely in transit, a three-day journey from one mission area to another. Faye ventured to give an answer that would evade the man's question.

"We are waiting for a suitcase," she said.

"Oh," he looked surprised. "Do you not have all your luggage? What's missing?"

"We just arrived on the flight from Madras. We're lacking a suitcase just like this one." I pointed to the raspberry-colored Royal Traveler beside me.

"I'll go and search for it," the stranger assured us. Moments later he returned, suitcase in hand. "I found it still on the airplane. It had lost its tag." Had this man not located it, we would have lost that piece of luggage. We expressed our gratitude. However, then came the loaded questions again.

"Is somebody meeting you?" he asked. Again we tried to avoid a direct answer.

"We'll be traveling on," I said.

"There are no more flights tonight," he informed us.

"Ah...yes, we know. We will be going on by train."

"To what town?"

"To Bilaspur," we admitted.

"That train will not be leaving until noon. You will need a place to stay for the night. Come with me." The man snatched up our two suitcases. My heart was in my throat, wondering where the stranger would take us. He was still talking as we all headed for the exit.

"We can catch a bus into town and find a hotel," he said. At least public transport sounded safe enough. We rode in silence into Nagpur knowing that small talk could be misconstrued as flirtatious. When the bus stopped beside a small hotel, the gentleman again took our bags, indicating for us to follow. He spoke with the desk clerk, then turned to hand us a key.

"Your room is just down this hall. Lock the door. You will be safe. Breakfast will be available after 7 A.M. I have also arranged for a taxi to come for you so that you will not miss your train. If you need any further help, here is where you can reach me." He handed us a business card.

Feeling assured that the man had only good intentions, I reached into my shoulder bag to locate some rupees for a tip. The man immediately held out a hand in protest.

"Please," he said. "Don't insult me. I'm a Christian, and it looked like you needed help."

A Christian! Only one percent of India's population is Christian. We reflected on God's power and His ability to help us—this time through a fellow Christian.

"Let all the inhabitants of the world stand in awe of Him." (Ps. 33:8)

16

Impossible!

∼ by Faye ∼

Storm clouds blackened the already dim skies of dusk. The Colorado Springs Airport was at a standstill. We were eager for our Australian tour, but if we missed connections in either Phoenix or Los Angeles, what then? We passed the time making light conversation with our parents, yet nervously keeping an eye on the clock. With each minute that ticked by we were losing precious time. An announcement confirmed our fears —our flight was canceled. They booked us on a later flight, but that also meant a later one out of Phoenix and a tight connection in Los Angeles. If we miss connections, would we have to reroute at greater expense or cancel the trip?

I walked over to the window. The pouring rain and fierce winds drove sheets of water across the empty runways. I looked up.

"Father, I know You don't want us to worry, but sometimes it's hard not to. Please make Your purpose clear so we may glorify You even in this present problem."

Finally our flight was called. Two hours had been lost. We said our good-byes. The look in Mom's and

Dad's eyes mirrored our anxiety. They promised to keep praying.

En route to Phoenix our plane was buffeted by the turbulence of the storm. Lightning flashed at intervals in the otherwise blackness of the night, creating an eerie glow on the clouds. Strangely enough through the fearsome display of God's power we felt clothed in His presence. In silence we savored the peace that settled over us. He who is the master of the wind and rain was riding with us through the storm.

Like a rude awakening, we snapped out of our reverie when a voice on the speaker system announced the times and gate numbers for connecting flights in Phoenix. The old worries surfaced again. Our connecting time was to be three minutes! The beauty of the peaceful assurance God had given us on the flight was discarded as we foolishly chose to cling to the tattered security blanket of our anxieties. At least the departure gate for our flight to Los Angeles was close. When our plane docked, Janice and I each sprang from our seats and made the mad dash.

Three minutes! As impossible as it had seemed, we made the change. As soon as we boarded the plane, a steward pulled the door into place and secured it. While the aircraft taxied toward the runway, I glanced out the window and murmured, "Good-bye, suitcases." There certainly wouldn't have been sufficient time for them to be transferred.

Upon landing in Los Angeles we barely had time to reach the international terminal. It was evident we were the last to check in. The only seats left were those in the smoking section. We would be separated from each other and would have seats that couldn't recline.

We clipped along at a trotting pace to the departure lounge. The flight was already boarding. At the gate we took time to call home and assure our parents that we had made the connections and were now boarding our flight to Sydney.

"Oh wonderful, our prayers are answered!" Dad said with a sigh of relief. "But I wonder how long it will take for your luggage to catch up with you." We had been concerned about that, too.

Later during the nonstop, fourteen-hour flight across the Pacific, I pulled the Bible out of my flight bag and began reading. One verse particularly fit our situation.

"A righteous man may have many troubles, but the Lord delivers him from them all," (Ps. 34:19 NIV).

Making my way out from my seat, I went back and shared the verse with Janice.

"Yes, I thank God we caught the flight," Janice reiterated. "But it is impossible for our suitcases to have made it."

After passing through immigration in Sydney, we proceeded toward the baggage service office with the intention of filling out a "lost luggage" form. The moment we entered the baggage claim area we stopped in our tracks, dumbfounded. There were our two suitcases alone on a carousel! How had they gotten there? That verse in Psalms may as well have been scrawled in bold letters across the sides of the cases. "A righteous man may have many troubles, but the Lord delivers him from them all." (Ps. 34:19 NIV). I turned to Janice.

"Maybe the Lord is reminding us that the word impossible is not in His vocabulary."

"For nothing is impossible with God." (Luke 1:37 NIV)

"You'll Never Make It"

At another time, around the world from Australia, the two of us walked briskly toward the baggage claim area of London Heathrow Airport. We were tired from our flight from South Africa. While Janice waited for our luggage, I telephoned the shipping lines to book passage on the ferry bound for Norway. I was informed that if we could get to the Liverpool train station by noon, there would be a train going directly to Harwich on the east coast, and it makes a connection with the ferry. With luggage in hand, we scurried to the underground subway station in the airport. We felt some relief to settle into a seat and be on our way. I glanced at my watch. It was 10:55 A.M.

"Good, we should have plenty of time to reach Liverpool station by noon." I noticed that the distinguished-looking gentleman seated opposite was leaning forward with a scornful look.

"You expect to reach Liverpool in an hour? Ha! You'll never make it!" The strong British accent only accentuated the sharpness of the disparaging onslaught of words. "I have ridden this line often enough to know. Good luck to you, but you'll probably only reach Holburn by noon. From there you'll transfer to another subway to go to the Liverpool Station. It's doubtful that you can get there before half-past twelve." The man pointed to the subway's route map located above the windows. Holburn was the twelfth stop. The man continued in his mocking tone.

"London is a big city, you know. You can't expect to get anywhere in a matter of minutes. You'll never make it!" With that, the man settled back and flicked open his newspaper.

We felt hurt by the cutting words and sat mutely staring at the floor. We wondered what we should do if we would miss the train and consequently also the ferry. That particular ferry direct to Norway went only once a week. We didn't have sufficient funds to book a flight instead.

The subway came to a stop at the first station. I checked my watch. Twelve minutes. Eleven more stops to the Holburn connection.

"The man was right," I murmured in whispered tones to Janice. "At this rate we won't even get to Holburn by noon." Her response showed resolve.

"God specializes in the impossible, doesn't He? Let's pray." She closed her eyes.

After praying, I kept a check on my watch. The next station came in six minutes, then four, then two, each stop shaving off a few more minutes so that hope again crept into my being.

By the time we reached Holburn it was 11:32. We were poised, luggage in hand so that when the doors opened, we shot out as though propelled from a cannon. Along the platform, through a corridor, and down a long flight of steps we flew, taking no time to stop and rest. Just as we arrived at the lower level of the underground, a subway train appeared from its tunnel. The moment it stopped we boarded, the doors snapped shut behind us, and we were on the move again even before we had taken our seats. Time: 11:36.

Minutes again ticked away as the subway sped through the subterranean passageways, stopping briefly at stations along the way. At 11:55 we reached the Liverpool Station. When the doors snapped open, we were off and running toward the exit stairs. We had two long flights to climb to reach ground level with no time to spare. It felt as though our suitcases became increasingly heavier as we steadily trudged up the seemingly endless staircase. Upon reaching the top, I spotted a clock. 12:00! Time had run out! Just then an announcement echoed through the huge edifice.

"...train connecting with the ferry for Norway now departing from platform #14." We were by platform #1.

"Oh no, we can't miss it when we're this close," I said. Without a moment's rest, we pressed on. By the time we reached platform #14, the sweat was rolling, our mouths were dry, every muscle ached, but joy flooded over us—the train was still there.

"Oh thank you, Lord!" We swung our things up into a car and climbed aboard. Just then the train gave a jerk and began to move. "Wow!" I sighed, "If only that Englishman could see us now! He said we would never make it, but with God's help, we did!"

"Yes, but without his strong words we wouldn't have hurried," Janice said. "Perhaps God prodded that man to give us the sense of urgency so that we could make it."

1979: Janice and Faye's grandparents immigrated
to America between 1898 and 1904.
The twins have returned to the land
of their forefathers numerous times.

17

Norway, Land of Our Heritage
~ by Janice ~

———◉———

The ferry eased away from the docks at Harwich. We watched from the deck, each of us engrossed in thought. Norway! We were going back for a second visit. For the first time since our mad dash through the London subways, we allowed ourselves the luxury of dreaming.

Faye and I reminisced about our first tour of Norway two years earlier in 1979. We sang in Oslo as well as cities along the rugged west coast. However, since our family's heritage is Norwegian, our greatest joy was to meet our relatives. Nearly eighty years had passed since our grandparents had sailed from those shores.

We had traveled by bus into the valley called Setesdal where picturesque farms were nestled against the mountains. The friendly driver recognized us, having seen our photo in the local newspaper. He dropped us off near a church beside a fjord. Olav Rostveit met us. By his appearance and mannerisms, he looked like dad's brother instead of a cousin. We felt instantaneous warmth of kinship and greeted him with a hug. To a stoic Norwegian, Olav later admitted that such a show of affection had totally surprised him. Yet, at the same time he felt loved and accepted.

"That's the Aardal Church. Your grandparents, Ole and Anne, were married there before they left for America," Olav said, before driving us to his farm.

I gazed at the octagon-shaped chapel in its pristine condition.

"That very building?" I asked, "They were married in 1902."

"That was built in 1827," Olav said.

Norwegians are experts when it comes to building and maintaining log structures.

That afternoon we met Olav's family and were shown keepsakes and old photo albums. Ingebjorg, Olav's 87-year-old mother, pointed to the cliff that bordered the eastern side of the farm. She spoke no English, but we understood her to say that our grandfather used to cut timber on the mountain, then ski off the cliff to come home. Each night we slept to the sound of a waterfall cascading from the cliff.

When we were alone with Ingebjorg, we appreciated the opportunity to augment our Norwegian. She was a patient, loving teacher. Since her eyesight was poor, we read aloud from her Bible. If we would mispronounce a word, she would not only correct us, but she would proceed to tell the entire Bible story.

Olav showed us around the farm. "Your great grandparents moved here in 1893. They came from the Rostveit farm forty miles east of here. ("Rostveit" is the original spelling of our surname.) It took them three days by horse and wagon. Your grandpa was fifteen years old then."

"What is the meaning of Rostveit?" Faye asked. "Is it rose vale?"

"No, *tveit* could be a vale or a small clearing in a wilderness area. However, *ros* was an Old Norsk word meaning horse. So, Rostveit is a small place for grazing three or four horses." With a grin he added, "I'm sorry I can't promise you a rose garden."

Each day we met more of Dad's cousins. Paal Vollen took us up the valley to Bygland to give a program at the high school. They appreciated our efforts to speak and sing in Norwegian, but they especially enjoyed our ventriloquist dolls. From there, Paal had taken us to his home higher up the hillside overlooking the fjord.

"This whole area has been home to your ancestors for hundreds of years," Paal said. He gave us a book that told the history of each farm throughout Setesdal. With this we were able to trace our genealogy to the early 1400s. What a treasure!

We walked to the adjacent farm owned by one of Dad's uncles, Eivind Sandnes. The lanky ninety-eight year old cheerfully greeted us. His son Olav and daughter Gunhild lived with him. Gunhild spoke some English. We were fascinated with all the wooden items in their home that were colorfully rosemaled (rose painted): trunks, bowls, cupboards, boxes, and several *kubbestols* (chairs carved from tree trunks.) Olav had done the carving, and Gunhild had rosemaled them.

Gunhild took us upstairs where she had two *bunads* (local costumes) for us to wear. Of all the *bunads* throughout Norway, Setesdal is known to have one of the most unique styles. The dresses had two layers of thick wool felt. They were as heavy as packs! When Gunhild heard us commenting about the weight of the dress, she shocked us by telling us that with a third layer it would become a wedding dress.

Our next adventure was to ride to Bygland to view a folk museum. Still clad in all the bulky woolen layers, we laughed hysterically as we crammed into Uncle Eivind's miniature car. Paal Vollen was eager to take pictures of us clad in the local attire. He wrote articles for the Setesdal newspaper. To walk among log buildings dating from the 1600s made us feel as though we were experiencing Norway's past, especially while we were wearing the costumes. One of the old log homes had rosemaled trunks, a built-in intricately-carved bed, a heavy table, and a cradle.

"This home used to be in our family. My older brother slept in that cradle when he was a baby," Gunhild said.

It was fascinating to hear how the art of rosemaling first became popular. In the 1600s, homes were dark and gloomy. Log walls were blackened by soot from a central fire pot. Smoke was released through a vent in the roof. In the early 1700s, the idea was introduced to decorate the interiors of churches. Elevated pulpits, railings, and altars were carved and painted in bright colors. At the same time lead-glass windows came into fashion, filtering sunlight into churches and homes. Charmed by the beauty in the churches, people began carving rose and scroll designs on cabinets, storage chests, and built-in beds. Rosemaling was most popular from 1725 until 1875.

Varying emotions surfaced when we saw the humble cottage where our grandmother, Anne, had been born and raised in Lauvdal. Gunnar Vollen, our second cousin who speaks flawless English, told us that Anne's father was known for his faith and often was the singer at the church in Bygland. When Anne, the eldest of seven children was eighteen, her father died in a logging accident. Three years later, the mother died, leaving Anne to care for her siblings until they were separated into homes of relatives and neighbors. The little cabin, barn, and storehouse have been maintained as a museum representing a "Cotter's Farm."

We had never met Grandma Anne. She died when Dad was only twelve. By meeting her relatives in Norway, visiting her birthplace, and learning of her history, we felt as though we knew her. The hardships she endured at an early age helped her face the rigors of pioneer life when she and Ole immigrated to the wilderness area of northern Minnesota.

The relatives in Norway had kept letters from Anne. She had missed her beloved homeland. She had hungered for a taste of *multe* (a yellow berry that grows high in the mountains.) She had longed to see her siblings and their families. It was Anne's faith in God that sustained her.

One of our Dad's memories of his mother was that of sitting on her lap in a rocking chair and listening to her read from her Norwegian Bible. Anne's Christian heritage had also been passed on to us.

"One generation shall praise Your works to another, and shall declare Your mighty acts." (Ps. 145:4)

We felt a keen sense of belonging especially when singing in the church where our great grandfather used to sing.

On the Lord's Day, with a sense of reverence, we entered the Bygland church and sat in one of the boxed-in pews. We admired the workmanship of the interwoven logs in the cross-shaped sanctuary. The worship service began with organ music echoing from the balcony. As we made our way to the platform to sing, I eyed the lone pew beside the altar. A hundred years ago the church singer, our great grandfather Paal Gun-steinson Lauvdal, sat there along with his family. What an honor to sing in the same place, bridging the decades.

We had come to love our relatives, many of whom had a genuine faith. Before we left the area we were touched by what Gunhild had expressed.

"Your grandmother left here nearly eighty years ago, and now you have come. What a joy that you have not forgotten God."

❧

Our reminiscing ceased. By this time the ferry had reached open waters, out of sight from England's shores. Overcast skies blended with the choppy, gray waters of the North Sea. A chilling wind had picked up. With a shudder and a glance of agreement, we took refuge inside. Finding a place to relax, our conversation turned to the days ahead. We eagerly discussed our dreams for this second visit to Norway. We voiced six specific desires:

Desire #1. To share our faith with one whom on our previous visit had exhibited a frankness, openness, and a perceptive awareness of spiritual matters.

Desire #2. To buy a double-knit wool sweater for our father.

Desire #3. To acquire a certain book we had seen in a shop window on our first visit. We could still visualize the picture of people in traditional costume painted on its cover.

Desire #4. To purchase a silver brooch, a type peculiar to Setesdal, as a gift for our sister, Laura Jean.

Desire #5. To meet our Great Uncle Paal Lauvdal,

the only remaining sibling of our grandmother, Anne.

Desire #6. To see the original Rostveit Farm—and even see inside the house.

As we discussed these desires, we knew it would be highly improbable to achieve or receive any one of them.

#1. The relative with whom we desired to share in spiritual matters indicated in a letter that he would not be as open as he had been previously. Knowing the reserved nature of Norwegians, we determined not to initiate any witness. Better that one be drawn into the kingdom than pushed. Pushing can be like forcing a rosebud to open prematurely. We would wait on God's timing.

#2. The cost of the sweater we wished to buy was prohibitive. When in Norway before, we had found them to be in the $100-$160 range. We wished they could be around $25, but knew it was an unrealistic expectation.

#3 and #4. Securing the book or the silver brooch also seemed impossible because we would be staying on a farm and would not be near any shop.

#5. An opportunity to see our great uncle seemed out of the question. We would be staying with relatives on the other side of the family.

#6. There was no sense in hoping to see the Rostveit Farm as it was forty miles from where we would be staying and gasoline costs were high.

We held no expectations of receiving any of these desires.

Upon landing in Kristiansand we were met by Olav Rostveit. He apologized because he could not park his vehicle closer to where we disembarked. We would have to walk about three blocks. In the second block, I spotted a sale rack of sweaters that had been set out on the sidewalk. As Faye and Olav were about to circumvent the rack, I took a quick look at a tag to calculate what the price would be in dollars. To our advantage the U.S. dollar had gained a better rate of exchange on the European market since President Ronald Reagan had taken office.

"Please wait," I urged. "These sweaters are the equivalent of only $25!"

Moments later we were riding inland into the valley called Setesdal, the road paralleling the clear waters of Byglandsfjord. At one point I glanced down from watching the scenery to admire our new purchase. The sweater was even the color we had desired. Psalm 37:4 came to mind, "Delight yourself also in the Lord, and He shall give you the desires of your heart." We marveled that God had granted one of our six desires—even at the price we had assumed impossible.

Within the day we were talking with the relative with whom we had hoped to share in a spiritual vein. Contrary to what he had told us in a letter, he was immediately very open and filled with questions. It was as though his reticent nature wished to keep his feelings hidden but God's Spirit, at work in his heart, would not allow it. Again we thought of Psalm 37:4. God had granted two of our six desires, this being the most important of them all, for which we thanked Him.

The following morning we received a phone call from Ommund Vollen, Dad's cousin. He invited us to their home for coffee. We enjoyed our midmorning visit. When it was time to leave, Ommund rose from his chair.

"We have something to give you." Our gaze fell upon the book in his hands—the very one we had seen on our previous trip. My jaw dropped open with amazement! Faye thumbed through the treasured gift. Our obvious pleasure was a delight to our relatives. A few days later another of Dad's cousins called.

"Have you ever met your great uncle, Paal Lauvdal?"

We hadn't. He offered to drive us the forty miles eastward to the valley where the Lauvdals lived. So we were granted yet another of our desires. Great Uncle Paal, though 91 years old, was delightfully young in heart. His son Olav's family also visited with us. At one point his wife, Ingebjorg, pondered, "Rostveit. Rostveit. Isn't there a farm named Rostveit?"

"Yes," I replied, "it should be just a few kilometers from here, near Dølemo."

"Is it still in your family?"

"No, an elderly lady by the name of Signe Baas lives there now."

"Signe Baas! Why, I know her, but I haven't seen her in years," Ingebjorg exclaimed. "Why don't we go and visit her?"

We could scarcely believe our ears! Within minutes we were on our way to the Rostveit Farm. Signe greeted us warmly and invited us in. As we stepped through the doorway into a part of our past, we were as excited as children at Christmas. To think, a century ago our grandfather was a toddler in this very home!

Surpassing the joy of sharing in this piece of heritage was the thought that God had orchestrated the events so that we could be there. He had allowed us to see the inside of the home—something we had imagined impossible. God knew this desire even before we had voiced it aboard the ferry.

"Before a word is on my tongue you know it completely, O Lord." (Ps.139:4 NIV)

With our limited knowledge of Norwegian, we found it difficult to follow the conversation between Ingebjorg and Signe, so we were content to sit in silence. Why was God being so good to us, granting us our dreams? I thought again of one of Dad's sayings, "I think God delights in doing these little things if they don't interfere with His bigger plans." I smiled while silently praising God. "Lord, I need not know why You give at some times, or hold back at others. I need only to know You and to delight in You!"

To add to our joy we discovered that Signe was a Christian. Faye and I sang, "*Han er min sang og min glede. Han er min Herre og Gud.*" (He is my song and my joy. He is my Lord and God.) Signe was overjoyed! She clapped her hands in delight and her eyes glistened. The smile from her heart gave her wrinkled face a youthful appearance. When we joined in prayer before leaving the farm, Signe's cheeks were stained with tears. We embraced the dear lady. The Rostveit farm was still in our family after all—in God's family.

Our days in Norway passed quickly and all too soon it was the last evening. At 8 P.M. Faye and I retreated to our bedroom to do some packing so that we would not feel rushed the following morning. With a contented sigh, Faye picked up the sweater, shaking her head in disbelief.

"It is incredible that we received five of the six things we had named on the ferry! Let's see now, what was the sixth thing?" Then she answered her own question, "Oh yes, it was the silver pin."

I paused momentarily from my packing and turned to the window. Billowy clouds floated overhead, rolling their shadows across the lush dandelion-studded fields of the farm. The late evening sun's rays shone upon the pine-covered slopes that framed the nearby fjord. While viewing the beautiful scene, I sensed God's presence. Not intending any irreverence I gazed heavenward and candidly asked, "Where's the brooch, Lord?" God must have a sense of humor. The words were scarcely out of my mouth when the doorbell rang. The two of us went into the living room to see who had come. The man at the door was a local silversmith.

"I heard you have some American visitors. So, I thought I would drop by with some jewelry items I have made and see if your guests would be interested in any of them." He opened a box displaying several items. There lay the exact brooch we had wanted to buy for our sister.

I could imagine God was smiling with amusement and pleasure. He had indeed chosen to give us all six of our hearts' desires.

Several times at Twin Conventions, Janice and Faye have won trophies or medals for the "Most Identical."

18

Twin Incidents

∼ by Faye ∼

———————○———————

At times we forget what confusion we cause by being identical twins. Here are a few incidents in our travels—what we prefer to label "twincidents."

"What Now, Lord?"

"Should we do something to help her?" I had stopped Janice during our brisk morning walk and had pointed out the teenage girl on the park bench. "As we passed, I saw she was crying."

"What can we say to her? We don't speak Portuguese," Janice said. Our three-month tour of Brazil had only begun. We had learned songs in Portuguese and were giving concerts each evening, but any attempt at speaking had to be done in Spanish. Here in the city of Goiania, we enjoyed a walk before breakfast. We usually stopped in the park to have a time of prayer before returning to the Kennedys' home. I gazed once more at the girl whose back was turned, head bent. Maybe it was no accident that in that brief second when she had turned our way, I had seen the glisten of tears, illuminated by the early morning sunrays.

"I can't ignore her. Maybe she understands Spanish. She might just need some comfort."

"You're right; we can at least try," Janice said.

As we approached the girl, her problem became obvious. She was pregnant and in extreme pain. We sat on either side of her, listening as she explained her dilemma. We understood the gist of her story—she was walking to a home where she worked as a maid. When the pains came, she felt she could go no farther.

Leaving Janice to pray with the girl, I ran across the road to find a telephone and call the Kennedys. Jerry worked with their mission's mobile medical unit, so I hoped to get some immediate help. Aleta answered the phone. My heart sank. Jerry had already left with the mobile unit for the far side of the city. However, Aleta went on to say that there was a hospital only two blocks beyond the park. Returning, I gave Janice the news. In the meantime, she had learned the girl's name was Lydia. She was eighteen.

When I asked Lydia if she could walk two blocks, her dark eyes, still brimming with tears, cast a frightened glance in my direction. Without a word, she shook her head.

Lord, what next?

As rare as it was to see anyone in the park that early in the morning, a motorcyclist stopped nearby. I asked him if he would take the pregnant girl to the hospital. He understood my Spanish and helped Lydia to get seated sidesaddle on the back. He drove slowly as we trotted alongside. As the girl was being helped into the hospital, it crossed my mind that perhaps they would refuse to admit her without payment.

"You stay with her, Faye. I'll run back to the Kennedys to get our money," Janice said.

With the girl still weeping, I spoke to the receptionist. I wasn't understanding the lady's replies, but one thing I did understand—she was refusing to admit Lydia.

"*Yo voy a pagar* (I will pay)!" I was growing frustrated with the delay.

Lydia, knowing the reason for the refusal, turned and walked back outside.

I continued to try to reason with the lady, but finally was made to understand that this was only a children's hospital and they didn't handle deliveries. I found Lydia seated on the lawn, moaning with pain. I sat beside her, put my arm around her and looked heavenward.

"What now, Lord?" Would I be delivering a baby on the lawn of a hospital?

Just then a taxi driver approached, signaling for us to come to his car. I didn't understand what he said, but Lydia got up and motioned for me to follow. She eased herself into the backseat of the taxi, but I refused to enter. I tried to explain that I had no money and had to wait for my sister to come. The driver was still urging me to get in. I had no idea where he was intending to take us.

With a pained expression, Lydia suddenly pleaded in Spanish, "*Tenga prisa* (hurry)!"

Reluctantly I slipped into the front seat. As we sped away, I glanced back in hopes of seeing Janice. She was nowhere in sight.

A few minutes later Aleta Kennedy and Janice arrived. Seeing no sign of Lydia or me, Aleta, speaking in Portuguese, asked the receptionist where the pregnant girl went. Aleta was confused when the lady pointed to Janice.

"Ask her," she said

"No," Aleta tried to explain. "We just got here. A pregnant girl was brought here a few minutes ago. What room is she in?" With impatience, the receptionist turned to face Janice.

"The girl was with you. You tell her where she is!" Janice, who had been struggling to understand the lady's Portuguese, now got the picture.

"Aleta, don't you get it? She thinks I'm Faye."

Aleta couldn't help but see the humor in the situation. She tried in vain to convince the receptionist that Janice was a twin. The lady, still confused, looked accusingly at Janice.

"You went outside with the girl. What did you do with her?" Aleta and Janice stepped to the doorway and surveyed the grounds.

"Where could they be?" Aleta said.

A guard at the entrance had witnessed the whole drama, first me with the girl, and now Janice and Aleta. He surprised the two when he spoke up.

"I can tell you!" The grin on his face betrayed his amusement over the twin confusion. "They left in a taxi."

"Left in a taxi? Where did they go?"

The guard only shrugged.

Meanwhile, Lydia and I had ridden a couple of miles through the city. Lydia was trying to explain where we were going. It was something about a government medical facility for the poor. Arriving at the hospital, the driver motioned for me to remain in the taxi. Then he gently led Lydia inside to get her checked in.

When he returned, he drove me back the way we had come. As we rode, I understood the driver to say, "I could see that you, a foreigner to our country, were being a good Samaritan to this girl." As we pulled to the curb by the children's hospital, the driver did a double take to see Janice standing on the lawn.

Janice, thrilled to see me, was eager to learn where I had been. There would be plenty of time to explain later. I offered payment to the taxi driver, but he refused, indicating that he would be a good Samaritan along with us.

That night we prayed for Lydia. We longed to learn of her condition. Yet, we had no idea how to locate that government hospital. What if there was payment needed? We had failed at our duty. The Biblical good Samaritan had promised to return and take care of any costs.

"'Look after him,'" he said, "'and when I return, I will reimburse you for any extra expense you may have.'"
(Luke 10:35b NIV)

While riding with Jerry and Aleta the next day, I recognized an intersection. "I was here in the taxi! We turned down that street."

"Let's see if we can find the hospital," Jerry said, eager to follow up on Lydia. He steered the car down each street I indicated until the hospital loomed ahead.

At the front desk, a man told us that two teens named Lydia had checked in the previous day. I wished I had thought to ask her surname. The man was curt, insisting that only family members were allowed to visit patients. Beyond the desk was a locked, barred gate leading into the hospital. We all felt the disappointment of not being able to enter.

Just then a tall nurse came striding down the hallway on the far side of the gate. A smile swept across her face as she called out, "Hello, I'm so glad you have come." At first I thought she was speaking to someone else, but it was obvious that she was looking at us. Bewildered, I glanced over at Jerry.

"Is she someone you know?"

"No, I've never seen her before," Jerry said.

"Please come in." The nurse was unlocking the gate. As we all walked down the corridor, Aleta explained about Lydia. Reaching the maternity ward, we learned that Lydia was no longer there. With medication they had successfully stopped her premature labor. Her husband had come for her by evening.

We were glad to know that all was well. Although we would never see Lydia again, we continued to pray for the remainder of her pregnancy.

"Let each of you look out not only for his own interests, but also for the interests of others."(Phil. 2:4)

At the Tourist Attraction

When we sang at the Flying W Ranch Chuck Wagon Suppers (mentioned in Chapter 3), we also worked in some souvenir shops before the mealtime. One day a man shopped in Janice's store, then came up the steep hill to my shop. When he spotted me, he looked bewildered.

"Didn't I just see you in that other store?"

"No, my twin works down there," I said.

"Yeah, sure. That was you! You must have come up a different way." Without giving me a chance to reply, he added, "I'll prove it." With that, he turned on his heels and dashed down the hill.

If he wouldn't believe me, I decided two could play his game. I picked up the intercom that linked the shops.

"Janice, no time to explain, but a man is running down to your store. Breathe heavily as if you've been running."

Janice, though baffled by the message, obeyed. She was puffing when the young man burst in the doorway. He pointed.

"Aha, I thought so, I'll beat you back up the hill." Then he dashed out again.

My intercom buzzed. "I don't know what's going on, but he's coming back your way," Janice said. I was emerging from a storeroom when he entered.

"So—is that where the back entrance is?" he asked. "I will prove somehow that there is only one of you." Once more he was heading down the hill.

"He's coming again," I repeated over the intercom.

This time he stationed a friend with Janice, telling him not to let her out of his sight. Then he trudged up the hill for the third time. I was busy with a customer at the cash register when he came in.

"Aha, you do have a twin!"

"I tried to tell you." I shrugged.

"So you did," he grinned good naturedly, "and I've worked up an appetite for supper."

The Puzzled Policeman

On a highway in southern Texas we came to a routine police checkpoint. An officer approached and asked to see my driver's license. I handed him both of ours, assuming it was a check for illegal aliens, and that he wanted to see everyone's identification.

"Why do you have two licenses?" he asked as he stared at the identical photos. His question had taken me off guard, so I gave a quick reply.

"Oh, because there are two of me."

Leaning to look in at both of us, he laughed, "I can't wait to tell my wife about this one."

South Africa

On the 20th floor of an apartment building, Janice and I stood by separate elevators.

"I'll beat you to the lobby," Janice said.

My elevator arrived first, but stopped on another floor. A man stepped in and talked amiably with me. As we neared the bottom, the man turned to face the doors.

Meanwhile, Janice's elevator had taken her directly to the lobby. She had stepped out and stood facing my elevator.

When the doors popped open, the man stared at Janice, obviously wondering how I could have gotten out of the elevator. Then he whirled around and was equally shocked to discover I was still behind him!

How Did She Do That?

On a long flight over the Pacific, Janice went to use the lavatory. Moments later I went down the aisle. As each door registered "occupied," I stood to one side. A man joined me in line. We talked while waiting. When a lavatory on the left became available, I went in. Just after I had closed my door, Janice came out of the one on the right. The man stared at her as she passed. Later, in the airport, he saw us together.

"Oh, there are two of you!" He explained what he had seen on the airplane and admitted thinking, "How did she do that?"

Australia

I was already well out of sight in the large church in Perth when Janice entered the building. Glancing from side to side, she wondered which way to go. A bewildered teenage girl stood nearby.

"Didn't you just come by here?" she asked.

Janice's eyebrows raised. "I did? In that case, can you tell me which way I went?"

⌒⌒⌒⌒⌒

We have always felt deeply honored for the privilege of being twins. Our individuality has never felt threatened, but rather is personified by our plurality. Here is a twin song we wrote.

♪ ♪ IT'S GREAT TO BE A TWIN ♪ ♪

Now I'm a twin, as you can see, for as you look,
    there's two of me,
And that's a fact that no one can deny.
When we're together, we're aware that people
    often stop and stare,
Now could that be an indication why
Twins are a fascination all across the nation?

With twins there's no mistake,
People do a double take.
Which is which, and who is who?
"I am me, and you are you!"
I can say, "It's great to be a twin."

"Now I am glad that I am two."
"God chose to make me just like you."
For our genetic makeup is the same.
"I was born the new creation."
"I must be the duplication."
We wouldn't have it any other way.
It's fun to cause confusion. We are no illusion,
We are simply two of a kind.
A better friend we cannot find.
Just like two peas in a pod.
Our Creator we applaud!
I can say it's great to be a twin.

It's double pleasure, double fun.
To be a twin, we're two-in-one.
The mirror image is no accident.
Though others tend to scrutinize,
Eventually they'll realize,
The bond we share is no coincidence.
Twins are a dual creation, not a freak mutation.
Twins have not been cloned by man.
They are made by God's own plan.
We give God double praise.
To Him our voices raise,
We are glad that God has made us twins.
"Thank you, God. It's great to be a twin!"

♪ ♫ "Thank you, God. It's great to be a twin!" ♪ ♫

19

Music and Nature

∿ by Faye ∿

"For since the creation of the world His invisible attributes are clearly seen being understood by the things that are made, even His eternal power and Godhead, so that they are without excuse." (Romans 1:20)

Many times in our travels, we have seen animals respond to music—not only pets in people's homes, but wild animals as well. While we have been singing in buildings where windows are at ground level, squirrels, birds, or rabbits have drawn near to peer in and listen. Here are some unusual incidents.

Deer

Once while hiking in the Rockies we spooked a deer. As expected, it quickly bounded away. But, to our amazement, music stopped him in his tracks. The deer returned and stood motionless through an entire song.

Then it slowly ambled off. We sat down on a log and in ten minutes composed a song entitled "In a High Mountain Meadow."

A deer goes leaping across the high meadow.
    It's summer in the mountains so high
My heart is leaping with joy everlasting,
    for Jesus has given me life.   ♪   ♪

So I'll sing o'er the mountains, through the
    meadows, or wherever I'll be,
Yes, I'll sing, sing o'er the mountains,
    for Jesus has given me life.

The flowers are blooming in the high mountain
    meadow, all colors in brilliant array.
They turn my attention to God up in heaven,
    Who has taken my burdens away.
                                          ♪   ♪

It's peaceful and quiet in the high mountain
    meadow, with fresh air and blue skies above,
I run through the meadow with singing and
    laughter, my heart overflowing with love.

Chipmunk

While standing atop a high hill in New Mexico, Janice suggested we sing before making our descent.

"Isn't it most fun to sing praises to God when He's the only one listening?" She had voiced my sentiments exactly. But God wasn't our only audience that morning. As we began to sing, a chipmunk scampered to a rock just three feet in front of us, raised up on his haunches, and listened intently through the entire song.

Silver Fox

In the far northern coastlands of Norway a similar thing happened. It was night. We were seated on moss-covered rocks, watching the midnight sun—its rays shimmering across the Arctic waters. We sang softly and were astounded to see a silver fox cautiously approach us. He settled down within arm's length, content to stay as long as we kept singing.

Marmot

Janice and I enjoy opportunities to go mountain climbing. One time far above timberline we spotted a marmot on a boulder. The large, rock-dwelling rodent eyed us warily.

"Good morning, marmot. Would you like us to sing for you?" At the sound of my voice, the marmot backed away cautiously to hide behind a rock. However, when we began to sing, it crept back out into view, its bushy tail making an occasional contented swish.

By the time we were singing a third song, it had altogether lost its cautious stance and was stretched out with its front paws extended, one lapped nonchalantly over the other. I momentarily took my gaze off the rodent to take in the magnificent view of alpine meadows and ranges to the west. The morning sun touched the peaks with a golden hue. Then Janice nudged me. To my astonishment, not one, but two marmots were giving us their full attention.

Later after having gone to the summit and back, we stopped at the same spot.

"I wonder if Mr. and Mrs. Marmot are home," Janice said. "I don't see them."

"There's one," I pointed. He was far down the rocky crevice, nearly out of view. "Marmot, if you'll come home, we'll sing another song."

The marmot perked up, then came scampering up the rocks. It didn't pause until it had reached the same boulder on which we had seen it earlier. Looking up as if to say, "Okay, I'm ready," it settled down to listen. We sang and then bade our friend farewell.

As we hiked on, we discussed how animals always live in fear of predators. They must long for the day when they can live in harmony, as is written in Romans 8:22.

"We know that the whole creation groans and labors with birth pangs together until now."

We all await that glorious day when the lion will lie down with the lamb. In Colorado, the mountain lion will lie down with the marmot.

Fish

One day in the tropics we were snorkeling over a coral reef. Fish in a myriad of colors swam in schools. I yearned to reach out and touch them, but they kept their distance. Then we tried an experiment of singing through the snorkel tubes. The higher tones drew the fish. They swam so close that they were touching our arms, swimming between our fingers, and staring at us eye to eye through our goggles. What fun!

Cockatoo

The country was Papua New Guinea. After an hour and a half flight in a small aircraft and a six-hour boat ride on winding rivers, we arrived at the village of Girin. We were the first American guests of Bible translators Dan and Rosalind Wilcox. Nationals lined the river bank to greet us. As Janice stepped from the boat, a white cockatoo swooped down and landed on her shoulder. The bird had joined the welcoming committee.

During our days there, the cockatoo possessed a jealous claim on our friendship. Each time we were outside, he would fly to us. We would pet it and talk softly as we walked. Whenever we retreated into the Wilcox's home, the bird put up quite a squawk.

Worship services were held daily. The meeting hall had waist-high bamboo walls, then an open space to the palm-thatch roof. Janice and I sat on a bench by the wall. Our friendly cockatoo always came to worship. He would perch on the wall beside us, tip his head down to touch us, vying for attention.

One afternoon when we walked to the front to sing, the cocky cockatoo hopped along the wall to stay close to us. He proceeded to augment our duet to a trio. The audience snickered as the bird squawked with every song. During the remaining days, our little friend sang with us. He never did learn to harmonize, but we had to give him credit for "making a joyful noise to the Lord."

Chickens

One of the most humorous incidents took place in a remote village of Zaire, Africa. It is not uncommon during village church services to have dogs wander in and out, but on this occasion the special visitors were chickens.

Bible translator Mark Huddleston had introduced us. We stood to face the congregation. The church building at Bomili, a mud-walled structure with thatched roof, could comfortably seat about 150 people. Two doorways at the far end afforded entrance to the men's and ladies' sides of the sanctuary. There was one other doorway about halfway up the ladies' side.

As we proceeded to sing in Kibali, the local language, the people smiled with appreciation. Our attention, however, was drawn to a drama unfolding outside. In the open space near the main doors were two chickens pecking in the dirt. The moment we had begun to sing, they perked up, turning their attention toward the church. Then they broke into a clumsy run, crossed the open area, and momentarily disappeared from view. Skirting the side of the building, they once again caught our attention as they appeared at the side entrance.

Screeching to a halt in the doorway, they folded their

wings into place, glanced cautiously around, then slowly, should I say, reverently entered. A lady seated near the entrance kicked at the intruders, trying to shoo them out, but the two scurried past her and reached the main aisle. Looking both ways, they turned and strutted toward the front. Finding the front bench empty, the two fat hens hopped onto it eager to hear the concert.

The two of us had to suppress the urge to laugh as the contented chickens sat there looking up at us and listening to each song. Several times a lady on the second row leaned forward and tried to shoo the hens away. The two would just ruffle their feathers, give an annoyed glance in her direction, and again turn their attention to us.

When we finished singing, the chickens looked at each other as if to say, "I guess that's all." Then they hopped down. Slowly, in a rather dignified way, they walked down the aisle and to the side door. As though released from the confines that demanded reverent behavior, they tore into their wobbling canter, returning to the open space from which they had begun.

Dove

One year, Janice and I had taken the challenge to memorize the book of Luke. No matter where our schedule took us, early mornings provided the best time for working on a few verses. As we were returning from a trip to Japan and Taiwan, we had an overnight stop at a hotel in Honolulu. We set the alarm for 5 A.M. to assure us ample time with the Scriptures before we would have to return to the airport. The dawn was lovely. We sat out on the balcony of our room. A portion of the Scripture to memorize was,

> "What is the kingdom of God like? It is like a mustard seed, which a man took and put in his garden; and it grew and became a large tree, and the birds of the air perched in its branches," (Luke 13:18 NIV).

We found it easier to put the entire section to music. As we were singing, a bird landed in a tree near our balcony. Soon another joined it. Since the song required repetition for retention, we sang it softly over and over. It amazed us that more and more birds kept arriving. The grand finale came when a beautiful white dove gracefully descended, as if floating in slow motion. It hovered, suspended momentarily in midair, then landed right in front of us on the balcony's railing. We sat captivated in silent wonder.

When the dove flew away, we resumed our memorizing. As we were finishing the final verse, a soft, white feather floated down toward us, wafted here and there by a gentle breeze. Then it came to rest on the open pages of the Bible that Janice held. She slowly closed the book upon it, a fitting ending, and a precious souvenir of the dove, a symbol of peace.

Many times creatures have reacted to music. Here, a toucan bird in Brazil is perched on Janice's hand.

PART IV

Reflecting on God's Solutions to PROBLEMS

Just as pruning to a rosebush, strong wind to a tree, or the firing kiln to a piece of pottery, we are strengthened through trials. When enduring difficulties, one may ask, "Why, Lord?" God may not choose to reveal reasons, and that is His prerogative, because He is God. Let us remind ourselves,

> "Strengthen the weak hands, and make firm the feeble knees. Say to those who are fearful-hearted, 'be strong, do not fear! Behold, your God will come,...He will come to save you.'" (Isa. 35:3,4)

When we reminisce, is it not the trials we often remember? Without them we'd have little to talk about, or even laugh at. In this section, we marvel as we reflect on times when God answered our calls for help during travel trials.

> "My brethren, count it all joy when you fall into various trials, knowing that the testing of your faith produces patience. But let patience have its perfect work, that you may be perfect and complete, lacking nothing." (James 1:2-4)

STRANDED! When the twins got off the train,
no missionary was there to meet them.
Instead, they faced the scrutinizing
stares of the local people.

20

Stranded

∿ by Janice ∿

───────────⬤───────────

Little did we know when we awoke aboard the Indian train that by evening we would be stranded. The steam locomotive with its cloud of smoke was puffing rhythmically, and a light film of coal dust covered the metal slab bunks in the sleeper car. My face felt gritty. I sat up and brushed soot from my cheek. I stretched to relieve the stiffness from the night on the hard bunk.

In the dim light of India's predawn, I could see that Faye, too, was awake. She had already straightened her sari so that it was draped properly. We climbed down from our third-tier bunks and found available space to sit near the open window. The sun was nearly ready to break over the horizon. Smoke from early morning fires rose to redden the skies, and silhouettes of villages revealed the movement of inhabitants who had long been bustling about their daily tasks. We watched the passing landscape with its sights, sounds, and smells so peculiar to India.

My attention was drawn to a Hindu Temple perched on a hilltop. The sunlight highlighted its unique architecture, with its walls a busy configuration of intricately-carved gods and goddesses. I tried to perceive what my outlook would be if I had been raised in a country where one would develop a dependency on having images to worship. With a concept of a multiplicity of gods, how would one perceive the message of one all-sufficient God who demands that no images be made to represent Him—One who does not live in temples made with hands.

"So many hills here are dominated by shrines or temples. It must have been much like this in Israel, when for many generations the infiltration of pagan influences displeased the Lord," I said.

"Their land is also full of idols: they worship the work of their own hands." (Isa. 2:8)

"They also built for themselves high places, sacred pillars, and wooden images on every high hill and under every green tree." (I Kings 14:23)

I wondered if the Psalmist was looking at shrine-covered hills when he penned, "I will lift up my eyes to the hills—Where does my help come from?" (Not from these temples with their idols) "My help comes from the Lord, the Maker of heaven and earth." (Ps. 121:1,2 NIV)

My thoughts were interrupted when a family struck up a conversation with us. Learning that we were singers, they asked us to sing. Their request resulted in a spontaneous concert, using our repertoire in Hindi. Out of curiosity, other passengers gathered around. More requests were made for various Indian languages: Oriya, Telugu, Tamil and others. At least in this small way, we were conveying the message of our living God.

Our concert ended when the train pulled into a large station. Excusing ourselves, we retreated to our upper bunks to escape the usual pandemonium. The commotion commenced. People scrambled to enter the *bogi* (train car) while others were trying to exit. They were equally vocal toward each other. Coolies in faded red uniforms pushed their way through the press to secure the jobs of carrying people's *saman* (baggage and bedrolls). Beggars, hands outstretched, reached through open windows chanting in a nasalized drone, "*Bachsheesh, Ama. Bachsheesh, Ama*" (a pittance, Ma'am). Peddlers shouted in a monotonous tone, "*Garum chai! Garum chai*" (hot tea)! By the time we rolled out of that station, our "audience" had changed considerably and the opportunity to sing did not present itself.

The remainder of the day passed quickly as the train rumbled past miles of rice fields and humble villages. After sunset we made sure to check the sign at each station, so as not to miss our stop. The missionaries' letter assured us that they would meet us at the Bargarh station.

"This is it, Faye," I pointed to the station's sign, "Bargarh Road." I reached for my flight bag.

"Wait! The letter simply said Bargarh, not Bargarh Road!" Faye was apprehensive. "It might be the wrong station." The seed of doubt sprouted a moment's worry, but then I checked my watch.

"It's nine o'clock. That's when we were scheduled to arrive. Come on." I flung the flight bag onto my shoulder, grabbed an instrument, and made my way toward the door.

"How often are Indian trains on schedule?" Faye murmured, still hesitant. But she hefted a suitcase and followed.

We inched our way through the press of incoming passengers and breathed a sigh of relief to step down onto the station platform. We glanced around, scanning the crowd in search of familiar faces. No one was there to meet us!

Locals scrutinized us with curiosity. This out-of-the-way station was obviously not frequented by tourists, so we were now on exhibition. At least being twins, we are accustomed to people staring. The eyes of the on-lookers followed us as we made our way to a bench.

With the departure of the train, the crowd thinned. Some left the station, while others settled down for the night. It is common for Indians in transit to curl up and sleep at the station. The station manager, an elderly man, locked the door to his office. Catching sight of us, he looked concerned and approached to ask what our plans were. Though his accent was heavy, the man could speak English. When we reassured him that a family was coming for us, he looked relieved, politely bid us good night, and headed for the exit.

Minutes dragged like hours. Several times we heard a vehicle and Faye sprang to her feet to see if it was the missionaries' jeep. Each time she returned bearing the same disappointed expression. Nagging doubts kept gnawing at me. Could we have gotten off at the wrong station?

By 11 P.M. we were nodding with drowsiness and decided we might as well get some sleep. We unrolled our sleeping bags and joined the carpet of sleeping humanity on the station's platform.

At first light, we rolled up the sleeping bags so we would be ready when the missionaries arrive. We needn't have rushed. Again we were left to wait and wonder. By midmorning, we were hungry. The small, village-area station had no venders offering deep-fried *samosas* and other spicy or sweet goodies. We recognized the white-haired station manager when he came for work. As he spotted us, his face took on an expression of concern.

"Oh, the family never came for you! What a pity that foreigners to my country should be stranded at my station! Please, please, come. Have a cup of tea and some biscuits in my office." We gratefully followed. On the way, the man unlocked a storeroom where he placed our luggage.

As we sipped tea, we talked with Mr. Chukra. Since we still wondered if we might be at the wrong station, Faye ventured to ask, "Sir, could there possibly be another railway station by the name of Bargarh?"

"Oh yes," the man replied with the Indian sidewise wobble of the head, an affirmative gesture. Faye and I exchanged worried glances. Mr. Chukra was turning in his chair to point to a map on the wall. When he pointed to a place in Uttar Pradesh, another state, we breathed a sigh of relief. We were certain we belonged in the state of Orissa, so we no longer doubted we were at the correct station.

Our conversation became a discussion of beliefs. Mr. Chukra was a staunch Hindu and tried explaining the reincarnation cycle, that life is like one climbing a stairway trying to reach the top by one's own goodness. If by the time he dies he has not attained perfection, he comes back in one of the other seven forms of life: fish, birds, insects, or various classifications of animals. We contrasted his thoughts by telling about Jesus, who rather than being a man who became a god, was God who became a man. He lived a perfect sinless life, demonstrated His divine nature through many miracles, died as a sacrifice for our sins, and resurrected from the dead.

"Oh yes, I believe Jesus was God's son. We Hindus are taught not to disbelieve anything," Mr. Chukra admitted. It was one thing for him to accept Jesus among his many gods, but yet another to accept Him as his only Lord and Savior. He expounded further.

"We are all trying to reach the Supreme Being. There are many ways to reach Him: we Hindus through our gods, the Buddhists through Buddha, Moslems through Mohammed, and Christians through Jesus."

Although I am not convinced that logical arguments in themselves do much to change one's ingrained beliefs, I posed a question.

"You said that you believe that Jesus is God's Son, right?"

"Yes," he replied, giving us his full attention.

"Wouldn't you think then that Jesus, coming from God, would have more authority than all the others who were but good men attaining 'godhood'?"

He nodded again in the affirmative.

"If we accept that Jesus has superior authority, shouldn't we believe what He says?" I asked.

Again Mr. Chukra followed the logic and agreed.

"You say there are many ways to reach the Supreme Being, yet Jesus, who is God's son, says, 'I am the way ...no one comes to the Father except through Me.'" (John 14:6)

The Indian gentleman raised his eyebrows pondering the thought, as if to be saying, "You have a point." Perhaps a seed was planted. By the time our discussion was drawing to a close, we had been in the office over two hours. We stood to leave, thanking the station manager for his kindness and generosity. As he escorted us out, he asked, "What will you ladies do now? Where will you go?"

"We don't know," Faye said with a reassuring smile. "We must trust in the Supreme Being of whom we have been talking. He knows where we are, and He knows where the other family is. We will just keep waiting." The old gentleman smiled, apparently pleased that we weren't fretting.

"Here is the key for that room where I left your luggage," he said. "You can return it to my office later. But meanwhile, if you should want to leave the station area, your baggage will be safe. There is a tea stall across the road where you can get something to eat when you are hungry."

That afternoon we ambled over to the tea stall, a small mud-walled structure with a corrugated tin roof.

Attached to the back was the kitchen, a smoke-filled lean-to. We seated ourselves at one of the three small tables. What does one do in a restaurant where there is no menu and where the waiter speaks no English? Our first attempt at ordering was to use some words in Tamil or in Hindi for particular foods. That didn't work. The man apparently spoke only Oriya. We knew just a few words in Oriya and some songs—of little value in this situation. I pointed toward the kitchen and then to the mouth like a beggar would do. We hoped he got the message—to bring us something to eat. Anything.

The man gave some order to the person in the kitchen, then took two glasses from a shelf and poured hot tea for us. Oh nice! A large ant was floating belly up in mine. Faye leaned over to look.

"Hey, no fair, you got some protein." I flicked the ant out onto the earthen floor and proceeded to drink.

We watched with curiosity as the man picked up five dirty glasses from another table and carried them toward the entrance. Just outside the doorway was a Brahma cow with her nose in a water pail, slurping noisily. The man nonchalantly leaned with his shoulder to shove the cow away, then bent down to dunk the glasses a time or two in the bucket. The "washed" glasses dripped as he came back in and placed them on the shelf.

"It's not exactly a AAA restaurant, is it?" Faye said.

A man brought us a meal of rice and curried vegetables. His expression read, "Will this be all right?" We accepted with a smile, managing to say "Thank you" in their language.

When we finished, we held out money, trusting the man to collect the amount needed. Then we returned to the station. Taking the key Mr. Chukra had given us, we entered the storeroom and closed the door behind us. The room had one small window. Its panes were so dirty and paint streaked, they were nearly opaque. A ceiling fan was a welcome sight, but it was no surprise that it did not work. To the left were two rickety chairs with broken armrests. The only other piece of furniture in the room was a table upon which our luggage had been placed.

We seated ourselves in the chairs. Discouragement settled over us as we wondered what had delayed the missionaries. They had a long distance to drive. Had they had an accident? What would we do if they never came? In the flight bag nearest me was a paperback Bible. I drew it out and read Psalm 33. Many verses related to our situation. This paraphrased verse became our personal prayer.

"Lord, we are trusting in Your holy name. Let Your constant love surround us, for our hopes are in You alone." (Ps. 33:22 Living Bible)

We bowed our heads in the silence, grateful to have the little room for the privacy of a prayer time.

"In the day when I cried out, You answered me, and made me bold with strength in my soul." (Ps. 138:3)

While we were praying, we heard a bird. The chirping didn't sound faint enough to have come from outside so, we looked up. There on the ceiling fan was a sparrow. The Holy Spirit brought to mind verse 24 from Luke 12. It was as if the sparrow was giving us a reminder:

"Consider us birds: we do not sow or reap, we have no storeroom or barn; yet God feeds us. And how much more valuable you are than birds!"

Faye and I resumed praying, grateful for the sparrow's reminder that God knows our situation. We need not worry; but we must wait and trust. We marveled when, at the conclusion of our prayer time, there was no sign of the little sparrow. Where had he gone? How could he have gotten out? Only God knows.

We ventured outside for a moment. Near the end of the platform was a large bush loaded with sparrows! We enjoyed hearing the orchestrated clamor of their joyful singing. Another verse came to mind, "Do not fear. You are of more value than many sparrows!" (Luke 12:7b) Faye, with a glint in her eye, said, "Okay Lord, we get the message."

Returning to the storeroom, we pulled out our instruments and composed a song, the words of which were taken from Psalm 33:

LORD, WE ARE TRUSTING ♪ ♪

Lord, Lord we are trusting,
   we are trusting in Your holy name.
Let Your constant love surround us,
   for our hopes are in You alone.
God is pure and just.   ♪ ♪
He is worthy of our trust,
He is watching over us. We will praise His name,
To the Lord we cry,

On His love we will rely,
His protection He'll supply.
We will praise His name   ♪ ♪
All in one accord,
Everyone in all the world,
Let us love and fear the Lord, and stand in awe!
When the world began,
It appeared at His command,
See His works throughout the land,
     and stand in awe!

Time passed and soon darkness fell. When it was almost 9 P.M., time for another train to arrive, we realized we had been stranded at Bargarh for one full day. Suddenly in the gathering crowd we spotted familiar faces. The missionaries looked surprised.

"You're here already!" They had accidentally circled the wrong day on their calendar, so thought they were arriving just in time to meet our train. They apologized when they learned we had been stranded so long, but we assured them that we felt God had a purpose in the mix up. We had learned a lesson in trust, giving inspiration and incentive for writing a song. Then, too, we had a meaningful discussion with the station manager.

Some months later we learned that the seed planted in Mr. Chukra's heart was taking root. He wrote us a lengthy letter, remembering the day we were stranded at his station.

"You had complete trust in your God. I cannot forget your devotion to this Jesus and I want to know more about him." We kept up correspondence until the man retired and moved away. When we lost contact, we prayed that God would direct another to water the seed that had been sown. One plants, another waters, but God causes the seed of life to germinate and grow to maturity. "I planted, Apollos watered, but God gave the increase." (I Cor. 3:6)

21

Not By Our Plan

∼ by Faye ∼

───────●────────

"I'm exhausted!" I flopped onto the couch. "I wish we had more days to stay at home." We had just driven through the night returning to Colorado Springs and had a mere two days to repack for a trip to Taiwan.

"I agree." Janice was thumbing through the stack of mail that had accumulated in our absence. "We could stand to catch up on some of this correspondence."

"I'd better call the travel agent and let him know we're back in town. He still has our passports." I forced myself to rise from my comfortable position.

"Your passports?" Barry's voice indicated alarm (name has been changed). There was a long pause, "...I'm sorry, Faye, I shelved them and completely forgot to get your visas."

"What can be done?"

There was silence as he contemplated a possible solution. Finally, with a tone of urgency in his voice, he asked, "Can you be prepared to leave on a flight for Los Angeles within the hour? You could get your own visas before leaving the country." The idea sent my thoughts whirling.

"I'm afraid it would be impossible," I stammered. "We have just arrived home and haven't even begun to unload the car, much less pack for Taiwan."

"You're right. It was an absurd idea. Tell you what—I'll catch that flight myself, get your visas, and be back by tomorrow."

Barry did return the following day, but not with good news. He had missed his connecting flight in Denver so was late reaching Los Angeles. He had rushed to the Taiwan Consulate, arriving just as they were locking the doors. Though Barry had pleaded with them to reopen the office long enough to process our visas, they had refused. To add to his frustration, the office would be closed two additional days because of a Chinese holiday.

Depressed and guilt ridden, Barry returned to Colorado Springs. He feared we would be angry, but we felt sympathy that his noble effort had been made in vain.

"Don't blame yourself, Barry, perhaps there is a reason. Often when things do not go as planned, God has a purpose for the change," Janice said. "Besides that, we will appreciate having a couple extra days at home."

We sent a telegram to missionary Ted Skiles, who had invited us, informing him of our delay. It was interesting to learn later that Ted had been sick at the time. He had prayed, asking God's clear guidance, as he felt too weak to make the long journey to the airport to meet us. So our telegram had come as welcome news.

On our original departure date, we received a phone call from a Christian friend, Bob Stephenson. At the time, he was a Colorado state representative. He had a friend in the senate who wanted to get a letter to Taiwan. Bob asked if we would be willing to hand carry it. We felt honored. Perhaps this was God's purpose for our delay.

The following morning Bob brought the letter addressed to Taiwan's Public Relations Director Miguel

Huang. Janice tucked it into a zippered pocket of our flight bag.

Departure day came, and our flight to Los Angeles arrived on schedule. Both of us had dreaded the task of finding the Taiwan Consulate, but God knew that. Like a piece fitting perfectly into a puzzle, Shirley Lewis entered the picture. Shirley, who had heard us sing, had recently begun to correspond with us. She had asked when we would be coming to southern California. Eager to rendezvous with us, Shirley was at the airport, ready to take us wherever we needed to go. She would have no problem locating the Taiwan Consulate. She was a cab driver, and she knew the greater Los Angeles area like the back of her hand.

We gave thanks to the Lord. How better could He have orchestrated the circumstances, allowing an otherwise frustrating day to pass with ease. By evening we were back at the airport with our visas in hand.

Upon arrival in Taipei, we informed Ted Skiles of the official letter we were carrying. Arrangements were made to deliver it immediately. To our amazement, the following day a government courier delivered an invitation for us to attend a VIP dinner with all the heads of state. We had been slated to sing for a Bible study that evening, but the missionaries excused us.

"We don't want you to miss this opportunity. We'll be praying for you," they said.

Donning the nicest dresses we had packed, the two of us went to the government building. We were welcomed and escorted up a wide, slightly curved, marble stairway. The smooth steps reflected the glistening lights of the large chandelier overhead. We felt ill at ease in such elegant surroundings. Uncertainties dominated our thoughts. What was official protocol for greeting heads of state? Do we offer a handshake, or do the Chinese bow when being introduced? If so, is it a bow of the head, or from the waist? Should we bow lower than the man, or for a longer period of time?

At the top of the stairs Miguel Huang met us and thanked us again for having brought the letter from the senator. He directed us into a sitting room where we could enjoy a cup of tea while waiting for others to arrive. They filtered in: the speaker of the house, the vice-speaker, and the secretary general. We observed how each of them greeted one another, a slight nod of the head as well as a handshake. When Miguel Huang introduce us, we used the same manner of greeting and trusted we had done the right thing. Everyone received us graciously.

More guests arrived, this time fellow Americans— eight delegates of the Michigan legislature. We learned that the evening was a welcoming dinner for these visiting senators and representatives. Although we felt out of place among all the dignitaries, we considered it an honor.

One of the Chinese officials expressed formal words of greeting, then distributed gifts to each of the guests. We were surprised to be included. We received lovely jade necklaces, a book about Taiwan, and a paperweight bearing the government seal. Miguel explained that it was Chinese custom to give three gifts, rather than one.

We were ushered into the room where dinner would be served. There were eight Chinese officials, making eighteen of us in all, seated around a large circular table. Clams, shark fin soup, shrimp, crabs, sweet and sour yellow fish, roasted duck—one by one the seventeen-course meal, mostly seafood delicacies, was placed before us.

A Chinese meal, of course, would not be complete without chopsticks. Janice and I were thankful we were comfortable using them. Thinking back to our youth, we remembered the special occasions when our family would eat at a local Chinese restaurant. We had fun attempting to eat with the chopsticks. It was a game for us at first, but eventually we had mastered their use. Now, finding ourselves in a real Chinese environment with no fork to which we could resort, we were grateful for the training. God had used our childhood fun to prepare us for such a time as this.

Conversation was minimal. Occasional comments passed between the Chinese men and the United States legislators concerning the hopes for continued good will between our nations. When the evening had ended, Miguel offered to take us home.

"I have arranged for you to sing on a nationwide television program tomorrow. The program coordinator has requested a Chinese song, rather than English," Miguel said.

When we entered the apartment of Phoebe Rees and Debbie Mehrens, several participants of the Bible study were still there. Everyone was eager to hear about our evening's experience. After relating details of the dinner, we mentioned the arranged television appearance. Although it was late, the young people lingered, eager to teach us a song. Since we had not sung in the Mandarin language, we gladly accepted their help. The song they chose had some lines that were repetitious, yet others that were confusingly similar. It would take much practice to get it memorized. Even after the young people had gone, we rehearsed the song many times before going to bed.

The next morning at the studio we were briefed on the order of the program. First, we were to be interviewed by the program hostess, after which we would sing our song. The hostess was a beautiful Chinese lady with dainty facial features. She greeted us with a winsome smile. When all the details had been worked out, the program director suggested a practice run. The

interview went well. Then it was time for our song. One mistake after another rolled off our tongues. The attempt was a complete disaster. We were embarrassed, but grateful that the cameras weren't rolling.

As the studio crew took a break, Janice and I stepped to the corner of the large room, hiding from view beside some studio props. There we prayed, asking the Lord to clear our minds.

"Ten seconds to program time." We returned to our places beneath the bright lights, the cameras were rolled into position, and a signal was given. Again the interview went smoothly. Then we directed our gaze solely toward the cameras and began the Chinese song. With confidence our voices rang out, blending as one, and the words flowed with ease. We made it through the entire song without making a single error! As the large cameras swung away to focus on the hostess, we were free to step quietly from our places. We praised God for answering our desperate prayer.

The television exposure brought requests for concerts in civic halls. The invitations our schedule would allow were accepted. None of these opportunities would have opened to us had it not been for the official letter we had carried to Miguel Huang. The Lord's promise proved itself again and again, "All things work together for good...." (Romans 8:28)

For a month our home base became Lotung, a town on the east coast of the island. Ted and Beverly Skiles ran an orphanage there. It was well named "Home of God's Love."

When it neared time for us to leave Taiwan, we were excited about yet another opportunity. A four-month-old boy was being adopted by a family in America. With the legal papers finalized, we would have the privilege of carrying the infant on our homeward journey.

As we rode to Taipei, Bev held little Michael in her arms. She knew she would have to relinquish the baby to us as soon as we reached the airport. She cherished these last moments of holding the sweet little boy she had lovingly cared for since his birth.

"I hope you don't miss your flight," Ted said, pressing harder on the accelerator. "When I calculated what time we should leave home, I forgot to consider your need of extra check-in time because of the baby. You will have to produce his papers at every desk to prove your legal right to take him out of the country."

As soon as Ted pulled the vehicle to a stop by the terminal, Janice leaped out to get the luggage out of the back. Bev handed the baby to me, then helped Janice with the luggage. Together they rushed into the terminal with me close on their heels. Suddenly I was startled when a man stepped toward us, signaling for us to stop. I tensed and held Michael tighter. Then I breathed a sigh of relief upon recognizing Miguel Huang, the government official for whom we had carried the letter. He greeted us warmly. As surprised as we were to see him, he was equally puzzled to see a Chinese baby in my arms. I made a quick explanation. Mr. Huang smiled to learn that the baby's name was Michael Huang, so similar to his own.

I fidgeted, knowing we needed to be getting checked in. This man was delaying us! But God had His plan. Soon we realized that Mr. Huang's influential presence would be of great benefit. He helped us through immigration and customs. By merely flashing his authoritative government identification at each counter, we passed through in record time. He accompanied us all the way to the departure lounge. We had not needed to produce the baby's papers even once. Truly a blessing!

Thirty hours later we touched down in Colorado Springs where we saw the familiar faces of our parents. We noted the couple standing beside them. With tears in their eyes and outstretched arms, we knew they were to be little Michael's new mother and father. What a joy!

Later that day, we made a special trip to the travel agency. Barry greeted us as we entered.

"We came to check on arrangements for our next trip. We need to leave for Costa Rica in less than a month."

"You mean you are still willing to do business with me?"

"Sure!" We shared with him the many doors of opportunity the Lord had opened, primarily resulting from the letter we had delivered. Barry had tears in his eyes realizing that what had begun as his error, God had turned into blessings.

"The Lord works out everything for His own ends." (Prov. 16:4a NIV)

22

Airport Adventures

~ by Janice ~

We had been in overseas travel for more than a decade with our suitcases seldom being unpacked for more than a week. Now we welcomed a change of pace —eight months of studying the Spanish language in San Jose, Costa Rica. Missionaries from all denominations as well as families of businessmen from various nations made up the student body at the language institute.

1980: During this time, the twins' singing continued as they were invited to many churches and had an opportunity to go to Columbia, South America.

On the first day, every student was given two exams: one to determine existing level of Spanish knowledge, the other to ascertain language-learning aptitude. Faye's test results were predictably identical to mine, so we were told we could be placed in the same group if we desired. All our lives we have preferred to do everything together. However, because we assumed that having different experiences might augment our language learning, we opted initially to be assigned to separate rooms. That caused fellow classmates to do a double take—like an incident on the first day involving a student from Taiwan.

Mei Fu Chen was in Faye's small classroom situated up the hill from mine. When the teacher called the roll, she realized that Mei Fu did not belong with that group. The class to which she was then escorted just happened to be mine. When she entered the room and saw me, she stared, puzzled.

It was a week later before Mei Fu spotted the two of us together and discovered that we were twins. Her bewildered reaction amused us. Since we had recently been in Taiwan and remembered some vocabulary, we nodded and uttered the Mandarin word for twin. She was equally overjoyed that we had spoken a word in Chinese.

Teachers, too, were confused. Faye and I, without conferring with each other, had each chosen the fourth chair from the door in our conversation classrooms. When Faye's group went to a different room for her phonetics class, she first took a seat nearest the door. Upon noting a glare on the blackboard, she switched to the farthest chair by the window.

The next hour my group was slated to be in the phonetics classroom. Like Faye, I took the closest chair to the door. When I found it difficult to read the blackboard, I moved to the seat by the window. The teacher later confided that she wondered why that same student had come to her class two successive hours and then even had repeated the mistake of sitting in the wrong chair.

Faye and I were to attend grammar class at different hours. The room had thirty chairs. We wondered why the teacher continually confused our names. We discovered, just as in the other classes, we had unwittingly chosen the same chair. It's a twin thing, I suppose.

In time, being in separate classrooms proved to hinder rather than help our language learning, so Faye was allowed to transfer into my class. Our class became the envy of the institute. We had a great teacher, and we all laughed our way through our conversation sessions. It always helps the learning if you can laugh at your own mistakes and can allow others to find the humor in it, too.

Teachers learned that we sing, so we were often invited to their churches for concerts. Midway through our studies there was a three-week break. Faye and I, along with classmate Audrey McKean, would spend the time in Colombia. Wayne and Cathy Thomas, Wycliffe Bible translators who had completed their language course, had invited the three of us to accompany their family.

San Jose Airport

Audrey, Faye, and I each brought only one flight bag to the airport. The Thomases with their six children would be traveling with many duffel bags of personal and household items. We packed lightly so that when checking in together, the Thomas' overweight luggage charges would be less. Wayne was relieved it was only $40. When the flight was delayed, we were detained over the lunch hour, so the airlines gave a meal voucher. We all smiled to see the amount of $44.

Bogota Airport

Missionary Chet Bitterman met us at the airport in Bogota and transported us to Wycliffe's guest house in the city. We had trouble cashing traveler's checks, so Chet loaned us money to tide us over until the checks cleared through his account. We were touched by that kindness. We sang in a church in Bogota and then were to fly to Wycliffe's mission center at Loma Linda.

Cargo and passengers were carefully weighed for loading the single-engine aircraft. Seats were removed so that we could fly along with the Thomas' six children. Seated on Faye's lap was five-year-old Patty. With eyes filled with wonder, her comments and questions during the flight were delightful.

"Are we in Heaven now?" "Can Jesus hear me?" "If we open a window, will a cloud come in?" While I watched the clouds, I silently prayed that the Lord would fill my eyes with wonder like a child. Oh, to always behold the beauty God has made and be aware of His presence.

After a few days of singing in Loma Linda, we bade farewell to Wayne and Cathy's family.

Villavicencio

Before flying to Villavicencio, a message was sent via ham radio to inform missionaries Phil and Kathy Banta of our estimated time of arrival. There was only one problem. The Bantas, who were temporarily in Bogota, assumed the message meant we were coming there. Needless to say, when we arrived at one o'clock, no one met us. We took a taxi to the Banta's home, only to find it locked. We waited on the porch.

Curious children began to gather. By the time there were twenty children, we seized the opportunity God was providing. We sang several songs and produced our ventriloquist dolls from our luggage to tell a Bible story. The dolls were always good tools for gathering a crowd and sharing stories about Jesus. They were also useful for improving our Spanish grammar as children felt free to "help" the dolls with vocabulary.

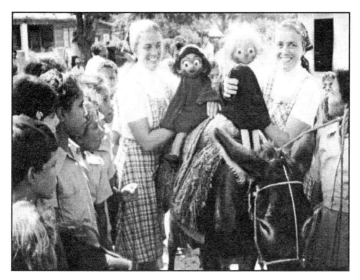

The boys and girls were enthralled. By supper time, the children scattered to their homes. When Phil and Kathy Banta returned, they were apologetic about the mix up, but we knew that our time with the children had not been wasted.

After singing in their area, we boarded a bus to return to Bogota. When the driver personally passed out sick bags, we knew we were in for a wild ride. It was frightening to speed down the mountains, often being in the oncoming lane on blind curves. We prayed and visualized our guardian angels getting frayed wings.

Once back in Bogota, we again saw the Bitterman family and repaid the money Chet had loaned us. Little did we know the trial the Bittermans would soon face. A few months later, terrorists broke into the guest house and kidnapped Chet. His pregnant wife and two daughters would never see him again. After about six weeks, Chet was fatally shot, but not before his faith had made a powerful impact on his captors. When considering the uncertainty of life, we are challenged to maximize our opportunities.

"Lord," I prayed, "when we have onetime touches on people's lives, help us to remember we may never pass this way again."

Cartejena Airport

As we left Bogota and landed at Cartejena on the north coast, we were apprehensive. Would Wanda Lumpkin be at the airport to meet us? We were arriving twenty-one hours late. There had been no way of warning her that our flight had been canceled and the airlines had housed us overnight in Bogota. As we feared, Wanda wasn't there. She had come to the airport on the previous day and had met incoming flights. When we had failed to arrive, she had returned home to wait for us there.

Wanda had written a letter to give us directions to her home. What she didn't know was that we never received that letter. A feeling of helplessness swept over us as we stood in the nearly vacant airport. We checked the correspondence from Wanda and were disappointed to find no street address—only a box number. Our mood lightened when I made a ridiculous suggestion.

"We could camp out in the post office until she checks her mail."

Faye rolled her eyes. She went to the check-in desk to inquire if a message had been left for us. There was none. Audrey spotted a public telephone and volunteered to search for a phone number. Thumbing through the directory, she found no listing for Wanda.

"There are three numbers for Latin American Mission," she said. With a small piece of paper in hand, she jotted down the numbers and the suburbs listed with them. Then she dialed. With hopeful anticipation, the two of us stood listening.

"*Hola, esta Wanda Lumpkin? Wanda Lumpkin... una enfermera con Mission Latino Americano. Somos amigas en el aeropuerto...No?...gracias...*" When the conversation ended, Audrey turned with shrugged shoulders.

"He didn't know Wanda. I'll try the second number." A lady answered this time. She also knew nothing of our friend. Audrey dialed the third. Later we learned that this was the number for the school where Wanda worked as a nurse. However, being a holiday, no one was there. With a shrug, Audrey hung up the receiver.

"Let's pray," I said. "We should have thought to do that first." Why do we often exhaust our human resources before we think to pray? Sitting in a corner of the terminal, we committed our situation to God. No sooner had we finished praying, when we saw a gentleman walking toward us, motorcycle helmet tucked under one arm.

"Excuse me," he said, speaking in Spanish. "Are you the girls looking for someone with Latin American Mission?"

"Yes! Wanda Lumpkin. Do you know her?" Audrey said, eyes bright with renewed hope. This man's presence seemed such a direct answer to prayer.

"Well, no, I don't, but after your phone call I thought about it. I might know where she is. So, I decided to come to the airport and help you find her." Reaching for two of our suitcases, he asked, "May I help carry your things? You can get a taxi and follow me."

Alvaro, as he had introduced himself to us, rode on his motorcycle, leading the way. We passed the ruins of a picturesque Spanish fortress as we wound our way through the town. Finally our guide stopped near a building on a hill. When we emerged from the taxi, our eyes caught sight of two ladies approaching. One was Wanda, the other an older lady. We ran to greet them. After a few minutes of excited chatter, Alvaro interrupted to inform us that he needed to leave. We thanked him again. He smiled as he donned his helmet.

"I was glad to help," he said. Then he turned his motorcycle toward the road.

"Who was that man?" Wanda inquired as we all watched the cyclist descend the hill.

"Alvaro. He is with Latin American Mission."

"But I don't know him," stated the older lady.

Audrey took from her pocket the piece of paper upon which she had written the three telephone numbers. Pointing to the first, she said, "He answered at this number."

"Latin American Mission has only one number." The lady took the paper and puzzled over it. "I've been with Latin American Mission in this town for thirty years. I know everyone who is with the mission, but I've never met that man. In fact, there is absolutely no mission work in the area of town you have written beside this number." She paused, nodding her head in bewilderment, then added, "As far as I'm concerned, these first two numbers don't even exist."

"Then who was he?" We all echoed, pointing to the end of the lane where the cyclist was just disappearing from view. Joking, yet perhaps absolutely correct, I suggested, "Maybe angels ride motorcycles these days."

"Are not all angels ministering spirits, come to serve those who will inherit salvation?" (Heb. 1:14 NIV)

San Andres Airport

Singing at various gatherings in Cartejena, the days passed quickly. Back at the airport we caught a flight to the Island of San Andres. Little did we know that once again no one would be there to meet us. By the time all other passengers had collected their bags and had exited the terminal, we were left alone.

"This is a repeat of our experience at Cartejena," Audrey commented.

"Yes," I said, "and this time we don't even know so much as a post office box number."

"Well then, why don't we pray FIRST this time," Faye said.

We all agreed and made our way over to one side of the room. There we sat on our luggage and bowed our heads. As we prayed, I pictured the man in Cartejena crossing the terminal toward us. I longed for the same quick answer to our prayer.

I could hardly believe my eyes when we raised our heads and saw a man striding toward us with purposeful steps. He was tall, lanky, and wore the uniform of a customs official. As he neared us, he stretched out his arms.

"Welcome, welcome, girls," he said with a broad smile. "It's good to see you. What brings you back to our fair land? Are you only passing through again?" For a few seconds we were too stunned to answer. How had the man remembered us? We had only had a brief flight stop there on our way to Colombia three weeks earlier.

"Ah, we are here for the weekend. A pastor in Bogota arranged for us to sing here. Right now we are waiting for a lady to pick us up."

"And who might that be?" he boldly inquired, maintaining his cheery nature.

"We don't know her full name. We were told she is called Trini."

"Trini! Why I know dear Trini. That is short for Trinidad. Don't you worry, girls, I'll telephone her, and she will be right out to get you," the man said. As he strode away, we bowed our heads again.

"Oh Lord, once again you have shown your promise to be true. You are always with us. Thank you for answering our prayer." Trini did arrive, and we had a good weekend there before returning to our studies in Costa Rica.

"Let them give glory to the Lord, and declare His praise in the coastlands." (Isa. 42:12)

1980: Faye and Janice by the Pacific shores of Costa Rica

23

Short on Time

~ by Faye ~

"I feel like a packhorse," Janice muttered as we puffed our way uphill the six blocks to the bus stop in the suburb called Guadalupe. We were back in San Jose, settled into the routine of catching a bus at 6:15 A.M. to get to the Spanish language institute. I glanced at Janice and smiled. Besides her usual shoulder bag of books, she sported an overnight bag, an instrument, a camera, and an umbrella. I was equally burdened.

"Such is our life," I said. We climbed aboard the city bus; its springs were shot from years of overloading. A cloud of black diesel fumes blew our way. With all our extra gear, we were glad to find available seats.

It wasn't until we had reached the institute nearly an hour later, that Janice gasped, "Oh no! We forgot our lunch!" If it had been an ordinary class day, we wouldn't have thought a thing about it, but today was to be different. It was a Friday. In the afternoon after classes, we would be going for the weekend to sing in a small town four hours to the north.

We recalled the previous evening when Isabel, the Costa Rican lady with whom we boarded, was making sandwiches. She had gone to the expense of purchasing special buns and lunch meat. No doubt she would be disappointed when she would discover that we had forgotten to pack the sandwiches for our trip.

We decided that after classes one of us could go back to Guadalupe to get the lunch. The other would carry most of the heavier things and go straight through the city center to reach the interstate bus terminal. I opted to take the Guadalupe detour. If buses were on time, I calculated I could make it. As soon as classes ended, I headed off campus. Before reaching the bus stop, I was hailed by a teacher.

"I'm going to Guadalupe. Would you like a ride?" Overjoyed, I readily accepted. No one had ever offered us a ride before. While riding through heavy traffic, I thanked the Lord and thought of the verse,

> "And we know that all things work together for good to those who love God, to those who are the called according to His purpose." (Romans 8:28)

The teacher took me right to our home. I checked my watch. Nerves tensed anew. It would still be a push to reach the bus terminal in time.

Snatching the lunch sack from the refrigerator, I made a hasty explanation to Isabel, and turned to leave. Just as I reached the front door, Isabel stopped me, "*Espere, espere*" (wait). She insisted I drink a glass of papaya juice. "*Buena para la salud*" (good for the health), she added with a cheery smile. Healthful or not, I didn't want to take the time; yet not wishing to offend, I accepted the glass. While I swallowed as fast as I could, trying to mask my frustration, Isabel kept up a monologue of the most rapid Spanish she knew how to produce. Since my knowledge of the language was still limited, I had difficulty understanding her. She was saying something about a small bus from Moravia. I didn't even want to understand. I just wanted to leave.

Finally I nodded as if I had understood, said good-bye, and hurried out.

I quickened my pace, knowing that a bus labeled Barrio Pilar occasionally would stop just around the corner. If I could catch that one, it would save me the six-block walk to the main Guadalupe bus stop. When I rounded the corner, my heart sank. The bus was pulling away. I had just missed it! If only Isabel hadn't detained me with all of her chatter. Resentment clouded my mind as I watched the bus rumble away ahead of me.

It was uphill all the way, six blocks of uneven sidewalks, and there I was struggling with sandals in which I couldn't run. I felt as though I would slide out of the back of them with each step. Filled with self-pity, I grumbled to myself. All things work together for good? What good could possibly come from this? To make matters worse, I remembered that the Guadalupe bus would drop me off in the center of San Jose, a mile short of my destination. I muttered aloud that I might not make it in time. By now Janice would surely be wondering why I was taking so long.

Finally completing the six blocks, I reached the corner where several buses were lined up. Among them was a small bus, not much bigger than a van. The sign on the front read "Moravia." I reflected on Isabel's words, "small bus from Moravia." Perhaps she had been advising me to take this bus. I knew they all ran to the center of the city. I ran to it, got on board, paid my fare, and sat down. There were only five other passengers.

The bus then wound its way through traffic, going faster than usual. A few blocks farther on we passed the Barrio Pilar bus, which I had hoped to catch near the house. It was moving slowly. I thought again of Romans 8:28. "Oh Lord, why is it as soon as things go wrong, I am quick to doubt, worry or grumble? All things do work together for good!"

This small bus sped on, not even stopping at the usual bus stops. As we passed each one, I could see people waving, trying to flag us down. With only the six of us on board, the little bus was weaving recklessly in and out of traffic, at times even swerving into the oncoming lanes to pass some of the slower vehicles. In record time we were nearing downtown San Jose. What usually took twenty minutes had taken only ten. What was going on? Why weren't we picking up other passengers? I had never yet been on a bus that didn't stop at all the regular stops. Was this driver in a hurry for some personal reason, or had God ordered him to take me to the end of the line as fast as possible? Whatever the reason, God sure had my attention.

As if God were further demonstrating His faithfulness, the bus passed the area that was the usual end of the line for all buses. Block after block we traveled westward until we had gone ten blocks farther. It left me with only a two-block walk, rather than twelve, to reach the bus terminal where Janice was anxiously waiting.

The muscles in my ankles were tense and sore as I struggled to keep my shoes on and yet run as much as possible, but this time I didn't voice any complaints to the Lord. Janice smiled with relief when she saw me come into view. The bus was already loaded and ready to leave for Guanacasti. We quickly climbed on board and even before we had reached our seats, the bus eased out of the station. Whew! That was close!

It felt wonderful to settle back into the soft seat and to finally allow my tired muscles to relax. As we rode along and ate what seemed to be the most delicious sandwiches, I had plenty of time to tell Janice of the lesson I had learned. I should not doubt God's Word. I was grateful He had shown His faithfulness through Romans 8:28. "...all things work together for good to those who love God, to those who are the called according to His purpose."

24

Victor Vega Rodriguez

∼ by Faye ∼

"No pueden salir del pais!" (You can't leave the country), the Costa Rican immigration officer curtly stated without lifting his gaze from our open passports. *"No tienen visa de salida."* (You have no exit visa).

"Exit visa! I didn't know we needed one," I said, struggling to use Spanish.

"How can we obtain one?" Janice asked.

"You can't now. It's late. The immigration office is closed for the weekend. You will have to wait and go to the downtown office on Monday." With a wave of his hand he motioned us to one side and began to process the passports of other passengers in line.

Panic. Somewhere in my confused whirl of thoughts, I asked God for help. Trying to mask my frustration, I glanced over to the seating area of the terminal where we had said good-byes to the Rodriguez family. They were still there!

As I looked their way, Victor rose to his feet. The shoulders of his husky frame were squared, giving him a taller appearance than his medium height generally portrayed. His thick mustache covered the thin line of his lips as concern was etched on his face.

When our eyes met, my apprehensions faded. Frequently during our eight months in Costa Rica, we had been invited to the Rodriguez's home. They had played a key role in augmenting our Spanish language studies. But above all, we treasured their friendship.

All too soon our departure day had arrived, and we had checked in at the airport for our 2 P.M. flight. Many Costa Rican friends were there to see us off, but when it was announced that there would be a substantial delay for our flight, we encouraged them to return to their homes. Victor and his family had insisted on remaining until we were safely on our way. Victor was his usual entertaining self, helping the hours to pass quickly. Hazel, his wife, was a quiet, beautiful woman with an infectious smile. Deep dimples would form at the corners of her mouth, and her eyes would sparkle as she laughed at her husband's antics.

Now it was after 11 P.M. I marveled that Victor and Hazel with five small children would wait with us so long. For more than nine hours they had kept us company in the airport, and now here we stood with the dread of a possible further delay. When the rest of the passengers had proceeded toward the boarding lounge, we again stepped up to the immigration desk.

"Sir, isn't there some way we can get our exit visas? We must be in Mexico by Sunday." We knew that our schedule was not his concern. He was just doing his duty.

"Sorry, nothing can be done until Monday," he simply stated. Our hearts sank. Victor noticed we were being detained and assumed we were having difficulty speaking Spanish. He approached the desk.

"What seems to be the problem here?"

"These ladies don't have their exit visas," the official replied, matter-of-factly.

"Can't you take care of it for them?" Victor inquired.

"The immigration office is closed."

"Where is the immigration office?" Victor asked.

"Well, there is one here in the airport."

" Why can't you open the office and process these passports?" Victor prodded.

"The office closed at 5 P.M. It is closed for the weekend." His curt tone communicated obvious annoyance at the barrage of questions. Victor, determined to get some action, came on even stronger.

"It would be a very simple matter for you to open the office and grant the visas so the ladies can catch their flight," he said, further irritating the official.

"Who are you anyway?" the officer blurted out.

With shoulders squared, Victor slowly crossed his muscular arms over his broad chest. Sternly and distinctly, rolling the R's with added finesse, he replied, "My name is Victor Vega Rodriguez!" Immediately, the expression on the officer's face changed.

"Yes, sir! Yes, sir!" He sputtered nervously, "I can open the office right away." He frantically snatched up the passports, "I'll process these immediately. Please follow me." He turned and walked briskly down a corridor.

Amazed at the sudden turn of events, we looked at Victor and whispered, "What authority do you have?"

He gave no verbal response, but his expression communicated volumes. The raised eyebrows, the rolling eyes, the mouth turned down at the corners, and the shrug of the shoulders disclosed his equal bewilderment. His thick mustache served to magnify the comical expression. We had to smile. Regaining his dignified and authoritative composure, Victor winked at us.

"See what pull I have?" He motioned for us to follow the official who was by then well ahead. Hurrying down the hallway and descending a flight of stairs, we reached the immigration office. The man had already unlocked the door and was rummaging through a desk drawer.

While the officer was preoccupied with stamping our passports, we glanced around the room. Victor was the first to notice the large plaque on the wall. He nudged us, calling our attention to it. Now we understood why God had kept the Rodriguez family at the airport those many hours. The plaque's inscription showed that the head of the immigration department of Costa Rica was none other than VICTOR VEGA RODRIGUEZ. The very same name, but not the same man! No wonder the officer had demonstrated a sudden change of heart. He must have assumed that Victor was his head boss, whom he had evidently never met. The Lord works in mysterious ways!

"He performs wonders that cannot be fathomed, miracles that cannot be numbered." (Job 9:10 NIV)

What's in a name? God had His purpose for one called Victor Vega Rodriguez to be at the airport.

25

Getting Into a Restricted Area

∼ by Janice ∼

Would some call this a step of faith, or had we made an unwise decision? We were leaving America and returning to India without the special permit we needed.

Political unrest and Hindu-Moslem violence caused India's northeastern states to be cut off from the public. Foreigners were not being allowed entry: not as tourists, not to visit friends, not for Christian work. Nevertheless, Phillip Ho, a Tibetan refugee involved in medical and evangelistic work in Meghalaya, invited us to come for six weeks.

Phillip Ho as a medic treats a child who has a burn on the leg.

"It won't be easy to get in," Phillip had warned. "You'll have to apply for a Restricted Area Permit."

We had applied for the permit. When our departure date neared and we still had not received it, we faced the dilemma: either cancel that first six weeks of our four-month tour in India, or step out in faith and go, hoping to secure the permit in New Delhi. We had opted to go.

It was well past midnight when we arrived in India. We inched along waiting to pass through immigration, too tired to even contemplate where we might stay for the night. Silently I prayed, "Please help us, Lord. All I want now is a bed."

Someone gently tapped my shoulder. I turned to face a college-age youth, her sweet, innocent face filled with anxiety.

"Excuse me. I've never been out of the United States before. I see you are wearing saris, so I assume you might be accustomed to traveling in India. May I stay with you until we get through customs, so I can know what to do?"

"Sure. Glad to help."

The girl's eyes scanned the onlookers. "There is supposed to be someone here to meet me, but what will I do if they're not here?"

"Don't worry. If they don't come, you can stay with us," we assured her. "We'll take a taxi and find an inexpensive hotel. Then tomorrow we can help you locate your friends."

"Oh, thank you. By the way, my name is Kathy." We learned that Kathy had come to India to help in some mission work. Her luggage arrived before ours. With apprehension she walked toward the waiting crowd. We watched as an American lady stepped forward to greet her. Kathy turned to catch our eye. Her lips formed another, "Thank you."

When our luggage finally arrived, we made our way out of the terminal.

"Wait! Wait!" The lady who had come for Kathy was running toward us. "Please stay with us tonight instead of trying to find a hotel at this hour." She brushed aside a lock of her sandy hair. "I'm Sis. Kathy told me that you are missionaries, too." Sis Kimbril, whose husband was away on an evangelistic tour, had a small apartment, but a willing spirit to share. The fellowship was precious and a good night's rest was an answer to prayer.

The following day, we rode to the center of the nation's capital in an auto-rickshaw. The open three-wheeled motorcycle taxi allowed wind to whip at the yardage of our nylon saris. When we stepped onto the sidewalk in front of the government building, we took a deep breath. With a prayer on our lips, we climbed the flight of steps to the imposing edifice.

"This is the place." I pointed to the sign above the office door that read, "Department of Internal Affairs." A stern gentleman rose to his feet as we entered the room. He motioned us to take a seat, resuming his position behind the desk.

"What may I do for you ladies?" We explained our desire to go to Meghalaya.

"That's in a restricted area. There is too much tribal unrest and warfare in those states for us to allow foreigners in there now."

"We realize that, sir, but we have an invitation and would like to get a permit if possible."

He remained businesslike. "In that case you will have to fill out an application form and wait up to two weeks for it to be approved."

"But, sir, we applied months ago and have been waiting for its approval," Faye said.

"Oh, is that right?" He pushed his chair back and stood to leave. "If you will excuse me, I'll go check on it."

"It does not look very hopeful," I whispered. "Let's pray." We sat in silence until the man reappeared, our application in hand. As he flung it onto the desk our hearts sank. Scrawled across the front in bold red letters was NOT RECOMMENDED FOR ENTRY. Was this a similar experience to the Apostle Paul's being hindered from entering Bithynia? If we would not be granted the permit, where would we go for the six weeks? I shoved those worries from my mind. For now, we needed to keep a positive attitude and cling to every thread of hope.

Now seated, the gentleman took the application in hand and scanned it. His expression revealed nothing of his thoughts. Without taking his eyes from the paper, he asked, "Why do you want to go to Meghalaya?"

"To visit friends who have medical work in Shillong and to sing in the area churches."

"I see. That is what you have stated in your application. As a Hindu nation, we do not tolerate Christian work," he met our gaze with a cold stare. "How long did you desire to stay?"

"Six weeks," I responded confidently.

"Bah! Impossible! Totally out of the question! It would not be a restricted area if we were letting people in for six weeks!"

"Could we possibly be granted four weeks, Sir?" Faye ventured boldly.

"Absolutely not!"

"Three?" I bargained hopefully, still cheerful, thinking that any moment the man might give in. We watched expectantly for the slightest change in the official's countenance, but saw none. I wondered if he ever exercised the muscles of his face. He remained quiet, stern, unmoving. If he was waiting for a bribe, it never crossed our minds. We just sat quietly, patiently waiting. Finally, there came that slight wag of the head.

"I will grant you a permit for seven days."

Seven days! I suppose we should have been elated

to receive a permit at all, but only one week? We tried not to show our disappointment. I contemplated that maybe we could get an extension after we reached Shillong. As if reading my thoughts, the man pointed an accusing finger.

"And don't try to extend this permit after you get up there!" He pushed away from the desk and strode from the room. We did not see that man again. A different gentleman returned with the permit. As he handed it to us, he glanced around quickly, then spoke in a hushed tone.

"If you extend this permit after you're in Meghalaya, just don't let the central government here know about it," he said. We nodded, thanking him as we tucked the permit away.

The following day we flew to Gauhati, Assam. The moment we stepped off the airplane, two officials approached us to inspect our permit. Upon approval we were waved on. We knew Phillip Ho would not be there to meet us because of our delay in New Delhi. Just outside the terminal we located an interstate bus.

"Good afternoon, ladies," the driver motioned us to find a seat. "We'll be leaving shortly and should reach Shillong about 9:30 tonight. By the way, taxis won't be operating that late."

Shillong is a big city. We wondered how we could find the home of the Ho family.

"Their correspondence does not give us any directions," I said.

"It looks like another one for the Lord," Faye stated.

"He brought us this far, didn't He? Surely He won't leave us stranded. He has rescued us many times before." We bowed in prayer.

Some time passed. We began to wonder why the bus had not yet left the airport. The driver was sitting with one foot up on the hump of the motor cover. He finally apologized and said we were waiting for some more passengers from a Calcutta flight.

"God has someone coming from Calcutta to help us, and he will sit right there." I pointed to the seat across the aisle. Momentarily startled by my own confidence, I almost blurted out, "Why did I say that?" Yet I sensed that a deep calm had replaced my anxiety. We waited with an expectant anticipation to see how the Lord was going to help us.

Soon the people from Calcutta were mounting the steps of the bus. The seat I had pointed out across the aisle was not a likely choice for them to take. There was already one man seated next to the window, and there were plenty of other empty seats, so each incoming passenger passed by. The one whom God wants to sit there will take that seat, I thought.

Then came an unlikely prospect. A man burdened down like a packhorse struggled to mount the steps. A bulky flight bag hung from each shoulder. A satchel clamped beneath his right arm was threatening to slip, as the man hefted his travel-worn suitcase from step to step. The other arm cradled a clumsy box over which was draped his coat. And as if that weren't enough, he clutched in his left hand a plastic bag filled with water and a live fish! I assumed that this man would locate a seat where he would have ample space.

It amazed us when he took the seat across the aisle. The most unlikely one to do so! Was God showing that He was directing this situation? We were only five minutes away from the airport when this gentleman leaned across the aisle and struck up a conversation.

"I'm surprised to see foreigners up here. How did you get in?"

"We have a seven-day permit," Faye replied.

"I've been trying to get some friends in, but the government is very strict these days, not granting permission to anyone. By the way, where are you going?"

"We're going to Shillong," I said.

"But to what area, which suburb?"

Not knowing how to pronounce the particular area, I located one of Phillip Ho's letters and handed it across the aisle. The address simply read, "Ho, Mawlai, Syllaikariah, Shillong." He gazed at the envelope with curious interest.

"Ho? Would that by any chance be Phillip Ho?" he asked.

"Yes." Our eyes reflected hopeful expectation. "Do you know him?"

"Yes, he's a good friend of mine. We often work together, since I, too, am in Christian work. I am the president of a Bible college. Austin John is my name." When we reached Shillong, Mr. John directed us to the Ho's place. Both Phillip and his wife, Margaret, were surprised to see us.

"We have been praying, but really didn't think you had been able to get a permit," Phillip said.

We apologized that the permit was only for one week, but Phillip was not disappointed. He was happy for any amount of time since no one had been getting in lately.

Sunday we worshiped in a large congregation where words of amazement were expressed by an eighty-four-year-old preacher.

"People from other countries used to teach us and share their faith, but then our area was cut off from the outside world. Now, after three years of seeing no outsiders, these two ladies have been allowed to come. Surely God has sent them."

1982: Phillip and Margaret Ho
with their children Jerry and Christy

Yes, God had helped us to reach this restricted area. How long would we be staying—if but a week, where would we go for the remaining five? We would take it one day at a time and trust God with the rest. He is our capable travel agent. Speaking of agents, we were soon to be contacted by government agents and perhaps even spied on by a secret agent.

26

Agents

~ by Janice ~

It was our third day in Shillong when we were asked to sing for a wedding. Following the ceremony, two

men were eager to talk with us because they each had twin daughters. In the course of our conversation, one of them asked how we got permission to enter the area. We told them we had secured a seven-day permit in New Delhi.

"Is that how long you wanted to stay?"

"No, we applied for six weeks." My expression revealed our disappointment.

"I see." His eyes expressed sympathy. "It's a pity if we can't keep you up here longer. Would you like us to extend your permit? We are state government agents."

We brightened, yet I recalled the stern warning we had been given in Delhi. We explained about the two officials, one telling us not to extend the permit, and the other saying, "If you extend it after you're up there, just don't let the central government know."

The men nodded, exuding confidence. "Very well, we will extend your permit, and do just as they requested—not let them know." They instructed us to come to the government offices every Monday to receive permission for another week's extension.

Now that we would have more time in the Khasi Hills, Phillip Ho suggested we get at a filmstrip project and see how much of it we could get done. The filmstrips would be culturally applicable tools for teaching the gospel. We had done the photography for similar projects on other mission fields, so we knew the enor-

mity of the task. We would need to take more than three hundred pictures, many of which would necessitate posing certain nationals as actors. Phillip and Margaret already had the scripts translated into the Khasi language. We took up the challenge, sandwiching the picture taking between singing programs, and all went like clockwork. By the end of the second week, we had nearly half of the project completed.

One day, Margaret took us to a lovely city park to take some scenic shots. We walked on the paved paths through some trees and by some flowerbeds and snapped several pictures along the way. A slight breeze caressed our cheeks and played with the soft material of our long skirts. The quiet beauty washed over our spirits, bathing us in a refreshing peace. We didn't know that apprehension and fear would soon shatter the serenity. We approached a pond where we paused. I was preparing to snap another picture, framing the scene with an overhead branch, when Margaret leaned close.

"Nice perspective," she said, then whispered, "Don't look now, but I think we're being followed." We talked in our normal tones and walked nonchalantly as if we suspected nothing. As the three of us talked, at least one could usually see the man out of the corner of her eyes. It did seem that the man was trailing us. One minute he would be sitting on a bench, the next, leaning against a tree, or pretending to gaze into a fishpond. If we moved on, so would he.

At one point when I swung around in the man's direction, pretending to check out a camera angle, he quickly unfolded a newspaper and leaned against a handrail pretending to read. When we moved on, his newspaper went down as rapidly as it had gone up. It was almost comical how obvious the man was being, but we realized this was no laughing matter. When we were far enough ahead to be out of earshot, I asked Margaret who she thought he was.

"It's hard to say. He could be a secret agent with central intelligence. I don't think he suspects that we've noticed him. Let's try to ditch him."

We continued to stroll, appearing casual, while our minds sought an opportunity to escape. Crossing an arched footbridge that spanned a meandering wide stream, we paused in the middle to take pictures. Meanwhile, our shadow had ducked into a refreshment stand, a three-walled structure with its open side facing the bridge. It seemed to be the only place where he could sit inconspicuously and wait for us to finish crossing the bridge. I leaned against the railing and pointed toward the stream. Margaret and Faye leaned close as if to view the fish.

"Let's try to retrace our steps. The man will expect us to continue across the bridge. If we double back when the man's not looking, we could circle around behind the refreshment stand," Faye said. Margaret pointed to a fish.

"Look at that big one." Then she lowered her voice. "It could be risky, but maybe it's our only chance." Margaret and Faye moved away from the railing as they continued their animated conversation. Faye stood at an angle where she could watch the man and keep us posted. When our pursuer's attention was momentarily diverted by the stand's proprietor, Faye gave the signal.

"Now is our chance, let's go!" We made a mad dash. Once past the stand we scurried up the tree-covered slope behind it. When obscured sufficiently by brush, we paused, hearts pounding.

"You shall hide them in the secret place of Your presence from the plots of man." (Ps. 31:20a)

We watched as the man rushed from the refreshment stand. He sprinted across the bridge and stopped bewildered on the far side. Frantically he looked from side to side deliberating which path to take. We never did learn who the man was, or why he was tailing us. We left the park and felt relieved to return to the security of the Ho's home.

With the filmstrip project well on its way to completion, Phillip decided we had time to travel to outlying villages for services. That entailed another stop at the government building as permission would have to be secured. Even the residents of Shillong who wanted to travel to other areas had to fill out special forms.

Again we were amazed when the officials stamped on our permit that we would be allowed the freedom to travel to any village without having to fill out the specific forms each time. We thanked the Lord for this, another blessing.

These tours to the villages were very fruitful. It was unusual for foreigners to be present, so great crowds would gather for the open-air evangelistic meetings.

The people situated themselves wherever they could find a vantage point. Some sat on logs, on fences, or on the porches of nearby houses. Like Zacchaeus, others were perched in trees. We sang Khasi language songs. Then a local evangelist would preach. At the close of each service, there were some who surrendered their lives to Jesus.

One such trip was to the village of Shelley located near the river that forms India's border with Bangladesh. Only one Christian family was known to live there. To encourage them, fifty Christians from the large congregation in Shillong crammed into five jeeps to go to Shelley for a church service.

The jeeps snaked their way down the narrow, winding cliff-edge road out of the Himalayan mountains. Views of snowcapped ranges and deep gorges were spectacular. Losing control could mean certain death. During the five-hour drive, the foliage changed from pine trees to tropical palms, and the early morning's briskness gave way to muggy oppressive heat.

The meeting was held in the open where there was ample room for the scores of villagers who joined the nucleus of believers. On the fringes of the crowd, we saw many Indian merchants who were Hindustani, rather than of the Khasi tribe. In our part of the program we included songs both in the Hindi language as well as in Khasi. We were thrilled that we were asked to make a tape of Hindi songs. We prayed that the messages of our recorded songs would bring listeners to Jesus.

At the close of the service, several people accepted the Lord. It was good to know that now there were more Christians in Shelley to share fellowship. The crowd made their way to the bank of the river for a baptismal service. There was singing, praying, and testifying. By the time we witnessed the immersions, the sun was setting and the new converts were silhouetted against a fiery horizon.

Darkness was descending upon the valley as we left Shelley and started the long drive up the mountain. Ours was the last of the five jeeps to leave the village. Mr. Ho had switched on the headlights, but we had not gone far when the lights dimmed, making visibility difficult. Phillip had no way of fixing the problem if the alternator was out, so we continued at a slow pace, straining to see the road. We knew that soon the lights would fade entirely. It was a moonless night.

We were relieved when we came upon the fourth jeep. They had decided to wait for us, though they knew nothing of our problem. Sandi, who had a flashlight, volunteered to sit at the back of his jeep and shine the beam onto the road. The hours passed slowly as we wound our way upward around corner after corner, keeping our eyes intently fixed upon the small beam of light ahead.

At times the jeep in front of us would take a hairpin curve and the little flashlight beam would vanish completely from view. Phillip would steer the jeep in that direction, straining his eyes in pitch darkness for a glimpse of the road.

To add to our difficulty, we ascended into heavy fog. We tried keeping closer to the lead jeep, lest the flashlight beam be totally lost from view. Then Sandi would shut off the flashlight to save on the batteries, assuming we could see the headlight beams from his own jeep. The fog prevented that. Though we knew he could not hear us, one of us would say, "Sandi, you have the light—let it shine!" An idea for a song was materializing. Other songs have had a similar theme, but it came especially clear to us that night. No matter how dim our light may seem, we must let it shine.

YOU CAN BE A LIGHT

You can be a light for Jesus, let it shine,
You can be a light for Jesus all the time.
Do your best to shine it bright,
Shine it in the darkest night,
You can be a guiding light, so shine!

Those who live in sin are wandering aimlessly,
Groping in the darkness of the night,
And they cannot find their way,
To a bright and better day,
Unless you will become a guiding light.

There are those who say, "My light's too dim to shine,
Jesus can use others more than me."
But your dim light He can use,
There's no one He'll refuse,
Give your life to Jesus and you'll see,

You are the light of the world,
Let your light so shine,
that God will be glorified.

All were tired but grateful to reach Shillong late that night. The next day we returned to the government offices. We had completed three weeks, and we were going in for an another extension. We were directed this time toward the passport department. There we recognized the friendly face of Everland, one of the men from the wedding.

"Phillip Ho will take your permit upstairs. Meanwhile, will you give a program here in my department?" Now we understood why we had been requested to bring our instruments on this particular day. The department was filled with the employees' families and friends. It was a joy to give them a concert. Near the end other agents entered the room together with Mr. Ho.

"Here is your permit," one of them said as he handed us the valued paper. "You have your extension to the fourth week now, but we have also sent word to New Delhi to let them know that you are still here. We thought it best that we let the central government know that we have no objection to your being here. As it is, you have nothing to fear. Your papers are all perfectly legal. This way you won't have to fear that a federal agent will find you and will ask why you have stayed beyond your original seven days." As he spoke I had visions of the man who had been tailing us in the park. Had he been a secret agent?

"Come again in a week," Everland said. "If we've heard nothing from Delhi, we will grant you your final two weeks." It seemed strange that they would consider granting two weeks' permission, when the previous extensions had each been for one. Returning to the government office the following week, we were told that no word had been received from Delhi. They stamped our permits for our final two weeks.

Each week we had been thankful for the extended time so that we could accomplish more in the churches and in outlying villages. Now we marveled that we had been granted our full six weeks.

While riding back to the house, I spotted the "secret agent" who had followed us in the park. Maybe it was unnecessary, but Faye and I ducked down in the back-seat to avoid being seen.

We were delighted to complete the photography work for the Khasi culturally-oriented filmstrips. These would be produced by Good News Productions International and would be returned to the Khasi Hills for use there.

Five days after having been to the government offices, Everland came to the Ho's home. He had other business, but when he saw us, he said, "By the way, a telegram arrived from New Delhi the day after you were in my office. It said something like, 'Why did you give extensions when we granted those ladies only seven days? Get them out of the region immediately!'"

"What shall we do?" I fully expected that he would advise us to pack our bags and leave for the airport as soon as possible.

"Don't worry," the man shrugged nonchalantly. "The telegram sat on my desk a few days, and now it'll sit on my friend's desk for a few more. By the time we answer it and the officials in Delhi respond, you'll have had your full six weeks and will be leaving anyway." He smiled. Our tension eased somewhat.

"But will this cause any trouble for you?"

"None whatsoever. Everything has been entirely legal," Everland said. "The fact that you've been allowed to stay so long will be a positive factor on your records. It should help if you ever apply to return, and we certainly hope you will!"

There were no more signs of trouble, and we enjoyed our remaining time in Meghalaya, completing the six weeks. The day came for us to take the bus back to Gauhati and leave the restricted area. When we entered the airport terminal, two soldiers approached us.

"Janice and Faye Rostvit? According to our records your permit expired five weeks ago."

"We were given extensions, sir." Faye handed him the document.

He unfolded it onto his clipboard. One of the officers studied it for a moment, then stamped it. "Very well." He handed it back with a smile.

With a sigh of relief and a prayer of thanksgiving, the two of us sat down to await our flight's departure. We reflected upon all the incidents, which like a giant puzzle intricately fit together, had allowed us to have the full six weeks. We had wondered if it were common for people to gain entry and keep obtaining extensions as we had. Yet when we asked one of the agents in Shillong, he had informed us that only one man had been permitted to stay as long as four weeks, and he was married to a girl from the region.

> "Oh how great is Your goodness, which You have laid up for those who fear You, which You have prepared for those who trust in You in the presence of the sons of men!" (Ps. 31:19)

Time to reflect on the circumstances God had arranged for the twins to remain in the restricted area, the Khasi Hills.

27

Mediterranean Marvels

∽ by Faye ∽

———————————◦———————————

Even the best made plans can go awry. One European tour was plagued with travel problems. Yet, in every case, we marveled how God intervened.

GREECE—Too Late to Change Money

We had been singing for a month in Turkey where we were privileged to see many areas where the Apostle Paul had traveled: Tarsus, Iconium, Ephesus, Smyrna, Hieropolis, Pergamum, and others. While singing in Istanbul, we received our personal "Macedonian Call," an invitation to sing in Thessalonica, Greece. The Apostle Paul had crossed the Aegean Sea by ship, but we would go by rail across the isthmus.

Bill and Elfriede Hinderliter, the Christian couple who brought us to Istanbul's train station, slipped a five-drachma note into my hand. A thoughtful gesture!

"You might need this before you can change any currency," Bill said.

We assumed we wouldn't need it, since we were scheduled to reach Neapolis by two o'clock. But the border crossing took longer than anticipated, so we arrived well past 3:00 P.M. Banks had closed. We were thankful for the drachmas. We spent some of it for a taxi ride into town, the rest to buy a snack for supper.

What would we do for a place to stay that night? We located a small hotel and climbed the steps to its second-story lobby. We had just set down our bags when the lady behind the counter threw her hands up in a demonstrative show of emotion. Excited, she shuffled her way around the end of the counter, hands still raised, "*Didymes! Didymes!*" She came toward us, eyes beaming to match her smile. Our hearts warmed as this little lady, who scarcely reached our shoulders, gave us a hearty embrace.

"*Didymes!*" Janice whispered. "She's excited to see twins." The Apostle Thomas was called Didymus, (John 11:16) the Greek word for twin. Maybe the difference in the word ending indicated the feminine form.

Janice tried explaining our dilemma to the stout desk clerk. She inquired if we could stay the night and pay in the morning after changing currency. The lady only giggled with a puzzled expression, obviously not understanding a word of English. An Italian gentleman, who had been watching with amusement, offered to help us communicate. Though he also spoke no English, he understood when we made our explanation to him in Spanish. He then translated to the desk clerk.

The lady nodded with a smile, motioning for us to follow. We wasted no time gathering our bags and falling in behind like ducklings. The nonstop chatter continued, her hands expressly punctuating whatever she was saying. We assumed she was still fascinated by twins, since like spices in Grecian cuisine, her monologue was sprinkled generously with the word *didymes.*

The following morning after paying our hotel bill, we set off by bus to see Philippi. We then continued southward, following the Apostle Paul's route.

"When they had passed through Amphipolis and Apollonia, they came to Thessalonica..." (Acts 17:1)

The weekend spent with the church there was a delight. We knew some Greek songs we had learned from Greek immigrants we met in Australia.

The Apostle Paul commended the Thessalonians for their work of faith, their labor of love, and their patience of hope. To think that the church was established there nearly two millennia ago and that Grecian Christians carried the Gospel northward into Russia, as evidenced by the Greek influence in their alphabet. Paul did not know who among his converts might bear the most fruit. Only God knows the lasting affects an individual's or a congregation's witness may have over the centuries.

Our travel route south, then westward took us through Athens and Corinth and eventually to the coast of the Adriatic Sea. There we would cross to Italy. We had followed much of Paul's journeys, more by chance than by design. Now as we watched the windswept waves of the Adriatic, I thought of Paul's shipwreck.

"Let's not follow his experiences too closely," I said. Our next problem did come in connection with the ship crossing. The ferry's schedule had changed, departing from Patros six hours late. It was too late to warn our contact in Italy. As the huge ship rocked over the rough waters of the Adriatic, we wondered if anyone would meet us when we would dock at Brindisi.

ITALY—Now That We're Here, Where Do We Go?

It was 4:00 P.M. when our ship docked. As several other ships were also there, the wharf swarmed with thousands of people. By the time the crowds thinned, it was obvious that we were stranded. We prayed, then set out. The Christian camp where we were to sing was across the peninsula, the heel of Italy's boot, from Brindisi.

We located a railway station where we tried talking with the ticket agent, but he spoke no English. I then pulled out a map to show him our destination. He shook his head and pointed to another town—Frankavilla. Apparently that was as close as we could get by rail. It was only halfway. We decided to go since at least we'd be headed in the right direction.

It was getting dark by the time our train pulled into Frankavilla. We stood alone on the platform contemplating our next move. Janice again unfolded the map that the missionary had sent us. Noticing a Frankavilla phone number written on it, she made the call. Speaking Spanish, Janice made herself understood, but she caught very little of the lady's reply. Something was said about Charlie Brown...radio station and some numbers. Janice quickly jotted them down. She called that number and was delighted to hear the heavy Texas drawl of this Charlie Brown who worked at a radio station. He promised to come for us as soon as he could. Two hours later, he approached on foot and explained that his car had broken down.

"I will call the lady you telephoned and ask her to come for us," he said.

It was almost 10:00 P.M. when the lady arrived. She explained that she couldn't get her car started, so she had come by bus. Empathy was written in Charlie's expression as he listened.

"With all these problems, it looks like there's spiritual warfare going on here," he said. "Let's pray." After praying, we struck out to walk the two miles to the Browns' home. We had walked less than two blocks when a car pulled up. The driver rolled down his window.

"Hey Charlie, where are you going?"

Charlie introduced us and explained our need to reach the Christian campsite.

"That is where I'm headed now," the man said. "I will take them." God had provided a way. When we arrived at the camp at 10:30 P.M., everyone was thrilled to see us. The rest of our engagements in Italy went without incident. An Italian we had met in Thessalonica

extended an invitation to us to sing during a midweek Bible study in Rome. What a privilege!

We also took the time to detour from our travel plan to see the leaning tower of Pisa. It was rather frightful to climb to the top. We heard that shortly after we were there, the tower was permanently closed because of the danger.

1989: Faye and Janice by the Leaning Tower of Pisa

En route to Spain, our train was waylaid in France, putting us way behind schedule. Upon arrival in Barcelona, there was no time to change our money. We ran to catch our next train. Hordes of travelers crowded the platforms. When we reached the correct coach, we couldn't board. Young backpackers pushed and jostled, choking the doorways of the overcrowded train.

One young man, desperately trying to get off, pushed against the flow. Someone bumped him, causing him to drop a handful of coins. Janice and I picked up several coins that landed on the platform at our feet and handed them to him. He thanked us in German and hurried off. Then as we climbed the steps, I found one more coin just inside the coach. I picked it up and glanced down the platform in search of the man, but he had already disappeared into the crowd. With a shrug I slipped the coin into my pocket.

That night when our train pulled into Valencia, it didn't surprise us that Ginny Loft was not there to meet us. We were arriving seven hours behind schedule. Ginny had come early in the afternoon. She had stayed four hours meeting several trains. But when officials told her that no more were expected, she had driven back to her home in Murcia.

It was 11:00 P.M. I felt forlorn on the platform as I stood by the luggage waiting for Janice to return from the main part of the station where she had gone to exchange money. She returned with a grim report.

"The currency exchange places won't be open until Monday!" This was Friday night!

With visions of camping out on the station platform for three days without food or water, we acknowledged that this was one for the Lord.

While facing each other in the deserted depot, its silence accentuating our sense of desolation, we lifted our petition to God. With the final "Amen," I looked up. Janice's expression registered a glow of excitement.

"Is that an answer to our prayer?" she asked. Her eyes were fixed on something behind me.

What could be such a quick answer? I whirled around to look. There in blinking red lights was a notice which read, SPECIAL DESTINATION—ALICANTE —11:15 P.M.

"What makes you think that's an answer to prayer?" I asked, feeling the letdown.

"Maybe God wants us in Alicante!" Janice said.

"Our destination is Murcia, and Ginny told us that Valencia would be as close as the trains would take us," I reminded her.

"But that sign was not lit up before we prayed," Janice pointed, still hopeful.

I was too tired to find Janice's logic amusing. To appease her, I searched in the flight bag for the rail map. I thought it a waste of time, but I located the map and unfolded it. Janice leaned close, scanning the names.

"Here it is!" She pointed to a town. Seeing it was two-thirds of the way toward Murcia, my mood brightened.

"Good, let's take it!" I checked my watch. "Yikes, it's already 11:15. Hurry!" I snatched my share of the luggage and sprinted for the train with Janice close behind me. We boarded just in time, breathing a sigh of relief. In the past two days, all the coaches had been crammed full, but this time we had the entire car to ourselves.

When a conductor came through, we handed him our prepaid Eurail Passes, good for a month's travel on any major European rail lines.

"Do you know if there is any train from Alicante to Murcia?" Janice asked. "That's really our destination."

"I doubt it. I'm quite sure Alicante is the end of the line."

"What time will the train get there?"

"I don't really know," he paused. "Maybe 2 or 3 A.M."

"Don't you usually take this run?" I asked.

"It's not that. It is the train that doesn't usually go there. The route to Alicante is run only once or twice a year," he said.

Janice smiled at me, our thoughts obviously the same. God answered our prayer with this extremely infrequent train on the night we so desperately needed it.

> "Fear not, for I am with you; Be not dismayed for I am your God. I will strengthen you, yes, I will help you." (Isa. 41:10)

The conductor handed back our passes. Starting for the doorway, he paused. With a kind expression he said,

"Feel free to sleep. I will wake you when we reach Alicante."

We were sleeping soundly when the amiable conductor awakened us. Drowsily I checked my watch. Two o'clock. Disembarking, we once again found ourselves on a deserted platform. Although we were closer to our destination, fatigue set in and our spirits flagged. We plopped our luggage beside a bench and sat down. Approaching footsteps startled us. We looked up and recognized the conductor. He began to speak even before reaching us.

"I inquired for you concerning a train to Murcia. There is one. It's a commuter train leaving in two hours." He meant well, but as welcome as it sounded, we didn't get our hopes up.

"Our Eurail Pass isn't accepted on local commuter or subway trains," Janice explained. "And we have no Spanish currency yet for buying a ticket."

"I'll check on it for you." He headed again for the dispatch office. I turned to face Janice.

"You're wrong about not having any Spanish money, you know," I reached into my pocket for the coin we had found in Barcelona. "Did you forget about this?"

"Yes, I did," she admitted with a giggle, "but that's not enough for buying train tickets."

The conductor returned with a swift gait to his step.

"They'll accept your passes."

The news revitalized our languishing spirits. We thanked the conductor and in our hearts also thanked the Lord for His never failing care. Interesting enough, no one ever checked our passes on that commuter train.

We arrived in Murcia on Saturday at 7:00 A.M. God had safely brought us to our destination. He had even provided the means for contacting the missionary: that coin in my pocket was the right amount for making a local telephone call.

"Hello, Ginny," Janice said, "This is the twins. We're finally here."

"You're where? Valencia?" Ginny asked.

"No, we are in Murcia."

"Murcia! How did you get here from Valencia?" Ginny was clearly puzzled.

"By train," Janice smiled with amusement at Ginny's reaction.

"You couldn't have. Trains don't go from Valencia to Murcia."

"They did last night." With those words we were reminded God had done it.

PORTUGAL—The Express Train is Full

Our final travel glitch occurred when we realized we had accidentally booked our trip to Portugal on the wrong day. Ginny drove us to a travel office where our flight from Madrid to Lisbon was changed with no problem. Then she took us to the train station.

"If you can get seats on the express train to Madrid, you'll be able to connect with your flight."

We took our place behind the four people already in the line at the ticket window. The one at the window asked for a seat on the express train. The ticket agent shook her head. I turned to Ginny.

"Did you see that? That guy couldn't get a ticket on the express train." The next one in line also requested a seat on the express to Madrid. He, too, was refused and walked away disappointed. The next two people were also told that the express train was booked full. By the time we stepped up to the ticket window I was thinking, what's the use of trying?

Just then another lady entered the booth. We were left waiting as the former ticket agent took care of her cash drawer and turned it over for the incoming shift.

Finally the lady turned her attention to me, but

before I could speak, a man leaned in front of me to ask the lady for a seat on the express train.

With a wave of the hand she said, "It's full, sorry." Again she turned her attention to me. I asked for the same thing.

"May we please book two seats on the express train to Madrid?"

To our surprise she said, "Yes."

I was tempted to say, "Are you sure?" But I kept silent as I watched her make out the tickets.

"Oh Lord, You've left us marveling again!"

The twins look over ancient ruins in Philippi.

28

Out in the Night

∼ by Faye ∼

———————●———————

The day had been cold. The night was frigid. I turned up the collar of my lightweight coat after stepping from the train.

"Brrr!" Even with the woolen Norwegian sweater under the coat, I still shivered from the icy gusts of Arctic wind. Our hearts felt as heavy as our luggage. We had traveled all day from Holland with plans to board a ship from Denmark's north coast to Norway. But since some trains were behind schedule, we arrived too late to catch the day's final commuter to the coast. Janice checked the door to the train station. Locked! With a tone of desperation, teeth chattering, she muttered, "We've got to find shelter."

> "We are hard pressed on every side, yet not crushed; we are perplexed, but not in despair; persecuted, but not forsaken; struck down, but not destroyed." (II Cor. 4:8)

All was dark except for lights from one building a block away. We walked as fast as we could with luggage in tow. The building was a police station. Just inside there was a waiting area with a row of chairs. We

welcomed the warmth. Speaking in English to the uniformed officer behind a counter, we asked if he knew of
a hotel where we could stay. He only shook his head. I
pointed toward the chairs and asked if we could sit
there for the night. The officer gestured toward the door
and said something about it being against regulations.

I swallowed hard, fighting back tears. We could die
of hypothermia out there in the night. Speak in Norwegian, came a prompting from within my spirit. I turned
to the officer who was escorting us toward the door. *"Vi
har slekninger i Norge og vi hadde lyst til a ta boten fra
Hirtsals."* (We have relatives in Norway and we had
hoped to catch the ferryboat from Hirtsals.)

Immediately the officer's cold nature thawed, pleased
at my attempt to communicate in a language related to
his own. Now it was our turn to struggle to understand
his reply in Danish. We understood enough to realize
the officer had some work to do in Hirtsals, so he was
inviting us to go along. As he and another patrolman
took our luggage in hand and led the way to the squad
car, he explained that Hirtsals had a youth hostel where
we could stay.

Everything looked brighter again. It was a strange
turn of events for us to be riding through Denmark's
countryside in a police car. By the speed we were traveling, we wondered if the policemen were hoping to get
us to the coast in time to catch the ferry. When we
topped a hill overlooking the coastal town, we peered
with eager anticipation. Our hearts sank. The ship was
just pulling out to sea.

The squad car stopped at the youth hostel. All was
dark. We were by the coast where the frigid winds
whipped ferociously off the North Sea. We were grateful that the policemen did not abandon us. They rang
the bell, pounded on the door, aimed their powerful
flashlight beams in windows. The place looked de-

serted: vacant rooms, no curtains on the windows, no bedding on the bunks. I could see that the officers, like us, were shivering violently in the freezing cold.

"God, please help us!" Just then a man opened the door and showed us to a room. Again we thought it strange that our room had no bedding or curtains, but we didn't complain. We were glad to be in a warm building. We pulled extra clothing from our suitcase to use as covers. After the evening of roller-coaster emotions, we slept soundly.

The following morning we obtained the hostel's phone number from the man. If we needed to overnight on our return, we could reserve a room by phone. Within the hour we were by the docks, booking passage for the next ship. The schedule indicated that the return ferry would arrive near midnight and would not connect with our train, so we immediately telephoned the hostel to make a reservation. Strange! No one answered. We tried several times, then later from Norway. There was never a reply.

The following week when we returned to Denmark, the two of us walked from the dock to the youth hostel. We knocked and knocked, but to no avail. The place looked just as deserted as it had the previous week, but this time no one let us in.

"Lord, where are you? You took care of us last time, why not now?"

At last we gave up and decided to spend the night there on the porch. We settled in a nook where we were shielded from the wind, grateful that the night was not as frigid as it had been the previous time. We used papers, books, anything in our luggage that could serve to insulate from the cold of the cement, a hard "mattress." We put extra clothing on our heads, on our legs, and socks on our hands.

"You look like a real bag lady," Janice laughed.

"Do you think you look any better?" On the serious side I added, "Maybe God wants us to have some sympathy for the homeless." We lay with our backs together to ward off the chill. I was wishing I could drop off to sleep so the hours would pass quickly. Time dragged.

"Hey, Faye, are you asleep yet?"

"Are you kidding? Of course not," I replied.

"Then let's think of what Scriptures might apply to our situation."

"How about the book of Job." I snickered.

"Oh, we don't have it quite that bad."

"Let me think. The Apostle Paul had many trials: beatings, being stoned once, being robbed, even spending a day and a night in the deep. But we don't have it that bad either."

"That's true. I'm glad we're not shipwrecked on the North Sea." Then Janice added a verse, "My brethren (my twin), count it all joy, when you fall into various trials." (James 1:2)

"It is hard to find the joy when you are in the middle of the trial." I squirmed, shifting a book that poked my ribs. No position was comfortable.

"Here's another verse that is tough right now. "I have learned in whatever state I am, to be content." (Phil. 4:11b)

How about this one, Faye. "Foxes have holes and birds of the air have nests, but the Son of Man has nowhere to lay his head." (Luke 9:58)

"Wow! Jesus knows our discomfort. We're in good company." I soon fell asleep.

The next day we slept well on the train. We still questioned, "Lord, why did we have to sleep on the street?" When things don't go as we plan, many times it is because God has a different plan. It gives us an opportunity to see Him at work.

Thinking back on our "night out," we began to see the experience in a new light. We considered the abandoned appearance of the youth hostel: no lights, no curtains, no linens, no tenants, no one answering the phone. Perhaps the Lord had allowed us to sleep outside on the warmer night so that we would see that He did let us in on the bitterly cold night.

Would it be preposterous to consider that when we were in such desperate need, God had sent an angel to open the door?

Slow down from your rapid pace,
Take time for the human race, ♪♪ ♪
And you will be able to face,
All the trials the come your way.

When trials come and make life seem unfair,
And I can't see beyond the pain I bear,
No longer can I smile, while focused on my trial,
Then I hear Jesus say, "Come away."

"Come away, Come away," ♪♪ ♪♪
"Come and give Me full affection,
I will show you a new direction,
Come away, Come away."

PART V

Reflecting on God's Answers to PRAYER

Needs for prayer vary depending on the situation. Likewise God's answers vary, not according to our desires or expectations, but according to His will. We realize that this book with its emphasis on God's mysterious ways is filled with stories of His provision, protection, and guidance, but in this section we include some very specific prayers:

Prayer for renewal from "burnout"
Prayer for physical healing
Prayer for reunions
Prayer for rain
Prayer for a sign of God's will

We stand in awe as we consider that God would listen to us and answer our prayers! "What is man that You are mindful of him, and the son of man that You visit him?" (Ps. 8:4)

"For the eyes of the Lord are on the righteous and His ears are open to their prayer." (I Pet. 3:12a)

Another Lesson to be Learned: ∼ Be Still ∼

1976: During a busy eight-month tour, Janice and Faye
realize their need for solitude and find the
peace and strength that only God can give.

29

Be Still

～ by Janice ～

With our exciting life—the travel adventure to exotic areas where tourists have not been, the joy of seeing God's saving grace transforming lives, and the thrill of His guidance, protection, and provision in our own lives, one may think we are always content and eager to serve. I wish that were so, but it is not always the case. There are times when, like the Apostle Paul, we find ourselves admitting, "I have the desire to do what is good, but I cannot carry it out." (Rom. 7: 18b NIV)

One such time was on an eight-month overseas tour with the first month in Hong Kong and Thailand, the remaining seven in Australia. Faye was taken ill with amoebic dysentery near the end of our weeks in Thailand. We needed to wait until she had regained sufficient strength, so our flight to Australia was delayed three days.

When we reached Brisbane, it was as though we hit the ground running. The schedule of singing responsibilities was full. Faye, in her weak condition, found it difficult to cope with the pressures. Her heart developed an arrhythmia that she had felt only once before when under extreme stress. When more bookings were added to the already full schedule, I felt that others were being insensitive to Faye's needs. Resentment mounted. We felt powerless, or we lacked the desire to change our attitudes.

Preparations for evangelistic services were demanding. We were not accustomed to their order of service nor their songs. The hymns, though having the same lyrics, often had different tunes. Then, too, there was the emotional drain of facing cultural differences. Australians have a separate value system than Americans— not better nor worse, just different. We struggled to perceive their way of thinking and to conform so as not to offend.

> "If it is possible, as much as depends on you, live peaceably with all men." (Rom.12:18)

As the weeks of heavy schedule wore on, we wore out. Our attitudes grew increasingly negative; little things caused resentments to surface. We are warned, "Do not give the devil a foothold," (Eph. 4:27 NIV) but that is exactly what we were doing. Situations, events, and our reactions to them were sapping our physical strength, our emotional reserve, and our spiritual fervor. Scripture such as, "Never be lacking in zeal, but keep your spiritual fervor, serving the Lord," (Rom. 12:11 NIV) caused us to feel more guilt. We pressed on, keenly aware that we were working in our own strength, not in God's power. This made us feel hypocritical.

One night after a particularly taxing day, we retired to our bedroom feeling beat. Faye dropped off to sleep, but I lay awake, troubled in spirit. My thoughts drifted back to a day in Thailand when we were traveling with missionary Robert Morse to the Lisu village of Mipo. At one point on the winding mountainous road, Robert had swerved the jeep to avoid hitting a cloth-wrapped bundle in the road.

"What was that, a baby?" Faye asked, alarmed.

"No. Probably some appeasement for the spirits," Robert had explained. "It is possible that someone has died in the village."

Moments later, we stopped shy of our destination to share in a picnic lunch. When we had finished eating, we all started to gather everything to carry back to the vehicle.

"Wait!" Mr. Morse motioned for us to sit down. "Let's not be in such a hurry. Too often we rush about, keeping busy, perhaps thinking the faster we work, the more we'll please God. We only end up going in our own strength, which  is never sufficient. Let's have a prayer time. We need to remember we are involved in spiritual warfare. We must go in God's power."

That evening in Mipo, as we sat on the split bamboo floor of a dimly-lit village home, we saw evidence of the fear that grips people who live in an animistic society. The Bible study Robert was leading was suddenly interrupted by a great commotion—people yelling and the noise of sticks being banged against the walls of the adjacent house.

We stepped outside to investigate. Mr. Morse had spoken the Lisu language since he was a child, so he quickly understood the situation. As he had surmised, someone in the village had died. Now the people with sticks were driving the demons out of the corners of the homes in hopes that the spirit of the dead would not trouble them. Yes, we were involved in spiritual warfare. It felt reassuring to know we were on God's side.

My reminiscing stopped. An echo of Robert Morse's gentle admonition again stirred me: "Let's not be in such a hurry. Too often we rush about...we end up going in our own strength...we must go in God's power."

At that time our resolve had been strong to daily go in God's power. Now only weeks later, that resolve had melted away. We had been neglecting to take time for personal Bible study and prayer. It seemed there was never time. It left us plugging through a heavy schedule halfheartedly with our own strength ebbing fast. What is the solution, Lord? How can we slow down when others are in control of our itinerary? A tear trickled down my cheek, and I drifted off to sleep.

"The Lord lifts up those who are bowed down." (Ps. 146:8b NIV)

The following morning, time was once again at a premium. Faye and I discussed our plight as we dressed. We were aware that self pity and resentments were producing a bitter spirit. We have been cautioned, "...lest any root of bitterness springing up cause trouble...." (Heb. 12:15b)

We felt as the disciples who, caught in a storm on the sea, had strained at the oars all night, before Jesus came walking on top of their problem. Our prayer, though short, was one of desperation: "Lord, we have struggled in our own strength far too long, doing only what was our duty to do. Help our hearts to get involved, so that instead of merely coping, we may enjoy the remainder of this tour."

The day was tiring, but by evening we saw that Jesus was already answering our prayer. We met Chris, a lad in his late teens, whose spiritual depth reached beyond his years. Even while we were singing, his expression was indicative of one who sees beyond the surface—a gift of discernment. This quiet young man, who was undergoing misunderstandings himself, had developed patience and a deep sensitivity to the true inner needs of others. His nature was characterized by Isaiah 30:15b, "In quietness and confidence shall be your strength."

Following the service, Faye and I were separated from each other, talking with people in the churchyard. As one family bid me good night, Chris approached.

"Rather tiring to make small talk, isn't it?" he asked. I nodded and wondered how he could read my thoughts. Then he made a strange offer. "How would you two like to go fishing tonight?"

"Yes! That might be just what we need," I said, feeling better already.

"Righteo, I'll get everything ready and pick you up at your home." Chris thoughtfully checked with Noel and Jan Smith, our hosts, to make sure they had no objection. The crowd had thinned considerably when I broke the news to Faye.

"Fishing?" Her expression registered a threatened anxiety rather than eagerness. Tears filled her eyes, and she tried to blink them away not wanting others to notice. "I'm tired. I just want to go to bed. There is never enough time to get rested up." Despite Faye's initial reluctance, she readied herself and enjoyed the late evening's excursion.

The fishing, quite unlike the lake or stream fishing to which we have been accustomed, had us wading thigh-deep in a river, spearing eels. Though we never quite caught the knack of wielding the spear, the outing was successful in refreshing us.

The following day was another that would test our endurance. In late afternoon, we had just enough time free for our evening meal and to change clothes for the evening service. We took seats at the dining table and the plates of appetizing roast lamb and steaming hot vegetables were set before us. I wished that our work was done for the day. I wanted to relax and enjoy the meal without being pressured by the singing responsibilities that still lay ahead. Physically I was chewing savory food, while mentally feeding my bitterness.

We were one month into the seven-month itinerary and had not had one day free. We were busy most of the days from 7 A.M. to 11 P.M. As I lifted a forkful of lamb with mint sauce to my lips, a thought suddenly came to me. Jesus was so pressed that often He "…did not even have time to eat…." (Mark 6:31b) My fork nearly stopped in midair.

The Holy Spirit was reminding me that Jesus daily faced a heavier schedule of emotionally and physically draining activity than we ever have to endure. He was probably tempted to complain at times, too, for we know Jesus "…was in all points tempted as we are—yet without sin." (Heb. 4:15b) He did not yield to the temptation of becoming resentful.

While helping to wash the dishes, I related the thought to Faye. It was some comfort to know that Jesus had gone through our same type of stress—only worse.

"But how did He cope? How did He gain the strength to keep going?" We were back in our bedroom hurriedly gathering what we needed for the evening when Faye answered my question.

"Jesus often went to the mountains or wilderness areas to pray, even spending all night in prayer."

"That's what we need to do. But how can we get away when we are guests in someone's home," I said.

"God can make it possible," Faye said with a new resolve. "Let's pray."

That evening after the evangelistic service had ended and most of the cars had pulled out of the churchyard, Faye and I stood gazing at the picture-perfect moonlit scene to the west. The Great Dividing Range was framed by the gangly limbs of a bunya pine. I sighed. It seemed so improbable that we would be able to get away.

"It looks as though your thoughts are far away," broke in the familiar voice of Chris.

"Not very far, really," I said. "Just thinking of your mountains and how we would love to spend some quiet time there." Chris nodded with understanding.

"Few people know what peace there is in silence." Again his perceptive nature had looked beyond our faults to see our need. His non-condemning, sympathetic spirit gave us liberty to openly share our inner feelings and failures.

Chris arranged a mountain outing for us. Daylight and evening hours allowed us no time so, just as Jesus had done, we went at night. Chris and his sister, Lyndell, led the way up the steep incline. Sometime past midnight, we reached the top of the range, where Chris and Lyndell busied themselves building a bonfire. They understood when we wandered off alone for prayer.

The oily leaves of the eucalyptus trees reflected the silvery rays of the moonlight. At one point, we were startled by a sudden noise, but smiled to see some wallabies bounding away. The mountaintop was a picture of peace. In the stillness, our troubled hearts made confession to God.

The Australian evangelist who had arranged our itinerary had become the target for our resentment and bitterness. We had worked with this man of God in other places and had experienced a precious kinship of Spirit, a bond of unity. We had admired his strong commitment and had grown through his faith. We were fully aware that he had not changed. His deep love for the Lord's work was still a powerful motivating force in his life. Although his zeal was partly to blame in causing insensitivity to our needs, thus driving a wedge between us, we could not expect to change him. We could ask the Lord to transform our attitudes.

In the quiet solitude that night, we prayed that God would renew in us the love, the forgiveness, the strength, and the zeal we desperately needed. We hungered to serve in harmony and unity as we ought. Portions of Philippians 2 reminded us of our example, "Let this mind be in you which was also in Christ Jesus: who,... taking the form of a servant,...humbled himself and became obedient...."

Later we returned to the fireside and shared in fellowship with our friends. The friendship, though new, deepened and developed into a rich spiritual bond. The time for meditation also provided the inspiration for us to compose this song based on Psalm 46:10a.

BE STILL AND KNOW THAT I AM GOD ♪ ♪

Walking through a meadow or climbing a hill,
Sitting there in silence just being still,
God seems to speak there in a voice small and still,
"Just read My Word, and seek My will." ♪ ♪

Climbing up a mountain, and resting a while,
Looking all about us just brings a smile,
Standing on a mountain and feeling the breeze,
Listen to the birds singing in the trees,
Be still and know that I am God, be still, be still.

The night passed quickly and soon the daylight hours found us laboring again in the valley. Though we had lost a night's sleep, we felt alert and energetic for the day's full schedule. There was ample occasion for inciting stress, but we coped with ease. In late afternoon, we went to sing at a hospital, which snowballed into requests to sing from room to room. It was nearing time for the evening service. Ordinarily under such circumstances, we would have been fretting, feeling the stress of not reaching the church in good time. Instead a calm acceptance pervaded our spirits.

"We are learning the lesson of the Good Samaritan, that ministering to the sick and wounded is more important than hurrying away to our duties at the temple," Faye said.

This tranquility remained even when we entered the church building with only five minutes until service time. Chairs were being placed in the aisles for latecomers. We made our way to the front and entered the room off the platform where we always had a prayer time with the evangelist.

"Let me see what you have planned for tonight," the preacher said, taking the song service list from my hand. Then he began making changes—cutting certain hymns and requesting others. Australian pastors often choose the hymns that best correlate with their sermons. If this evangelist had last-minute inspirations, we should be willing to submit to the changes. Though we had always complied, it nevertheless had become a source of frustration. It necessitated our flipping nervously through hymn books to find the number changes. This time, it did not unnerve us. A peace prevailed that we could not comprehend. We felt no irritation as the preacher jotted his ideas on my paper. I chided myself for not turning the problem over to the Lord sooner.

When bowing in prayer with him, we at last felt the oneness, the unity in spirit and purpose that had been missing. God had restored the relationship. We were a team again.

Moments later, Faye and I were facing the crowd. We sensed a genuine freedom in Spirit. The song service became an overflow of joyous praise. The change in us wrought a marked difference in the audience's reaction as well. The joy in the eyes of Chris and Lyndell especially mirrored our jubilation. They knew the source of our joy.

When we sat down, we felt exhilarated rather than drained. As the preaching followed, we were filled with appreciation and a spiritual admiration for this evangelist. We thanked the Lord for removing the bitterness and replacing it with love. We reflected, too, on how busy the day had been. God had not changed the busy schedule. He had changed us so that we could face it as overcomers. Had not the Lord allowed the day to be extra busy to demonstrate to us that even under the most stressful pressure, we could give and give if dependent on His power, rather than our own? The often quoted verse, "I can do all things through Christ who strengthens me," (Phil. 4:13) took on fresh meaning as the result of spending a night on the mountain in prayer.

The remainder of our tour was not always a mountaintop experience. There were times when the pressures would again threaten to get the best of us, but we would not allow it to build up. Instead we would turn it over to Jesus. We also recognized the importance of not missing our morning quiet time, even if it meant having less sleep.

As months passed, we grew to love Australia, to marvel at the variety of flowers, the uniqueness of its animals, and the beauty of her coastlines. But most precious to us were the deep friendships that had developed. No more were we threatened nor offended by cultural differences. We had come to love the Australian people and to accept their ways.

On several occasions, our schedule took us back to the farming community where the Lord first turned our attitudes around. Each time, our friends Chris and Lyndell arranged an outing to climb the mountains. Knowing the joy and benefit of getting away, they usually invited several others to join us in the inspiring time for prayer.

When the seven-month tour came to an end, two memories we would forever cherish tugged at our hearts: our times alone with God on a mountain, and our times spent sharing in the faith with Christian friends. They still remain very dear to us. In our final concert the night before we were to fly back to America, we included another song that we had composed during one of our outings on the Great Dividing Range. We fought back tears before its conclusion.

A SONG OF LOVE ♪♪

I hear the wind a blowing,
But who knows where it is going?
I hear the birds a singing.
Who gave them a song?
Who placed the stars up yonder?
These questions you may ponder.
"God" is the answer to them all.

Now let me sing this song that's on my heart,
A song of thanks to God above.
Thanks for the joy He gives right from the start,
Now let me sing this song of love.

I feel the warmth of friendship, ♪♪
Who gives this bond of kinship?
Who draws us close together in spirit and love?
Who gave these friends to me?
I know they'll always be,
Deep-rooted friendships in the Lord.

A Need for Healing

India 1978: While Janice was hospitalized with
back trouble, Faye continued alone with
the schedule of singing in villages.

30

Lord, Please Heal Me

～ by Janice ～

———————————◖▭◗———————————

Although generally healthy, we have had occasional problems. We'll share specific stories where prayer obviously helped to facilitate the healing.

Back Injury

"If she takes another step she could be paralyzed!" The Indian doctor was speaking in Hindi to Missionaries Bernel and Joan Getter, but I detected the urgency in his voice. Joan translated his diagnosis to me. I tensed as I lay upon the cold metal surface of the antiquated X-ray table.

"This is serious. It's a ruptured disc. She must be hospitalized," the doctor said.

As papers were being made out for my admittance, Joan hurried back to the mission bungalow to inform my twin. This was the day we were scheduled to travel by train, a day's journey, to the Kulpahar Mission. Now Faye would have to go alone to perform concerts for the next eight days without me. She hurriedly repacked, leaving what items I might need.

The back trouble had begun before Christmas. Assuming it would get better in time, I had not checked with a doctor before departing for India in January. I suffered with the pinched nerve during two months of village evangelism. Jeep rides on rough trails and through riverbeds had caused the pain to intensify.

Now I was to experience life in an Indian hospital. I was put in skin traction, which meant a system of weights pulling at the legs. The ward was full, not only of patients, but also their relatives who slept on mats on the cement floor. The hospital did not provide meals, so the families were there to cook for the patients. With the use of small kerosene burners, they often caused the ward to be filled with smoke and the pungent smell of curry. Joan Getter pedaled her bicycle the mile from the mission bungalow to bring my food.

A cleaning lady swept the floor daily. I dreaded her coming. The dust she stirred up invariably caused me to cough or sneeze, resulting in excruciating pain. Self pity threatened to undo me. Most of all I longed for a bath. My feet were terribly dirty. There had been no opportunity to wash them since returning from the villages. Finally on the third day, after much persuasion from Mrs. Getter, the nurses bathed me and brushed my long hair. I felt human again.

I kept myself amused by watching birds fly in and out of the broken windowpanes. I didn't have much time to myself, though. Nurses often brought other patients to my bedside, requesting that I sing. I used Hindi songs and prayed that God would minister to them through the messages.

The leg traction did nothing to improve my condition. It only added to my discomfort by creating a pressure point bruise, as painful as a burn. After eight days I was checked out of the hospital and taken back to the mission bungalow. Later that day, Faye returned from Kulpahar. As the two of us have seldom been separated, we had missed each other. For a while there was non-stop chatter. We had plenty of catching up to do.

The following morning we rode with the Getters to the train station. My hospital ordeal with no exercise had left me weak. I fainted on the platform.

We had one more concert before leaving India. It was at a school for the blind in the Himalayan foothills. Silas Ekka, the director, brought a couch to the veranda where we were to sing.

"Your audience can't see you anyway. You might as well be comfortable," he said. I did appreciate reclining pain free for the concert, but Faye teased me for lying down on the job. From there we flew homeward via Europe and across the Atlantic. In New York we had a tight connection, so we had to run through the long concourses. With each step, pain shot through my sciatic nerve. Faye, running ahead, reached the gate in time for them to hold the flight.

As that plane finally touched down in Denver, I checked my watch. Late again. We would have to rush to make our connection to Colorado Springs. While the airplane was docking at the gate, I prayed, "Oh Lord, please send an electric cart so that I won't have to walk the long concourses." I rose to my feet and stood motionless, allowing the pain to subside; then I followed Faye into the terminal. There at the gate was an electric cart! The attendant who was assisting an elderly lady, allowed us to step aboard. As we glided quietly and speedily through the long corridors, I thanked the Lord for this obvious answer to my prayer. Without the ride, I doubt we would have made the connection.

After twenty-eight hours of travel from the far side of the globe, we circled over our hometown. Snow-covered Pikes Peak loomed majestic against the clear winter sky. Home. We were home at last. "There's no place like home." I whispered, as tears of relief spilled down my cheeks. We had only a week in Colorado Springs before a three-week concert tour of the Midwest. I immediately went to see a doctor.

"Rest as much as possible during this week, plus on your trip," the doctor said. "When you return, I'll run tests to determine whether you will need hip traction or surgery." Surgery! I certainly wanted to avoid that. If I were to be hospitalized, it would take of the time and funds needed for our next overseas trip. We were booked for an April through August tour to Australia shortly after the Midwest tour. We would have to delay our departure to Australia. Faye wrote a letter to Doug Willis, the Australian preacher who arranged our itinerary, asking him to cancel April's bookings. She explained about my back injury and of the possible need for surgery. We assumed we could still meet the commitments for four of the five months.

During our three-week tour of the Midwest, the back pain worsened until I could no longer bear to sit in the car. Faye did all the driving while I lay in the back seat. One evening when the pain was particularly acute, I took a pain pill before concert time. It made me almost too dizzy to sing. After that concert, a lady approached me to tell about her former back problem.

"I had a test that showed I had a ruptured disc and the doctor said I needed surgery. Then because of James 5, I called on the elders of the church to pray for me before I went into the operating room. The doctor was amazed that the disc was not ruptured as badly as the test had indicated," she said.

"That's wonderful, but you should have had the elders pray for you before your test instead of before your operation. Maybe you could have avoided having surgery," I said. Just as the words tumbled from my lips,

I realized how it applied to me. I would soon be having that same test. I read the James passage and determined to have the elders pray for me.

> "Is anyone among you sick? Let him call for the elders of the church, and let them pray over him, anointing him with oil in the name of the Lord. And the prayer of faith will save the sick, and the Lord will raise him up." (James 5:14,15a)

"Good morning, girls. It is a beautiful Lord's Day!" Mom's sweet voice aroused us from sleep. It felt good to discover we were in our own bed. "Janice, you may appreciate knowing that Dad was up praying for you in the night. He wouldn't have told you, but he prayed fervently, and he felt the Lord assuring him that you will be all right."

Following the worship service, the elders prayed for me. As I considered the loving prayerful concern that these men and our parents had shown, I again reflected on the Scripture that went on to say, "The effective, fervent prayer of a righteous man avails much." (James 5:16b) I felt no instantaneous total healing, yet I sensed an inner assurance that I had reached a turning point. Previously my condition had steadily deteriorated, but now I was on the mend.

The following day in the doctor's office, I felt a sneeze coming on. For the past three months, sneezes had always precipitated a paralyzing pain. "Ah..ah..ah." I quickly pressed a finger against my upper lip in a futile attempt to suppress it. Too late! "Ah..Choooo!" I braced myself. Nothing happened. I relaxed with a smile. Although I still felt a weakness in my back even after the elders prayed for me, I no longer had the excruciating pain.

"You seem to be improving," the doctor said after his examination. I agreed, explaining that the church elders had prayed for me.

"Praise the Lord! I also believe that God does heal,"
he said. I was dismissed from the doctor's office and
was told to wait and see. Surgery was no longer considered. That day our visas arrived, as if to say, "All
systems Go." We sent a telegram to Doug Willis stating
we would come in April as originally planned. Upon
arriving in Australia, we asked Doug if it was a problem
that we came on schedule after having asked him to
cancel the first month.

"Cancel the first month?" He looked puzzled. "I
never received any letter about canceling anything."
[The letter had been delayed in an Australian mail
strike, finally arriving five weeks late. God works in
wondrous ways.]

During April we were kept busy giving concerts in
schools, churches, and auditoriums. I had felt gradual
improvement in my back, but I was cautious with it. I
still felt a weakness with any unexpected jar.

One day, we had some spare time before our next
concert. Doug Willis steered the car onto a side road that
led into some hills. The day was beautiful. A slight
breeze whispered through the gum trees and the light of
the afternoon sun shone on the eucalyptus oil of the
leaves. Doug parked the car and suggested we have a
prayer time. We had always enjoyed praying with this
man, but for some reason, this time I desired to be alone.
Doug nodded, understanding. I headed down a trail,
strolling through the forest, praying as I went. Jesus
seemed very near.

I sat on a stump, my feet shuffled through some dried
leaves. I looked up through the branches overhead and
praised the Lord until tears filled my eyes. I lost track of
time because of being with the One who is not bound by
time. Finally, as one coming awake from a dream, I
realized I should be getting back. I started the long
return trek, being careful where I stepped to avoid

jarring my back. I had not gone far when I stopped in my tracks. What was that I heard? I strained my ears to listen. There it came again, "Ja..a..nice!" A faint voice; it was clearly Faye's, calling from a great distance. Then it came again. This time it was unmistakably Doug's voice, "Ja..a..a.. nice!" They sounded so far away. I considered calling back, but realized I was downwind from them. They wouldn't be able to hear me. If only I could run! I had not run in four months since I had first pinched the nerve. Then a passage of Scripture came to mind,

"Those who wait on the Lord shall renew their strength; they shall mount up with wings like eagles, they shall run and not be weary, they shall walk and not faint." (Isa. 40:31)

"Lord, I don't need the 'they shall walk' part, but I'd love to be able to run. Please give me the wings of an eagle! Help me to run," I prayed. I rose up in faith. Step after step I ran, feeling as though I were floating in an ecstatic dream. It thrilled me that the jogging was not jarring my back. My waist-length hair wafted in the gentle breeze, while tears of joy moistened my cheeks. At last I neared the car where Doug and Faye stood. Seeing my tears, Faye eyed me with concern.

"What's the matter, Janice?"

"Nothing." I brushed at the tears. "I was running. Didn't you see me?"

"Yes, but why?" She still thought something had frightened me.

"I had to hurry back. When I heard you calling my name, I knew you were worrying."

Both Faye and Doug, looking puzzled, jointly echoed, "We never called you." There was no one else around.

I concluded God had put the voices on the wind to cause me to rise up in faith and run. Since that time in 1978, my back has given me no more trouble.

A Stomach Problem

In every country we have always eaten whatever is put before us, not fearing for our health. "Nothing is to be refused if it is received with thanksgiving." (I Tim. 4:4) Yet, occasionally we have become sick. Recently in Poland I developed a stomach disorder causing me pain any time I ate. Food wouldn't stay down. As a result, I ate as little as I could tolerate without offending our hosts.

One Sunday morning, we had arrived at a chapel well before time for the service to begin. The pain suddenly came. I winced as I held my abdomen.

"Faye, I'm hurting again."

"It's been eight days, hasn't it?" Her expression reflected concern.

I nodded, discouraged. We were to sing for nearly an hour that morning. How would I cope? I then asked for prayer. During the church service, the pastor called me to the front for the special prayer time.

A hymn followed. I was trying to mouth the Polish words of the song when suddenly it dawned on me the pain was gone. As we gave our concert, I felt great! After the service, I was hungry. When we had dinner with a Polish family, I ate well, feeling perfectly normal. The prayer before the meal was praise for my renewed health.

Swollen Foot

I should have known better than to try "kicking up my heels." Others make it look easy. When I tried, the leap went fine—the landing was a flop! My right foot buckled under me and I fell in pain. I couldn't tolerate any weight on it. It was not only sprained but also had a chipped bone. The doctor wanted me back in a week, saying I would need a cast or crutches for six weeks. A CAST! I didn't want a cast or crutches. Within a week we were to go to India. How would I manage in the hot tropics? How could I walk on muddy trails, wade through rivers, or balance on narrow rice paddy ridges?

I had the elders pray for me. Immediately my foot improved. Though still swollen, it no longer hurt to bear weight. When I returned to see the doctor, he was surprised to find no problem with my mobility. I would not need a cast or crutches. I was pleased to walk away with only an ace bandage, quite manageable in India.

Malaria

Following a trip to Papua New Guinea, I succumbed to malaria. Malaria is not contagious. One gets it from the bite of an anopheles mosquito. Usual symptoms are chills, fever, headache, and depression that turn on and shut off in cycles. It was a warm day in Colorado Springs, yet I shivered in my bulky winter parka as I entered the medical facility. Because of the fever, my hair hung in sweaty ringlets.

Knowing I needed to get my blood tested while the fever was high, I walked past the receptionist. Precious time could be lost if I stopped to fill out papers. The young woman at the desk tried to get my attention, but I proceeded straight to the lab. Minutes later, my twin approached the receptionist. The young lady stared dumbfounded, then handed Faye the papers. When I returned from the lab, the lady threw up her hands and nearly fell off her chair.

"Mercy sakes alive, there are TWO of you! I wondered how you could look so sickly one minute and so normal the next." After we all had a good laugh, Faye handed me the paperwork.

"Would you mind completing this. I have a terrible headache," she said. It was soon evident we both had malaria. We were sharing the symptoms—it's a "twin thing." I had the chills and fever, Faye had the headaches and depression, each turning on or turning off every twenty-four hours.

Malaria struck again in 1993 when we were in Chile, South America. This time we reversed symptoms. Faye had chills and fever, and I the headaches and depression. We hadn't thought to bring any malaria medication with us. Doctors there didn't know how to treat it. Missionaries Ralph and Cindy Shead suggested that the various missionaries in Santiago gather to pray for us. One brought oil for the anointing mentioned in James 5:14-16. By morning all signs of the malaria were gone. In the near decade since, neither of us has had a reoccurrence. To God be the glory!

Chile: After being healed of malaria, the twins helped teach a children's session at a South America missionary retreat.

Broken Shoulder: A "Twincident"

While ice skating, Faye fell and broke a shoulder.

"I was doing a triple lutz," she joked, but admitted that she was just a triple klutz. As a loyal twin, I felt the pain. After the bone healed, she was to go through therapy. Interesting enough, my shoulder also froze up. I had no more movement than Faye, yet X-rays proved nothing was wrong with mine.

We called on the elders to pray for us. It did help to diminish the pain so that we could both endure the ten months of physical therapy. Is that carrying the "twin thing" too far? Others who heard about it laughed.

Oh well, as they say, laughter is good medicine!

31

Lost and Found

～ by Faye ～

---○---

A traveling ministry such as ours offers the blessings of acquaintances worldwide, yet occasionally we lose contact with distant friends. This chapter is devoted to those unusual circumstances of God's intervention to reestablish lost friendships.

Audrey Hughes

When we were seven years old and living in Hibbing, Minnesota, a young lady conducted a KYB (Know Your Bible) Club in our home. Every Tuesday we, along with other neighborhood children, would leap off the steps of the school bus and run into the house. With choruses, flannelgraph stories, and Scripture memorization, Miss Hughes made the Bible come alive. During each week our mother helped us learn new verses, so we could proudly recite them to Audrey: "For all have sinned and fall short of the glory of God," (Rom. 3:23) "Be kind to one another." (Eph. 4:32a) The verses we memorized in those early years can still be easily recalled, a clear example of the value of teaching children while they are young.

Sixteen years later, Janice and I were conducting after-school Bible clubs patterning our teaching after Audrey's example. We longed to see our childhood teacher to thank her for her influence. So, we asked God to get us in touch with her. Admittedly, we doubted as we prayed. After all, we had moved from Minnesota to Colorado when we were only eight years old. Besides, Audrey Hughes had been single. Doubtless she had since married.

Two months later, we were in Minnesota visiting Uncle Paul, our dad's eldest brother. Paul, whose first wife had passed away, had since remarried. We were becoming acquainted with his new wife, Hazel. While we were in their home, Hazel received a letter from a friend. A portion of it read, "I hear you have recently married a Rostvit. Is he any relation to the Ed Rostvit family in whose home I conducted KYB Club years ago?" It was signed, Audrey Bunker. For us to be there on the day the letter arrived was amazing. Coincidence? We prefer to label it as God's orchestrated coincidents, an answer to our prayer.

Dr. Charles Richards

In the chapter entitled, "Upon the High Seas," we mentioned a man who drove us through hectic traffic from the coast to the Los Angeles airport. While in Australia thirteen years later, we were reminiscing.

"Remember that man who met us at the docks. What was his name?" I asked.

"I don't know," Janice replied. "I only remember he was tall, thin, and had a big warm smile. Wouldn't it be nice if we could see him now to thank him again?"

"Why don't we pray about it?" I said.

"What good would it do? We don't even know his name."

"All the more reason to pray. God knows him. If He

could reunite us with Audrey, whose name had changed, why can't He reunite us with a man whose name we have forgotten? My confidence even surprised myself.

We did pray, and the answer was not long in coming. Four weeks later we flew from Australia to the Philippines. Our tour included time with the Itawes people. Bible translators Charles and Mickey Richards met us. Charles was a tall, thin man with a winning smile.

"You may not remember me. Some years back I met you when you came by ship to L.A."

We praised the Lord. He had done it again!

Kandasami and Shanti

On our first trip to India in 1971, Kandasami had been the driver who had taken care of me in one village when I was sick. When we returned for a second visit in 1973, we were disappointed to learn that Kandasami and his wife Shanti had moved. One day while we were walking to a village, a local preacher approached us.

"Do you remember Kandasami and Shanti? They used to live in my village. Kandasami asked me to give you his address if I ever saw you." He handed us a slip of paper. We were elated.

In the chapter entitled, "We Pray, Yet Worries Prey," it was Kandasami (Mr. Dass) who met us at the airport on our third tour of India in 1974. We enjoyed occasional visits with this couple whenever we passed through Delhi. Then on the last night before flying back to America, we met Kandasami's brother-in-law. He had recently purchased a Bible and was eager to learn of God.

The Lord was obviously touching this man's heart and had arranged for us to be there. We stayed up the entire night sharing the Gospel, answering his questions, and praying with him. The Lord had reestablished the acquaintance for a purpose.

In India, a lost acquaintance is found. Faye and Janice meet with Kandasami and have opportunity to teach his relative about Jesus.

Lost Address Book

In 1979 we lost an address book. Some names were retrieved from mailing lists, or through friends, but still others were irretrievable. In the ensuing weeks, we noticed that whenever we felt sadness at the thought of another missing address, that person would write to us. No doubt the Holy Spirit had urged them to do so.

Lloyd Lanyon, a pastor and a pilot, had requested two weeks of our next Australian tour so he could fly us into the outback for some concerts. Quite certain that Mr. Lanyon didn't have our address, we feared this to be a lost opportunity. To our amazement, however, a letter arrived from him, so we did later have the joy of ministering to those who lived in isolated areas.

One year after losing our address book, we thought of only one address still missing—that of Kandasami and Shanti Dass. This time no letter came from them. In 1982 when we again journeyed to India, we felt sadness knowing we would not see our friends. Although we had been to their home in Delhi on the previous trips, we had never paid attention to the location. While riding in a three-wheel motorcycle taxi, we passed through an intersection I recognized.

"Janice, that street looks familiar—Panscheel Marg. Isn't that where the Dass family lives?"

Hearing our excitement, the driver looked my way. I quickly motioned for him to stop. The Dass' home was only a half block away. They were as pleased to see us as we were to see them. Friends whose address had been lost to us for a second time had been found again. Joy unspeakable.

Uncle Clifford

At the start of a six-month tour of African countries in 1985, we had the unusual task of searching for a lost uncle. For two decades Uncle Clifford had worked at a mine in Liberia, returning occasionally to see his family. Don Stahl, Clifford's son, asked us to look for him.

"The mining company went bankrupt and none of us has heard from Dad in nine months," he said. "We're afraid he doesn't have the funds for a flight ticket home, yet we don't dare send money. The address may no longer be any good." We jotted down the name of the company.

When we arrived in Liberia, missionaries Ken and Carolyn Vogel met us and drove us ninety miles eastward. That evening they briefed us on our singing itinerary. Knowing we would be tired from our flight, the first full day had been left open. This would be our only opportunity to search for our uncle. Ken, who was teaching at a Christian school, would be busy with exams so he couldn't drive us to Monrovia. We would go by local bus.

As we lay in bed that night, we felt apprehensive about the next day's adventure. Liberia's tropical heat and humidity added to our exhaustion. Janice prayed, "Lord, we dread tomorrow's task. Please give us sufficient rest in these few hours, and help us…" I don't even remember hearing the "Amen," as I drifted into a sound sleep. The next thing we knew, Carolyn's voice was rousing us.

"Janice? Faye? Are you awake? The bus for Monrovia should be here in half an hour." I had set the alarm but must have shut it off during the night. We jumped up and dressed. The bus arrived fifteen minutes early. We snatched our flight bag, said good-byes, and were out the door.

As we rode in silence, we again prayed for God's help. By 9 A.M. we reached Monrovia. We checked first at the U.S. Embassy, hoping Uncle Clifford had registered, but he hadn't. The receptionist suggested we check with the Bureau of Mines. She scrawled the address on a piece of paper and handed it over the counter.

While we rode by taxi, I searched frantically through our bag for the mining company's address. In our haste to leave that morning, we had neglected to take it along. Moments later we entered the Bureau of Mines' office. We felt foolish voicing our inquiry to the secretary. We were looking for an uncle for whom we had no address, no telephone number, and who had worked for a mining company for which we had no name, and that no longer existed. How vague could our quest be?

Despite our lack of information, the lady graciously gave us access to the file cabinets where all mining companies were listed. We flipped through endless files. Nothing jogged our memory. After hunting in vain, we were ready to give up the search. Just then a man entered the room. He cast a suspicious gaze in our direction, then asked the secretary what we were doing at the file cabinets. We felt embarrassed as she explained our situation. The man's expression softened.

"What's your uncle's name?" he asked. When we told him, his face lit up. "Clifford Stahl? I know him. We worked together at a mine over on Mano River." Then he pulled a photo from his pocket. "Is this him?" It was clearly our uncle pictured in front of a large piece of machinery.

"Do you know where we can find him?" I asked.

"No, I haven't seen him since the company folded last August. I'm no longer mining."

"You're working here in the office now," Janice said, more as a statement than a question. It seemed obvious from the heir of authority he had displayed. His reply took us by surprise.

"No, I'm a taxi driver now. Business was slow this morning, so I just dropped in here for no reason," he said. No reason? I suspect God had His reason: to help us.

This man, who called himself Nelson, offered to drive us down by the docks. He explained that the company had a temporary office there for selling their remaining ore. In a few minutes we were at the harbor. A man seated at a desk answered our inquiry.

"Yes, Clifford comes in once a month to check his mail. Too bad you missed him. He was just here yesterday." At least we knew that our uncle was alive and probably living in Monrovia. But how could we find him? A lady who overheard the conversation spoke up.

"You might check with Bernard, a man who works on the second floor of a bank building downtown. I think he knows Clifford." Nelson drove us to our next lead. Bernard did know where Clifford lived, and soon the four of us were in the taxi with Bernard giving directions. It was a long ride. We rode through residential sections, first past some nice homes then more moderate ones. When we entered an area of small, drab, cement-block houses, I wondered if Uncle Clifford had been reduced to poverty. We proceeded outside the city limits and turned off the highway onto a dirt road.

Eventually we followed a mere foot trail. The path led down to a swampy area where there was a two-room clapboard structure. Bernard pointed as the car rolled to a halt.

"That's where he lives."

We stepped out of the car, staring at the shack. Poor Uncle. He must not have enough money to get back to America. I glanced at my watch; it was 10:00 A.M. Only one hour had passed since starting our search. Truly God had helped us. We meekly knocked on the door. No answer. Nelson, with more determination, forcefully thumped his knuckles on the warped plywood. Not being latched well, the door swung open.

"Hello-o-o? Uncle Clifford?" Silence.

Both Nelson and Bernard indicated they needed to return to their work. They offered to drive us back to town. We thanked them, but said we would wait for our uncle. We assumed if he didn't come, we could walk back to the main road and catch a bus. Janice reached in our bag to get money for the taxi fare, but Nelson refused to accept anything.

"No," he insisted. "Clifford was a good friend and I'm glad to help his relatives." (Later when we told the missionaries about it, Ken said, "A Liberian taxi driver refused payment? That is unheard of!")

Less than an hour later, we spotted Uncle Clifford walking down the trail. Or was it him? We knew he should be about age 68, but this man looked much older. He was our uncle, and who can say which of the three of us was the most surprised. The once strong broad-shouldered Swede was now thin and frail. As we talked for hours, Clifford explained his plight. The mining company had promised to give big bonuses to its long-term employees if they waited around. The months wore on, but the promises fizzled. As Clifford's financial resources dwindled, he had moved from company housing to a rented apartment, and eventually to this shelter. The company did provide a flight ticket for his return, but then Clifford's health failed. He struggled through hepatitis and later malaria. Now he was only waiting for summer before flying to his home in northern Minnesota.

About a month after our visit, Uncle Clifford did fly home. His daughter, Betty, a registered nurse, placed him directly in a hospital. With good care, healthful meals, and plenty of loving support from his family, Clifford regained his sturdy stature of former years.

Dag Pagander

During that same African tour, we had a short time in Nairobi, Kenya. One afternoon the family with whom we were staying had to leave to run errands. When the phone rang, I answered it. I found a scrap of paper on which to write the phone message. To my surprise, the name Dag Pagander was on the paper. Dag is the man who often arranges our itinerary when we have tours of Norway.

When the family returned home, we inquired about it. The Paganders were temporarily involved in mission work in Africa. We walked the short distance to their home and had an enjoyable visit. We thanked the Lord for the reunion. The Pagander family has since returned to their homeland, and we have seen them on our trips to Norway. It's a small world.

Kay and Carolyn

Our spiritual tanks were running on empty after three and a half months of concerts in Australia and New Zealand. Our personal devotions had been quite erratic during the busy schedule. We longed for that to improve.

"I wish we could set our minds to memorizing Scripture again. It would also be good if we had someone to be accountable to, who would also be memorizing," Janice said.

"Someone like Carolyn Barricklow?" Carolyn had been one of our best friends during college. She had been a missionary in Japan for ten years. After that we had lost track of her.

"Yes, that would be great. Or perhaps Kay Kendall." We did not know her well during college but had perceived her to be one with a consistent devotional life.

The last stop in New Zealand brought us into the home of John Fulford. Since he had attended our same Bible college in America, we reminisced about mutual acquaintances. At one point John asked if we knew Kay Kendall.

"Interesting you should mention her. Only days ago we were talking about her. We haven't heard from her in twenty-five years. Do you have her address, or that of Carolyn Barricklow?"

John didn't know, but God did.

A few days later we left New Zealand and returned home to Colorado. We received a phone call from Kay Kendall in Michigan. She had a three-way phone connection. Who should be the third party? None other than Carolyn Barricklow! Briefly, we filled one another in on the news of the past couple decades. Then Kay explained why she had made the call.

"Lately my devotional life just hasn't been what it ought to be. I need someone to be accountable to. I'd like to memorize more Scripture and encourage each other." She had echoed our sentiments. Kay and Carolyn have continued the phone contact with us ever since.

Collette Divine

In our teenage years in the early 1960s, Collette

Divine, professional singer, gave us voice lessons each week. Nearly four decades passed. In the year 2000 we tried to locate her but to no avail. Then one day in 2001 we were singing room to room in a hospice. We overheard one visitor say to another, "Wouldn't Collette Divine enjoy hearing these twins?"

"Collette Divine! Do you know her?" We echoed simultaneously.

What a joy to be given her phone number. Within days Collette had invited us into her home for a nice long visit.

Robert Rayl

In chapter 11 we told about the choir tour bus driver who came to the Lord in 1971. Many times in the ensuing years we've wondered how this brother was doing. God knows our thoughts and desires, but perhaps there are times He waits to act until we specifically ask. Finally in December of 1999 while driving to Minnesota for Christmas, we prayed, "Lord, will you please let us be in contact with Robert Rayl again?"

Two weeks later we returned to Colorado. The phone rang. It was Robert.

"Where have you been? I've been trying to call you," he said. "Two weeks ago I felt a strong compulsion to get in touch with you, so I searched the Internet and found your number."

"We had to celebrate and be glad, because this brother was lost and is found." (Luke 15:32 NIV)

In February of 2000, Janice and Faye again see the bus driver who drove for their choir tour three decades earlier.

God's methods of communication are marvelous. The reunions here are only a foretaste of the joys we will experience when we are reunited with our "family" in Heaven.

Lost Luggage

A chapter titled "Lost and Found" for travelers surely would not be complete without one tale of lost luggage. For our first thirty years of travels and over eight hundred flights, we had always boasted that we had never lost anything. Then came the tour when the old saying came true: "In this jet age you can have breakfast in Colorado, lunch in New York, supper in London, and your luggage in HONG KONG." We were on an extended tour with singing engagements in Iceland, Egypt, Ukraine, Belarus, Poland, and the Czech Republic.

We always had made it a practice to travel in dresses, plus have an extra dress in our hand luggage. That assured us we could manage for a while if our suitcases were delayed. On this tour we reasoned that Iceland is cold, and the ladies' dress is casual, so we decided to wear slacks for the flight. Bad choice! Our luggage was not only delayed; it was gallivanting all over Europe. We had checked three suitcases, two of which were filled with Christian teaching materials to be given away in the former Soviet Republics. Daily we checked with the airlines to no avail.

"Lord," I prayed, "I know when You sent out your disciples you told them not to take a bag, money, nor an extra tunic, but I don't know if we can manage with only one dress each for a three-month trip." There were no dresses for sale at the military base where we were singing, but several people loaned us clothing for the week. On the final day, Maureen Simms, a lady in the church, handed us a package. She had driven to the town thirty kilometers away to purchase identical dresses. She said she felt the Lord had urged her to do this for us. We were grateful to the Lord. Now that we had two dresses each, we could manage.

As we left Iceland, anxious thoughts still clouded our minds. Were the suitcases with the teaching materials lost forever? Despite the frustration, we had a wonderful time in Egypt, especially since our friend Carolyn Barricklow joined us for this part of the tour. Besides taking in some of the ancient sights, we sang where a local pastor had us booked. The Lord's mighty hand was evident as we saw Christians whose zeal of service was not deterred by persecution. It is faith building to see God at work through people of other lands.

Despite the frustration of lost luggage, Faye and Janice marveled to visit ancient sites that were seen by Joseph, Moses, and Mary, Joseph and Jesus.

At the end of our schedule, we returned to Cairo's airport. You can imagine our elation to see our suitcases. The customs officials opened the bags. When they saw all the Christian teaching material, their faces took on a grim expression.

"We are a Moslem nation. We will confiscate this Christian literature."

Confiscate it? Now that the lost had been found, were we to lose it again? We explained that people of Ukraine wanted the materials. We had no intention of leaving them in Egypt.

"But it is now in Egypt," he countered firmly.

"We are leaving Egypt today, sir. May we take them with us?" Silently we were praying.

After some deliberation, the officials backed down. With a slight nod of assent, they motioned for us to close our bags and go. We then realized God's purpose for having allowed the luggage to be lost for two weeks. If we had entered Egypt with all the teaching material, no doubt it would have been taken from us.

Later, it was a joy to distribute those materials in Ukraine and Belarus!

32

Pray for Rain

~ by Janice ~

A handful of Pokot men stood atop a ridge called Taraket. Penetrating sunrays of midmorning reflected like mirrors from their spearheads and glistened on their sweaty bodies. The African warriors watched as a helicopter, like a giant dragonfly, drew closer. It skirted close to the mountainsides, making use of the lift created by updrafts. While passing over the ridge, Mike turned from his co-pilot seat, shouting over his shoulder.

"This is Taraket. You'll be singing here later this afternoon." We took in the view of the semiarid region, the mountainous terrain of Kenya's border with Uganda. We were at the conclusion of a six-month tour of African countries. This work among the remote Pokot, a nomadic people, sparked our adventurous spirit.

Missionaries Mike and Karolyn Schrage had worked hard to learn the Pokot language and to understand their culture. Utilizing teaching and nursing skills, they had earned the respect of the people. With our coming, Mike had made arrangements for evangelistic work in several outlying areas, some of which he had not yet reached.

People called the Pokot had obviously never heard the Gospel before. They were eager to hear more about this God who created everything and who loved them.

Just beyond Taraket we descended into a valley, hovered, and eased into a clearing. When the dust stirred by the chopper's blades had settled, we stepped out. People stared wide-eyed from places where they had taken cover. A man and woman were lovingly helping their daughter to walk toward the helicopter. The girl was obviously in pain, her entire body covered with ghastly sores. George Lacey, the pilot spread a clean sheet over the backseat we had just vacated. He tenderly lifted the girl aboard. Her parents climbed in beside her. Within minutes the chopper was airborne and disappeared over Taraket ridge, bound for the clinic.

Meanwhile many people had gathered. We made our way to the area where women were congregating. Their apparel of dark, crudely-tanned cowhides contrasted with rows of colorful beads and copper coils that adorned their necks and shoulders.

One woman cradled two babies on her lap. They appeared to be twins. Faye and I squatted beside her. I motioned to the two with a questioning gaze toward the mother. Apparently understanding, the lady nodded and uttered one single word, "*Sela*." We deduced it meant "twin." Faye pointed to herself then to me and repeated, "*Sela*." A jubilant smile spread across the mother's face. "*Sela!*" She reached out to touch our arms. Turning to the other ladies she explained that we, too, were twins.

The interpreter introduced us, explaining to the crowd that we did not speak their language, but we knew some songs. Only a week earlier while in Nairobi, we had met a Christian studying in a Bible institute who taught us six Pokot songs. God's timing was perfect for equipping us  for work among these people. We could also use our repertoire in Swahili, the trade language. Expressions of astonishment and understanding swept across faces as we sang. The women at this meeting demonstrated more of a keen interest than we had seen at previous gatherings. Perhaps the small touch of communicating with the mother of twins had helped to open their hearts.

By the time the preaching had ended, the helicopter had returned. We were flown to Taraket. The pilot circled, then landed, but to our surprise no one came. Mike looked bewildered.

"Something's strange," he said. "I am certain that a messenger was sent to arrange this meeting. What could have gone wrong?" At other places 100-150 people had assembled.

When we were ready to give up and leave, five men arrived. They explained that because the helicopter had already flown over three times, the people assumed we would not be coming. The women had gone to tend their cornfields some distance away. The men urged us to stay and teach the handful of men still in the vicinity. We waited. The pilot felt to blame for the misunderstanding.

"Oh, it's my fault. On my way back from taking the girl to the clinic this morning, I hovered close over the ridge to decipher what spot would be best for this afternoon's landing. They must have taken that as a message," he said.

About twenty men came, all carrying weapons. The Pokot are an aggressive people who make raids on neighboring tribes to rustle cattle. Of course, they do not consider it as stealing since their legends say that in the beginning all cattle belonged to them.

When Mike Schrage preached,
he used illustrations from the
culture of the Pokot people.

When we had concluded our singing, Mike stood in the shade of a nearby tree to preach. His sermon illustrations culturally fit the people.

"Men, when you make a raid on the Karamazhang or the Turkana Tribes to take some cattle, and you kill some of the people in the process, what do you do when you return to your home village?" The men perked up, obviously amazed that this tall red-haired white man was familiar with their ways. Mike continued without waiting for an answer. "For one thing you make scars on your body, scarring the right side if you have killed men, and the left side if you have killed women." At least half of the men had scarred bodies, straight rows of marks made from thorns ripping the flesh.

"What else do you do after taking another person's life? You make a sacrifice, don't you?"

From my vantage point I studied the expressions on the men's faces—one of curiosity and astonishment mingled with suspicion. Some fingered the shafts of their weapons though not with any apparent intent of using them. A Pokot male was rarely seen without a spear or a bow and arrow in hand, ready at all times in case of retaliation from a neighboring tribe. Now each face bore the expression of one whose conscience was being stirred. Perhaps they were thinking back to their first kill, of having killed a young lad or a defenseless woman. Mike finally answered his own question.

"You sacrifice a goat to cleanse yourselves of the wrong of shedding blood." Some men nodded; others glanced at each other with raised eyebrows, as if to say, "He does know what we do!"

"What color do you insist on that goat being?" Mike asked.

This time the silence was broken by a couple of men. "Black," one said. The other said, "spotted." They were not speaking the truth. They were only testing the missionary.

"No, you insist on it being a white goat to symbolize purity. Isn't that true?"

Now the men did agree, and Mike kept their full attention as he related that all of mankind has fallen away from God. Our lives, like their bodies, are scarred by sin, and we have no way of personally removing those scars. But God in His love and mercy provided a sacrifice to cleanse us of all wrong—His own Son being that sacrifice. Instead of calling Jesus the Lamb of God who takes away the sins of the world, Mike referred to

Him as the "white goat" of God. The applicable message obviously stirred interest in many. After the meeting, a stream of questions followed.

"We have never heard of a God who would give his own son for a sacrifice. What tribe would dare to murder the Son of God?" one man asked. Mike did not say that self-righteous Pharisees instigated Jesus' death, nor that Romans carried out the crucifixion. He explained that Jesus willingly laid down his life and that through our sins, each of us is guilty of killing him. As Mike further taught concerning Jesus' resurrection, the Pokot men showed utter amazement.

News of Jesus' resurrection astounded the people.

"Our *shamans* (medicine men) have never told us of anyone having the power to come back from the dead. The things you tell us show this God of yours to be very powerful and also loving. Yet why should we accept what you say as true? You are young. You don't even have a white hair in your head," another said. Mike's answer was surely inspired by the Holy Spirit.

"Men, I, too, respect and appreciate the wisdom of the elderly, knowing they have gained much knowledge through the experience of years," he said. "But tell me, if you want to send a message to an area across the ranges, whom do you send? You send a young man who has the strength to go. I am but a messenger sent to give you this good news."

"I would like to believe in this God of yours, but how do we know He would send rain for our corn? When we want rain, we pray to that rock." The man gestured toward a large boulder. Then switching his gaze, "If the rains don't come, then we pray to that tree."

"Perhaps later this young man should return and spend a few days with us. Then we could have a contest. We will sacrifice a cow and pray to our gods for rain. If there is no answer, then he can pray to his God," another man said. He pointed toward Mike who acknowledged the invitation with a nod. Mike, translating everything to us, drew the same conclusion as we had.

"It's like a modern day contest of Elijah with the prophets of Baal." In time we walked toward the helicopter. George was still berating himself for having chased away our potential audience. Mike consoled him, feeling that God had turned the "mistake" into a blessing.

"I doubt that the men would have openly asked questions had the crowd included women and noisy children," Mike said.

A helicopter was a quick way to reach remote villages.

After climbing aboard the helicopter, I glanced back. One of the Pokot men was running toward us waving to get our attention. Mike swung his long legs out and stepped back onto the ground to give the man his undivided attention. After a moment he turned toward us to translate.

"The man asks if we will pray for rain tonight as proof that our God exists." We all assured him that we would. Satisfied, the man nodded and backed off into the brush, waiting to watch us lift off.

Meanwhile, we had second thoughts about the promise we had just voiced. On takeoff, the dust swirled around, obscuring the handful of warriors from our view. As we glided off the ridge, we took a good look at the sky. Not a single cloud was in view.

"And we just promised we would pray for rain?" I said. This arid region was south of Ethiopia during a time of great famine. How could we expect rain? Doubts were creeping in.

After sunset, when dim twilight was silhouetting Taraket ridge, Faye and I stood outside to pray. How wonderful it would be if God would send rain to show Himself to these people. The thought was but a fleeting one. We were praying because we had promised we would. Neither of us expected rain to come. Rather than displaying faith in the capability of our all-powerful God, we were still looking at the conditions: the cloudless sky, the dusty ground, and the season of famine.

It wasn't long after our prayer time that we climbed the ladder to our cozy quarters in the loft. We had just stretched out comfortably beneath the covers, ready for a good, quiet night's sleep when suddenly we were both startled by a deafening noise. It was rain! A heavy downpour was hitting the corrugated tin roof not four feet above our mattress. We felt humbled, ashamed for our lack of faith, yet elated as we lay there rejoicing.

Centuries ago, the disciples who were caught in a tempest on the Sea of Galilee looked at the conditions and thought the storm could not end. Now we had thought a storm could not begin. We were limiting God, yet He still has control of the elements. Jesus could just as readily have said to us that night, "Oh you of little faith." I'm glad that when God answers prayer it is not according to our faith, but according to His faithfulness.

"Your mercy, O Lord, is in the heavens, and Your faithfulness reaches to the clouds." (Ps.36:5)

[A few months later, the Kenyan government pulled all missionaries out of that border region to protect them from tribal unrest. The Schrages, though disappointed to leave, then concentrated their mission work in another area. Later, Mike met Pokot people from villages as far away as 200 miles who had heard the story that one great God proved His existence by sending rain during the time of famine. Many Pokot are now coming to the Lord because God prepared their hearts.]

1988: Each time Janice and Faye are in India,
they wear the local attire, the sari.

33

Ask for a Sign

~ by Faye ~

Determining God's will is not always easy. Concerning our bookings, we pray about each invitation we receive, asking the Lord's guidance in our decision. We often add a P.S. "Lord, if You don't want us to go, please slam the door." Occasionally when we have been in a quandary, we have asked God for a sign. Some may think of Matthew 12:39a. "An evil and adulterous generation seeks after a sign." But that Scripture refers to skeptical mockers seeking proof. As for us, we were honestly seeking clear answers for guidance. We will relate three such incidents.

Should We Go to India?

Two families invited us to India for January and February of 1988. We wrote to both families explaining that we already had been asked to be in Mexico during the first four months.

Several months later, the same two wrote again. Bernel Getter wrote, "Can't you possibly come to Central India? Any amount of time during the early part of the year would be wonderful." Our hearts were in turmoil. We turned them down a second time because of the prior commitment.

Not long afterward, Dean Cary, the man who had invited us to Mexico, wrote to ask if we would go with him to Honduras instead—and only during April. Our initial reaction was that January and February were now available to go to India. Yet, if we would offer them the time, would we be prying at a door the Lord intended to remain closed?

It was August 23. If we were to go to India, travel arrangements and visa applications would have to be made soon. Janice and I would be leaving September 2 for a three-month tour in the States. We asked the Lord to give a clear sign before September by having one of the missionaries invite us a third time.

The missionaries had no telephone or e-mail; they would have to write. Mail takes at least two weeks from India, and we were asking for a letter in nine days. This was a step of faith. Nothing is impossible with God. He could have placed it in the missionaries' hearts to write to us even before we prayed, or He could speed up the mail service.

Each day we eagerly checked the mail. Nothing from India. On the last day of August, God answered our prayer in the form of a postcard from Hong Kong. Sharon Getter, who taught in a university in China, had just been visiting her parents in India. She wrote, "My folks urged me to send you a note. They really want you to come next year. Is there any possible way you can go?" Her card was postmarked August 24. With the time difference, that would have been August 23 in Colorado—the very day we had prayed.

We did have a good trip to India, fulfilling both invitations.

Should We Go to the Township?

BOOM! We bolted upright in bed and staggered bleary-eyed to the window. In the early light of dawn, we scanned the city. A cloud of smoke and dust billowed where a bomb had exploded less than a mile away. It was a politically hot time to be in Durban, South Africa. The white populace was celebrating a holiday, while militant blacks sabotaged military installations.

Political unrest brought on violence to Durban South Africa, curtailing some scheduled plans for the Rostvits.

The following night, I awoke with an uneasy feeling. There were noises in the street: voices, clanging, and the sounds of metal being dragged across rough cement. I leaned out the window to peer below. Police cars had their lights flashing. Some people were being apprehended, and barrels were being loaded onto a truck bed. The vehicles pulled away and all was silent again.

In the morning we learned that the barrels removed from the adjacent building had been full of explosives. We weren't the targets, yet we came close to being victims of terrorism.

Missionary Floyd Stamm had scheduled us to sing in churches of various racial groups. During this holiday, we were to sing in a black township on the fringes of Durban. The political tone being what it was, officials had made the township off-limits to Caucasians, except by special permit. Mr. Stamm was determined to secure that permit. On the way to the office, we prayed, "Lord, if you don't want us to go, please stop us."

At the office, the official hesitantly granted the permit, but strongly recommended we not go until after the holiday. Permit in hand, Floyd drove toward the township, not fearing the actions of those who were militant. Suddenly the car screeched to a halt. The tie rod had broken. We'd be going no farther with that car. Floyd hoped to get it repaired so we could still get to the township. A policeman came along and gave us a ride back into Durban. Although he had no idea where we had been headed, he warned us not to go anywhere near the township that weekend.

When we arrived back at the Stamm's apartment, Floyd picked up his newspaper. The headlines read, MOTORISTS STAY HOME. He turned on the television. A devotional spot was on the air: "tarry in the city…until you are endued with power from on high." (Luke 24:49b) Floyd finally gave in.

"Okay! Okay! I hear You, Lord! We'll stay home." The Lord had used many circumstances to make His will clear.

When time came for us to leave the country, we had a very unusual takeoff. After lifting off the runway, the jet remained extremely low. It couldn't be overloaded as there were very few passengers. Suddenly the jet turned sharply, one wing appearing dangerously close to sand dunes below. After the hairpin turn, we tipped the opposite direction. One minute we were facing the ground, the next we stared up into the sky. Why the erratic turns? Still flying low, we headed out over the waters of the Indian Ocean, then shot upward in a steep ascent. We were shaken. It was later explained that the flying low, the snaking turns, and the steep ascent were all precautions taken to avoid being shot down by heat-seeking rockets. We may have our times of anxiety but must keep serving where we feel the Lord is leading.

"Search me, O God, and know my heart; try me and know my anxieties. See if there is any wicked way in me, and lead me in the way everlasting." (Ps. 139:23,24)

Should We Change Ministry?

In 1984 after sixteen years of overseas travels, the two of us thought we had reached a major turning point in our lives. Five years of struggling with stomach ulcers was taking the joy out of our ministry. We didn't want to quit traveling, but it was becoming increasingly difficult to sing when nausea and pain persisted. Certain foods would inflame our condition, and often we were far from medical help. Was this called "burn-out" or "burn-in"? A change of pace seemed inevitable.

We were due to travel to Papua New Guinea in the fall. Ulcers or no ulcers, we didn't want to cancel this opportunity. Since 1956 when we had seen the mission program about New Guinea, we had wanted to go there. If our traveling ministry had to end, perhaps the alternative would be to settle down as permanent missionaries. We could use our linguistic abilities as Bible translators.

How could we determine the Lord's will? We believe that God wants us to bring our choices to Him and seek His guidance. In Isaiah 7 we read about King Ahaz being asked by the Lord to seek a sign. When the king refused, saying he would not tempt God, the Lord urged him, "Ask a sign for yourself from the Lord your God; ask it either in the depth or in the height above,"

(Isa. 7:11). If nothing is too hard for the Lord, why not pray in specifics and seek a direct answer?

We were in a 747 flying from Hawaii toward the South Pacific when we determined what sign we would seek from the Lord. Since we would be singing in various areas of New Guinea and staying in homes of Bible translators, we asked God, "If you want us to become Bible translators, please have each of the missionaries clearly suggest it."

When we had been in the country of Colombia in 1980, many of the Wycliffe Bible translators had commented that we had an ear for languages. Several of them had asked if we had ever considered getting into translation work. Now in our prayer we reiterated, "Lord, please make it clear by having each translator we meet suggest it, or else NONE of them. Not half and half. Not nine out of ten. ALL or NONE." Were we being unreasonable in making such a request? Certainly if God did not want us to become translators, He could close the mouths of the missionaries to the subject of recruitment.

During the remainder of the flight, we discussed the pros and cons of changing from a singing ministry. Because of our ulcers, our hopes swung slightly in favor of translation work. But we determined not to steer conversation in that direction and not to share with anyone the sign we were seeking. We wanted the outcome to be truly according to God's will.

Our final flight took us to Madang. Missionaries who met us were strangers, yet we felt a warmth of kinship. Perhaps a new chapter in our lives was just beginning. We were filled with eager anticipation, wondering which way the Lord would answer our prayer.

34

Along the Ramu

∽ by Janice ∽

As the six-passenger Cessna sped down the runway, the lift off caused my senses to soar, delighting in the panoramic view of the azure waters of Madang Harbor. Pilot Bob Peaker banked the aircraft while the altimeter needle marked our steady ascent. We crossed over the range that separated Madang from the Ramu River valley. Bob's parents, who had come from Australia for

a short visit, were also aboard. Like a tour guide, Bob kept a running commentary going with his dad, who occupied the copilot's seat. We felt privileged to be on the same flight.

Bob Peaker, pilot with MAF (Missionary Aviation Fellowship), would often go out of his way to touch lives.

Papua New Guinea was the sixtieth country we visited, yet we gazed at the surrounding rain forest with a childlike wonder. How will God answer our prayer? Will we become translators, or keep traveling in a singing ministry? Admittedly we both were hoping for the change to translation. Will all the missionaries suggest that? Might this tropical island one day become our home? I prayed silently from our airborne perch that we would be willing to obey whichever way God directed. We both felt confident that God would make His will clear.

First stop—Gokta. The airplane eased onto the grassy strip situated in rolling hills at the edge of the highlands. When we had taxied to a stop at the end of the runway, Bob Peaker opened the doors. He offered a hand as we stepped out, then turned to greet the many nationals who had gathered. *"Moning, olgeta"* (Morning everyone).

We were following his example, shaking peoples' hands when my eyes fell on a man approaching. His skin looked like the hide of a crocodile. Is that leprosy? Scabies? Ringworm? Bob may have sensed my apprehension. He immediately clasped the man's hand in an enthusiastic handshake. Without taking his eyes nor his smile off the man, he said to me, "Don't be afraid. It's nothing catchy." I was touched to see this pilot's thoughtful nature. He cared about the man and about my feelings as well. I smiled as I extended my hand. This man's skin problem may not have been contagious, but Bob's enthusiasm was.

Australian missionaries Diana Catts and Fay Christensen welcomed us. Bob Peaker made sure our luggage and instruments were off-loaded, then prepared to leave. After takeoff, Bob circled back over the strip to vigorously tip the wings. We returned the wave. Diana smiled, leaning down to pick up a box of supplies.

"Bob is a great guy, always doing things for others."
We all climbed the hill by the airstrip to the small house
that would be our home for a few days. Entering the
house with our arms full, my eyes took in every aspect
of my surroundings, like a child exploring something
new. I had not expected to see a gas range, a kerosene
refrigerator, and a two-way radio with a battery pow-
ered by a solar panel.

Outside, a large tank stored rainwater from the corrugated metal roof. This was piped to a faucet in the
kitchen. Diana showed us to our bedroom. This home,
made of jungle materials, was a work of art! Walls and
ceilings were of intricately woven strips of bamboo—
each room sporting its own unique design.

As we ate lunch, we became acquainted with Diana
and Fay. Fay, like ourselves, was an identical twin.
Imagine our surprise to learn her sister's name was Jan.
She was doing mission work on another island. Fay was
working on translating Scriptures into the Rao language. Our ears perked up, listening for God's invitation for us to get into translation. However, conversation came to an abrupt end as a deluge of rain pounded
the metal roof.

"Good time for an afternoon nap," Diana yelled over
the din as she headed for her bedroom. With loud cracks
of thunder and bright flashes of lightning, sleep eluded
us. We sat up in bed and reviewed the forty songs we
had in the trade language of Melanesian Pidgin.

By late afternoon the rain slowed to a gentle patter.
Carrying our shoes, instruments, and an umbrella, we
made our way barefoot over slippery grass and through
water puddles to a local Bible institute. Approximately
thirty-five students and teachers gathered. Men were
arranging some bamboo poles of varying lengths at the
front of the room. When the singing began, one man
straddled the bamboo pipes and thumped the hollow

ends with the rubber sole from an old shoe. Beautiful tones spilled into the room from this jungle pipe organ. After their enthusiastic singing, we feared our songs would sound dull. Our fears were dispelled when the men begged us for more songs.

The meeting ended at 10 P.M. Back at the house, Diana lit a kerosene lamp while Fay put a teakettle on the stove. Before retiring, Faye and I each experienced our first "bucket shower." A metal bucket with a showerhead attached to the bottom dangled from a rope and pulley system in the shower stall. Faye added hot water from the teakettle. Ingenious—all the comforts of home!

By 5:30 A.M. we were awakened by the annoying buzz of a mosquito that had somehow sneaked inside the mosquito net over our bed. We dressed quickly and decided to take a walk before breakfast. The airstrip would be a perfect place to get some exercise before the sun's rays would intensify. We slipped out the kitchen door. Faye glanced to her left.

"Wait, Janice! What's that?" The movement of something dark in the shadows had caught her attention. In a husky whisper she gasped, "It's a wild boar!" I stood motionless for a few seconds, then nudged Faye.

"Come on, let's go. I don't think he sees us." We quickly turned and eased our way down the gentle slope to the airstrip. Once out of sight, we sighed with relief, assuming the boar wouldn't follow. Settling into a fast walk, we breathed in the cool fresh air. Occasionally we checked to see if the boar was in view. After we had gone a couple hundred feet, Faye looked back and gasped, "It's on the airstrip!"

"Don't panic!" I tried to remain calm. "He'll probably just cross to the jungle on the other side. We took longer strides hoping to put more distance between us and the intimidating swine. Faye glanced over her shoulder again.

"Yikes, he's coming this way! Where can we go?" The boar was no longer ambling along— it had broken into a trot, definitely making us its target.

"Run," Faye screamed. I was ahead of her. We ran as fast as we could.

"Hurry," I urged. "It's gaining ground." We were quickly tiring. My lungs were screaming with pain. "Look, Faye!" I pointed ahead to the few village huts I had spotted located to the side of the runway. One more backward glance revealed our pursuer running at top speed, its head down, its white tusks glaring menacingly in contrast to its charcoal body. The fearsome sight pumped fresh adrenaline into my aching limbs. Like rodents fleeing from a hawk, we exited the airstrip and burst into the clearing where five huts stood on high stilts.

Invited or not, I was going to climb into someone's home. Just then, the bent form of an elderly lady appeared on the porch of one of the huts. Seeing our dilemma, she motioned for us to come. We quickly climbed the ladder, which was simply a log with toe holes notched into it. With chests heaving, we reached the porch and looked back down. The boar was pacing back and forth at the base of the log, its piercing eyes glaring up at us. We thanked the lady and then watched in astonishment as she grabbed a stick and proceeded to descend the log ladder. What could this frail lady do against a wild beast?

She may have appeared frail, but this brave lady had evidently handled situations like this before. With fury she yelled and beat the boar with her stick, chasing it until both she and the boar disappeared into the jungle. We felt chagrin as we thought of our own fears.

When the lady returned and indicated it was safe to leave, we walked the airstrip back to the house, but not without frequent glances over our shoulders. At the breakfast table we told about our daybreak adventure.

"It would have made a more interesting story had our rescuer been a strong man with a spear instead of a feeble grandmother with a stick," I said. Everyone burst into laughter. One of the students from the Bible institute taught us some songs in the Rao language. They were useful in the days to come as we walked to nearby villages to sing.

"*Balus, balus*," people yelled as they ran past the house. Diana saw my startled expression.

"*Balus* means airplane. They must have heard it in the distance and are gathering at the airstrip," she said. Eager to watch the mission plane arrive, we quickly finished packing our things. Diana and Fay were planning to fly to the next area with us.

We watched as Bob Peaker emerged from the plane. The day was sweltering hot. Curious villagers crowded around, smothering any hint of a breeze. Bob took the time to greet everyone enthusiastically. He loved the nationals and missionaries alike. While Bob was loading cargo, we waited in the shade of the wing.

The pilot, knowing how to distribute weight, usually determined where each passenger was to sit. Fay Christensen, having flown often and knowing that with her slight figure she would be relegated to the back seat, decided to board. When Bob saw that Fay was heading for the door on the far side, he ran to the tail of the plane to play a trick on her. As soon as Fay climbed in and took her seat, Bob pushed down on the tail, making it look as if Fay's weight had tipped the plane. Everyone laughed, including Fay. She loved Bob's sense of humor.

The ten-minute flight brought us to Chungribu where an airstrip had been carved out of the thick jungle beside the Ramu River. For the next few days we went with Diana and Fay to various villages. We never knew whether we'd be walking through the jungle or going by canoe on the Ramu to reach our destination. We welcomed the boat rides. The 40-HP motor propelling us along created an invigorating breeze. We used the time to memorize songs in the local language. Many times submerged logs threatened to break the pin on the motor or capsize us.

One day we were going to the village of Angguna. On the way we saw a crocodile sunning itself on a sandy beach. The nearly ten-foot-long creature spotted us. With quick motions the armored reptile slithered to the water's edge and disappeared into the murky depths. I shuddered. I wondered how many submerged "logs" had actually been crocodiles.

There were no Christians at Angguna but two national preachers, Andrew and Yamri, had been holding regular Bible classes. In the afternoon as Faye and I sat in the shade of a tree practicing songs in Melanesian Pidgin, it wasn't long before a crowd of more than a hundred people were seated around us listening.

"Let's hold a meeting since everyone has gathered," Yamri said. The people listened intently as Yamri preached passionately with tears. [Two months later more than a hundred surrendered their lives to Jesus.]

Clouds enshrouded the craggy mountains while lush foliage of the tropical rain forests blanketed the valleys beneath us. Bob drew my attention to a cone-shaped island off the north coast that was venting steam.

"That's Manam Island. It's an active volcano." We looked forward to each flight with Bob Peaker. On this day we had several stops to make. Inviting us to take turns in the copilot seat, Bob pointed out various landmarks along the way, including a downed bomber from World War II. At Bunam we were to pick up two nationals plus some pigs and take them to Momonup. Faye and I took our instruments out and sang to the gathering crowd. The pigs were tied up and wrapped in burlap. Their squeals competed with our music as Bob and some of the men lifted the wiggling bundles into the cargo hold.

On the final leg of the journey, Faye was in the copilot seat. Below, the Ramu River snaked like a discarded ribbon on a lush carpet. Occasional villages could be seen situated along its banks.

"The Mbore people live near the mouth of the river. That's where you are headed." With a wry grin and a glint in his eye, Bob added, "Are you sure you want to go there? They used to be cannibals, you know." All too soon Bob was banking the plane and landing at Bunapas. Bob hopped out to begin his friendly ritual of shaking hands with everyone. Fair-haired, Bible translator Dave Parrish stood among the crowd. Bob grasped his hand firmly.

"G'day, Dave, how are you? Come to pick up the *Tupela Meri* (twin ladies), I suppose?" Bob said with a mixture of Australian lingo and the local trade language.

"That's right."

"Did Alice and the girls come?"

"Only Mandi. The rest stayed in the village." The

little four year old came out from behind her daddy and smiled when Bob tousled her hair. Missionaries always looked forward to "plane day," a touch with the outside world. While Bob busied himself unloading our luggage and some supplies for the Parrish family, he and Dave continued talking. Dave asked Bob if he had brought the all-important mail bag.

"If you forgot that, you might as well not have come," he teased. Bob had us all laughing as he rummaged around, pretending he couldn't find it. Finally he emerged with the welcome item.

"Take good care of my copilots now," Bob said as he climbed into the plane to leave. We stayed at the airstrip until Bob had taken off.

"He'll circle around and tip his wings. It's his way of waving good-bye. Even when he's busy, he takes time to add those special touches. The nationals love him. They call him, *Bob bilong mipela* (our Bob)," David said.

We all waved as the aircraft buzzed the strip and waggled its wings in Bob's wholehearted manner. We picked up our luggage and made our way down to the river. Once situated in the fiberglass canoe, we prodded Dave.

"Is it true the Mbore were cannibals?"

"Yes, up to a generation ago. They remained cannibals and headhunters longer than others because of their advantage of living at the mouth of the river."

"How was that an advantage?" I asked.

"They could paddle upstream to raid other villages. After filling their dugouts with booty and captives, they could make a fast getaway since the retreat was always downstream. They were a much-feared people; few dared retaliate.

"Following World War II, the Australian forces worked at suppressing the raiding. But the Mbore still kept on until the late fifties. Now only a handful of the older folks remember those times. No one wants to return to the old ways."

"That's interesting. It was about that time, 1956, we saw a slide presentation about New Guinea by missionary Alfred Cole. Although we were young, it sparked our interest in missions."

An hour and a half later we rounded a bend of the river where the village of Kabuk came into view. The sound of the boat motor drew people to the riverbank. They all helped carry the supplies. Their friendliness made it hard to imagine that the Mbore people had ever been vicious or fearsome.

The following day the Parrishes led us to the village meeting house for our concert. The large structure was decorated with fringes of sago palm fronds. From the center beam hung a decorated carving. Dave explained that the shield identified the particular clan, but that it also had some significance for their spirit worship.

Translator Dave Parrish loved the Mbore people.

People from neighboring villages were gathering and milling around. Suddenly a murmur came from the crowd. Two clan leaders in full ceremonial dress were approaching, their grass skirts swaying as they walked. Woven palm bark breastplates adorned with clamshells provided a percussion instrument against their necklaces of bones and pig tusks. Shells across their backs and around their legs rattled with each step. Colorful leaves woven into armbands shimmered in the afternoon sunlight. Headdresses of plumage from exotic birds crowned the men's painted faces.

Cannibals. A feared tribe. A feeling of uneasiness swept over me. "What's this all about?" I asked Dave.

"I know the men, but I have never seen them dressed like this before." Dave's uncertainty gave little comfort. He walked over to meet the men. Returning with a smile he introduced us first to the older man, Undai, then to Ngum. Dave translated as Undai said, "You have come all the way from America to sing in our village. This is a privilege. We have dressed up for this special occasion."

"Consider this a great honor," Dave said. Indeed we did. We also accepted a gift of grass skirts the men handed us. When they urged us to wear them for the concert, we were relieved that they allowed us to wear them over our own skirts. Dave's words "consider it an

honor" echoed through our minds, and we contemplated the importance of our singing ministry. Music can open hearts and touch lives. As we sang in the Mbore language, Ngum appeared to be deep in thought.

Undai and Ngum, leaders of the Mbore people, adorned themselves in full ceremonial dress to honor the coming of the Rostvit Twins.

The concert was finished by late afternoon. During the evening we had precious fellowship with Dave and Alice and their three sweet daughters. At one point, Dave began explaining the Bible translation process. He shared their vision for the Mbore clan.

"Even if there were only one family in this language group, we would spend our lives here to give them the Word of God. We truly love these people." We listened with interest, wondering if they would be suggesting we get into translation work.

Just then Undai and Ngum came to the house. Undai wanted to tell us about his life. Dave translated as Undai explained that he wasn't originally from the Mbore tribe. He had been born farther up river. His fun-loving boyhood days had been abruptly cut short when Mbore warriors had raided his village. They had come in their dugout canoes under cover of darkness to kill, headhunt, and steal fetishes. Undai remembers that frightful night: the yelling, the confusion, the screams, and the glint of the spears. Wide-eyed with terror, he watched as his mother was killed. Then a Mbore man with a painted face grabbed little Undai and smeared light-colored mud on his forehead and in his hair. He hadn't realized that the man had just marked him to be spared from death. He was to become a slave.

Undai and other boys who had been "marked to live" were carried to the canoes. The elaborately-carved dugouts were paddled downstream with their captives. When they reached the village of Kabuk, a lady took pity on Undai. To save him from slavery, she hid the boy in the loft of her home where ceremonial masks for spirit worship were stored. In the dark recesses beneath the palm-thatched roof, little Undai wept in silence until he fell into a troubled sleep.

When nightmares of the raid startled him awake, he bolted upright. The flickering light from the firepot below cast eerie shadows. He turned and gasped as he found himself staring into the demon-like faces of the masks. The hideous carvings gave a ghoulish reality to his nightmares. The lady kept Undai hidden for months and then raised him as a son. Undai told us how relieved he is that raiding and headhunting have ended and that people no longer need to live in fear.

We rejoiced along with Dave when that evening he learned a word that could be used to translate a key term in the Bible. Like Undai, we, too, have been "marked to live" or "redeemed" by the blood of Jesus.

When departure day arrived, we hated to have to leave. We stepped into the canoe with Dave and headed upriver. Alice and the girls were among the villagers from Kabuk who lined the banks of the river waving until we were out of sight.

At Garati, our next stop, our arrival created quite a stir. Villagers crowded around us, pointing to our eyes, clothing, and shoes. Some were touching our hair. Why this reaction? When missionary David Pryor had announced that twins would be coming, he hadn't considered that these people had never seen adult twins.

Because of superstitious fears, when twins were born
one would be taken to a faraway village and given to a
distant relative to raise. It was never divulged that the
infants were twins.

How sad! We so cherish our twinship! We could not
imagine the pain of being raised without each other.

David walked with us through the village. Along the
way we noticed a little boy with a ghastly sore on the
whole side of his face.

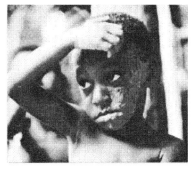

"What happened?
Did he fall into a fire?"
Faye asked.

"No. That's little
Max. The sore started a
few days ago and
spread rapidly, but we
do not know what
caused it. His father,
Buat, is helping me to translate the Bible into the Kire
language." David explained that unbelievers in the village were blaming Buat for having become a Christian.
They claimed that the boy was cursed and would die.
"But Max has been a brave boy. With faith he boldly
said, 'I won't die, Jesus will heal me.'"

At the far end of the village we came to the Pryor's
home. David's wife, Sharran, was busy home-schooling
their two children, John and Amy. The Pryor family
shared what the Lord was doing in Garati. Only weeks
before, Ruri, the leader of the ancestral spirit worship,
had become a Christian. Several in the village had followed his example.

During our week at Garati, we sang for their nightly
prayer meetings using both the trade language plus
Kire. On the final night we were asked to sing several
extra songs. A time of sharing followed. David translated what was being said. One man rejoiced that the

prayer meetings were keeping Satan from getting a foothold in their lives. A lady praised the Lord that none of their infants had died in the past six months. (Usually the mortality rate among newborns was 50 percent.) She then suggested continued prayer for Max. Little Max, seated by his father, managed a sweet smile. Buat then stood.

"This afternoon my son Max was sleeping. Suddenly he sat upright and said, 'Papa, you must listen!' I drew close to my son, unable to determine if the boy was truly awake. Then Max said, 'Papa, you know the twin ladies who sing in our language? The music they make—it's from Jesus.' Then without another word, Max laid down again and was fast asleep."

We felt humbled when another man reiterated, "Surely God has given these twins this special gift of singing in many languages, including ours."

[A month later we returned to Garati and found that Max's face was completely healed. Jesus had honored the boy's faith.]

Days and weeks passed quickly. Every new location became a diary full of experiences, every home a haven of fellowship, every journey an adventure. Each time we flew with Bob, we witnessed his example of selfless service. He went out of his way to cheer others.

One day he detoured from the flight pattern to fly over the village of Samban. Having learned that missionaries John and Bonita Pryor and their boys were all sick with malaria, Bob flew low and tipped the wings. It was a strange sensation to rock back and forth. Bob then banked the Cessna in a sharp turn to repeat the performance. By this time we could see the entire family standing on their porch waving in return. Tuning in on his radio, Bob talked with them.

"You get well now; we're praying for you."

"Thanks to you we feel better already," John said.

That same day we flew over the highlands where Steve and Rhonda Hayward lived. They were in such a remote area that they had to hike for fifteen hours over the ridges to reach their home. Again, Bob flew over and tipped the wings, then spoke on the radio.

"Keep up the good work. You're not alone out there. We love you," he said.

"Thanks Bob, you made our day," Steve replied. One time Bob made an unscheduled stop at a short airstrip in the mountains. He had heard that Vern and Natalie Ward's little daughter was having a birthday. Bob surprised them by flying in some ice cream for the party.

When translators William and Robin Butler had completed an airstrip at Likan, it was Bob who flew in for the first time, officially approving and opening the strip for use. He went the "second mile" by taking all the leaders of the village up for a flight, an experience they would cherish for the rest of their lives.

Bob loved to fly, but first and foremost he loved people. He touched lives by "tipping the wings" of his heart.

⚬⚬⚬⚬⚬

By the end of our months in Papua New Guinea, we knew the answer to the prayer we had made before coming. We had been in the homes of many Bible translators. If any of them had suggested for us to get into translation work, we had failed to hear it. Instead, most had encouraged us that our linguistic ability being used in a music ministry was unique and appreciated. Even the Mbore clan leaders, Undai and Ngum, and sweet little Max had confirmed God's will for us.

We were not disappointed with the outcome. On the contrary, we were lifted to heights of renewed joy. God's clear affirmation of our ministry and our acceptance of it also affected our physical condition. Our ulcers healed, never to trouble us again.

Just before leaving Papua New Guinea, we spoke on the two-way radio to say good-bye to all the Bible translators in the outlying areas. It was an emotional time. We sang a farewell song we composed for them. We were choking back tears as we sang it.

We're sorry we must be on our way.   ♪♪
It's hard to know just what to say,
Our hearts cannot express,   ♪♪ ♪♪
This feeling of emptiness.
Now it's time to say good-bye, we must travel on,
A never-ending reunion, will come later on.
Amid my tears there comes release.
A deep sense of God's own peace,
Just to know you feel the same.
We are one in Jesus' name,   ♪ ♪
Though our hearts are filled with pain,
A bond of love we share,
We'll be praying for you,
And leave you in God's care.

Several of the families thanked us for the song.

"We only wish Bob Peaker could have heard it, too," we said.

Then in radio lingo, Bob's familiar deep voice interrupted. "Break." We could hear the hum of the Cessna's engine in the background.

"Go ahead, Bob."

"G'day, *Tupela Meri*. Thanks for the song—I was listening in. God bless you on your homeward journey." We did have a fine trip home although we missed the friends we had made in Papua New Guinea. We had left a piece of our hearts behind, so it wasn't a difficult decision to accept an invitation for another singing tour two years later.

Faye and Janice in the village of Kabuk

Faye and Janice
singing in a
village church

The Rostvit Twins sang at each airstrip while flying with
MAF pilot, Peter van Zanen

35

Conflict in the Night

∽ by Faye ∽

———————◉———————

"What other nation is so great as to have their gods near them the way the Lord our God is near us whenever we pray to Him?" (Deut.4:7 NIV)

On our return tour to Papua New Guinea, we appreciated having intercessory prayer for one particular fearful situation.

The heat of the midday sun beat down with merciless intensity as Janice and I prepared for the five-hour trek from Pasinkap to Angguna. We strapped our instruments to our backs. Two men who would lead the way donned our backpacks. During the first hour we traversed hills where we had to watch our footing on muddy slopes. At one point in the tree-covered hills, I was startled to hear some popping and crackling sounds. Was it gunfire? The fleeting thought passed when I spotted smoke. My eyes widened. Would we be trapped in a forest fire?

The men kept walking, causing me to wonder if they hadn't seen the danger. The trail skirted near the fire. Our guides merely quickened their pace. It was life as usual for them. They knew someone was preparing a large garden by the "slash and burn" method. There was no danger of the fire getting out of hand, yet we did get close enough to feel its heat. When at last the trail descended into the dense rain forest, we welcomed the thick shade. We plodded steadily through the jungle, slowing only to cross small gullies or streams on single log bridges.

Halfway through the trek, we could hear the drone of the MAF airplane. The thick canopy of foliage overhead would hinder us from seeing the aircraft, but it warmed our hearts to know who was at the controls. No, it was not Bob Peaker. He was now stationed in Mt. Hagen. We had already enjoyed a week with his family, flying daily with Bob to various missions.

This year, the pilot in the Ramu region was Peter van Zanen, a tall handsome Dutchman.

Peter had been preaching before he felt called to become a missionary pilot. He had a gentle, compassionate nature, often sensing people's deep needs and taking time to pray with them. As a result, he earned the nickname "Pastor Pilot." It was easy to picture Jesus with this Dutchman's face. The sound of the Cessna faded, yet it had been a reminder that there were people out there praying for us. Peter, having flown us to Pasinkap a few days earlier, knew we were making this trek.

Four hours into the hike, we reached a larger river. Janice and I stood on the high bank overlooking the swift-flowing waters. Sizing up the log, I dreaded yet another crossing. The teasing words of one of the missionaries came to mind, "Don't worry if you fall off one of the logs. You won't drown. The crocodiles will get you first." This log was much longer than any of the other five we had traversed that day. My thoughts were interrupted as Janice moved toward the log.

"I'll go first this time, is that okay?" she asked.

"Sure, go ahead." I hoped that by watching her I could gain more confidence. One of the nationals led the way. Janice followed. The log gently bounced with the rhythm of their footsteps.

When they reached the far bank, the other man stepped forward, motioning me to follow. I couldn't put off the inevitable so I gingerly mounted the log. After a few steps, the bank dropped away. Any courage I had mustered began to wane. I wished I had removed my shoes so my feet could conform to the curvature of the log. Would mud on my soles make me slip? The narrower the log became, the higher my fears mounted. I thought back to childhood and to a missionary slide presentation. The scenes of log bridges with hand railings of woven vines had appeared so adventurous. But none of these logs today had hand railings! It was more adventure than I wanted.

About halfway across, I made the mistake of taking my eyes off the log. The swift movement of the muddy waters nearly made me lose my balance. I stopped, frozen with fear. How far below was that rushing current? Twenty feet? Thirty feet? Or was my mind exaggerating the distance? Now more than ever the log seemed like a tightrope. It still tapered endlessly toward the far shore. I wanted to turn back, but I knew that was not an option. Even if I did, I couldn't find my way alone. These guides would not agree to turn around. Not that the hike was too arduous for them, but they feared that evil spirits haunted the region now behind us. Even many of the local Christians doubted that God could protect them from the curses in that area.

It was probably only a matter of seconds that I stood frozen, but my panicked thoughts kept whirling. I couldn't quit! I visualized the faces of ones who knew we were on this trek: besides Peter, the pilot, there were missionaries Kyle and Kathy Harris back in Pasinkap and Martha Wade at the other end of this trail. I had to draw strength knowing they were praying.

My guide, sensing my fears, turned with a reassuring glance. I gave him a nod, trying to convince myself as well as him that I was ready to continue. I couldn't let my fears get the best of me. Then the man reached back, offering his steady hand. Slipping my hand into his, I told myself that this was the hand of Jesus. "For I, the Lord your God, will hold your right hand, saying to you, 'Fear not, I will help you.'" (Isa. 41:13) This New Guinean had walked this trail many times before. His legs weren't shaky like mine. It went easier as I focused my attention on the dark-skinned, well-callused bare feet in front of me, and followed one step at a time. Finally, with a sigh of relief, we safely reached the other shore.

As Christians, our walk through life isn't easy. When difficult times come, Jesus firmly takes us by the hand. It is only when we take our eyes off Him and focus on our fears that we fail to move forward. If we will faithfully follow our guide, He will safely lead us to the distant shore.

The trek continued. What little sunlight filtered through the forest's dense canopy overhead cast deceptive shadows on the barely distinguishable trail. Vines like giant pythons hung and looped in every direction. Unusual noises or shrill cries aroused our curiosity. We wanted to peer overhead to identify whether the sounds were birds, animals, or insects. Yet we couldn't take the time. Slippery roots or vines threatened to trip us if we took our eyes off the trail. Then too, the men walked very fast. If we lagged behind, we could lose sight of them. We welcomed a slower pace as we entered the intensely dark sago swamps. For perhaps half an hour we slogged through water or thick mud that tried to suck our shoes off. Going barefoot was not an option since the murky waters could conceal leeches or thorny sago fronds.

We had a five-hour trek through the rain forest to reach the village called Angguna.

Finally we saw the Sogeram River. We recalled having traveled up that river on our previous trip to hold some singing and preaching services there. That was before Martha Wade settled there to do Bible translation. We neared Angguna. To our surprise, men, women, and children lined the trail for the entire length of the village, reaching out to shake our hands. With our faces sunburned, hair wilted in messy ringlets, dresses soaked with perspiration, legs and shoes caked with mud, we didn't feel worthy of such a royal welcome. We felt like we had completed a marathon. At the far end of the line stood Martha. She greeted us with a smile, handing us each a glass of cold water. Ah, did that ever taste good!

I recalled one of our local language songs that spoke of walking on the trail that leads to the "heavenly village." When we do reach that heavenly home, we will receive a welcome far better than the one we had just received. There our clothing won't be stained, but will be spotless, washed in the blood of the Lamb. Forever we will drink of the water of life freely.

⚜

The steady rhythm of drumbeats filled the air. The chant-like chorus of the villagers' *singsing* (an all night social gathering) grew in intensity as darkness set in. By the warm glow of a kerosene lamp, five of us sat conversing in Martha Wade's home, sharing experiences in the Lord. Diana Catts and Fay Christensen had come upriver to join in the special activities. This being September 16, the country's Independence Day, Angguna had buzzed with festivities all day.

In the morning we had sung in a dedication service for the newly constructed church building. By afternoon nationals had converged on Angguna from neighboring villages up and down the Sogeram. We had watched with fascination as the men organized a contest of skills with their bows and arrows. Near sunset everyone joined in the feast of sago, tubular vegetables, and roasted wild pig. The locals were now concluding their celebration with an all-night *singsing.*

Following an evening church service, the Angguna Christians planned to congregate beneath the stars to have their own Christian *singsing.* Their gathering would be for praise and prayer. They had told us they didn't expect us ladies to attend. We had already sung in two all-night services that week. We would welcome a good night's sleep.

While the five of us visited, we could hear the din of the two meetings outside competing against each other. Around 11 P.M. Diana announced she was going to bed." Fay Christensen stretched and also headed for the back room.

The ominous pulsating music we had previously ignored now aroused my curiosity. It occurred to me that I was hearing only one *singsing*.

"Martha, why don't we hear the Christians?"

"Hmm, I don't know."

"Do you mind if we go outside to see what's happening?" Janice asked.

"Not at all, I'll go with you." Martha led the way toward the clearing near the new church building where a handful of discouraged believers sat. They explained that they had lost their crowd to the lure of the traditional gathering only a short distance away.

We three migrated toward the other group. Drums beat incessantly. Eerie shadows of dancers loomed like monstrous demons against the backdrop of the jungle's dense foliage. I stood on tiptoes, trying to see over others' shoulders. In the center danced men adorned in their finest *bilas*. Their grass skirts, breastplates of shells and pigs' tusks, feathered headdresses, plus arm and leg bands of woven colorful leaves bounced vigorously with the drum's pulsating rhythm.

As I strained to see, I was reminded of another incident in India. Similar to this occasion, we had paused on the fringes of the crowd, curious to see what was going on. In the center stood a Hindu who was selling some charms intended to ward off evil spirits. Suddenly he had stopped his sales pitch and pointed directly at us.

"You there—go away! You're hindering my magic." If Christians were a hindrance, then we knew his magic had an evil source.

A second incident in India also came to mind. One night Janice and I were approaching a Hindu temple. We had seen other shrines and temples, but this time a man was inside going through some rituals. The smell of incense wafted our direction. A red glow accentuated the hideous features of the idol. The Bible tells us, "...they sacrifice to demons and not to God, and I do not want you to have fellowship with demons." (I Cor. 10:20) We had intended to step closer for a better look when suddenly it was as if we had come against an invisible wall. Perhaps angels were there to stop us. Instinctively we knew we didn't belong in this enemy territory. Inwardly we said, "Yes, Lord," and took some steps backward, then turned and ran.

Now in Angguna I felt the same as we had in India. Although we had been at the edge of the crowd not more than two minutes, I felt the strong compulsion to leave.

"Let's go," I whispered to Martha and Janice. They readily agreed, admitting they felt the same urging in the Spirit. When we walked back in the direction of the church, to our suprise thirty or forty people followed us.

At the sight of us returning with a crowd, the Christians lost their downcast expressions. Getting to their feet, they began singing. We all joined in. After a couple of songs, a man with a hideous, carved mask suddenly leaped into the center of the circle. When he raised a bow and arrow just inches from my neck, I gasped. With a quick jerk, he pivoted to point the arrow at Janice's neck. The white mask with ugly features looked ghostly and terrifying in the night. Before I could do anything, he turned and leaped back out of the circle. It all had happened very quickly. I heard locals fearfully muttering "*Sangguma,*" "*Sangguma.*" Villagers were terrified of *Sangguma.* It is a term for Satan or for the one who carries out the death curse.

"Do not be afraid of sudden terror, nor of trouble from the wicked when it comes;" (Prov. 3:25)

Our momentary reaction of fear melted away as we thought of the Scripture, "He who is in you is greater than he who is in the world." (I John 4:4b) Perhaps, like the incident in India, we were spoiling or hindering their magic and powers over people. We took courage and sang on. More people migrated from the traditional *singsing* to join our group.

A few minutes later, the strange incident reoccurred. The man with the white mask again broke into our crowd. The Christians stopped singing. A deathly silence pervaded the circle of believers, all eyes on the intruder. As before, the masquerader pointed his bow and arrow toward me and then toward my twin. I thought, "Resist the devil and he will flee from you." (James 4:7b) If this was one of Satan's cohorts trying to put a death curse on us, we felt no fear. Jesus said, "...do not be afraid of those who kill the body, and after that have no more that they can do." (Luke 12:4)

Janice and I broke the silence by bursting into an Apal song that Martha had taught us. Its message was simply, "*Sangguma,* go away. We serve our big Brother Jesus." The intruder immediately withdrew, ducking through the crowd and disappearing into the darkness. When our short duet had ended, we sensed a change in the atmosphere, an electrifying faith in the crowd. The Christians burst into song with a spirit of enthusiasm and conviction—"Satan has no power. Jesus has defeated him. Jesus has overcome death."

Our desire for sleep had vanished, as had the masked man, who we never saw again. We felt compelled to stay with the believers, these villagers who were relatively new in the faith. We needed each other as we sensed that the spiritual warfare was strong.

> "For we do not wrestle against flesh and blood, but against principalities, against powers, against the rulers of the darkness of this age, against spiritual hosts of wickedness in the heavenly places." (Eph. 6:12)

As hours passed, more people from the traditional singsing drifted toward the Christian gathering.

Finally by 4 a.m. the drums of the other *singsing* were silenced. Their entire crowd, including those with the feathered headdresses, had joined ours. I sensed that our presence was no longer needed. Suddenly a tiredness I had not felt all night swept over me. Just as I was about to suggest to Janice that we go back to the house, one of the Christian leaders approached us.

"Thank you for being here when we needed you. Now you may go rest. God has accomplished His purpose."

We had three hours sleep before getting up for breakfast. When we shared the events of the night, both of the Australian ladies said that independent of each other, they had awakened in the night. Sensing that spiritual warfare was going on outside, they had each spent time in prayer.

Martha and all the villagers stood on the banks of the river waving as we headed down river with Diana and Fay. We loved the quiet rides on the winding rivers of the Ramu Valley. There was quality time to think, and to pray.

PART VI

Reflecting on God's Dealings with PEOPLE

People. God cares about people. In the previous sections of this book, we have marveled at certain aspects in God's care through orchestrating circumstances in life, His purposes through our trials, and His answers to specific prayers. Above all, He shows by all His dealings that He cares about people. We thank the Lord for all His blessings.

"Bless the Lord, O my soul, and forget not all his benefits." (Ps. 103:2)

Among the Lord's benefits heaped upon us, are special relationships with people. We realize that as He calls, equips, and blesses, it is our responsibility to mirror His purpose—reaching PEOPLE for His kingdom.

Bob Peaker

September 14, 1990: Bob Peaker telephoned from the MAF office in Papua New Guinea to wish his "twin sisters" a happy birthday. He, who often did thoughtful things for others, reached across the Pacific to give the Rostvit Twins the birthday gift they would always cherish.

36

Two Phone Calls

∼ by Faye ∼

———————————◼———————————

R-i-i-ng. "I'll get it." Janice reached for the phone in the kitchen. It was September 14, 1990, our birthday . It was probably the only time in twenty years that we had been home to celebrate the day.

"Happy birthday, *Tupela* (twins)."

She immediately recognized the deep voice. Excited, Janice held the receiver to one side.

"Faye, it's Bob Peaker!"

Only days before, we had been reminiscing about the flights we had taken with Bob in Papua New Guinea. We had marveled how he had treated us, giving more than the common courtesies that would be expected. Several times he had invited us on family outings so we could get to know his wife, Sharon, and sons, Michael and Tony. As we had reminisced, Janice had made the comment, "Bob has been such a true brother to us. I only wish he had actually called us his sisters." Now, only days after having said that, Bob was telephoning from the South Pacific.

"Sharon and I have decided to call all our brothers and sisters on their birthdays. We just want you to know you are IN. We love you. God bless, *Tupela*." The short but sweet call had been a perfect birthday present.

Our travel ministry has its physical and emotional stresses. It is not always easy to be the visitor, the interrupter of routine. Meaningful relationships need to be established in a short period of time. So, to be accepted and loved as family is a heaven-sent gift. Bob had joined the ranks of the special family Jesus promised in Mark 10:29,30.

> "There is no one who has left house or brothers or sisters or father or mother or wife or children or lands for My sake and the gospel's, who shall not receive a hundredfold now in this time—houses and brothers and sisters and mothers and children and lands, with persecutions—and in the age to come, eternal life."

The following week we were singing in a mission rally in Wheatland, Wyoming. We were alone in our host's home when the phone rang. It was Bonita Pryor, a missionary to Papua New Guinea whom we had seen on both of our trips there.

"I hate to have to break the news," she said, "but Bob Peaker's plane crashed…"

Only five days earlier we had heard Bob's voice and cherished his words. Now he was gone! His words still echoed from eternity. "You are IN. We love you. God bless, *Tupela*."

Our last mental picture of the Peakers was at the Mt. Hagen airport when we were leaving the country. "How long 'til we see you again?" Bob had asked with tears in his eyes. Then they each embraced us. When we took off, I had wished the pilot would tip the wings for the Peakers, as Bob had often done for others.

Now in Wyoming we felt very much alone. That night I slept fitfully. Each time I awoke I wished the phone call had only been a bad dream. Tears flowed as I prayed for Sharon and the boys before drifting back to sleep. Twice that night I experienced what may have been "night visions." In one, decorations filled the ceiling: colorful streamers, and tiny lights twinkling like stars. I sat up with a start. About a dozen dark-skinned people were seated around the bed. I felt frustrated.

"What are you doing here? And what's all this decoration?" I said. "Don't you know Bob Peaker just died?"

"Yes, we know. We're celebrating because he has gone to heaven. And we have come to sit with you in your grief." (At that time we were unaware of the New Guinean custom that friends sit up all night with ones who have lost a loved one.)

Later I was aroused from sleep again when I heard a noise. I was fully aware we were in the two-story home in Wyoming. Clearly remembering that our hosts were gone for the day, I wondered what could have made the sound? THUMP! There it was again, even louder. Could it be burglars? CREAK! CREAK! Oh no, someone was coming up the stairs! My heart raced. I dared not move. I wished we had closed our bedroom door, but it stood wide open. Dim light filtered in from a night light in the hall. Within seconds, I saw silhouettes of at least four men. One entered the room.

"Who are you? What do you want?" I called. To my own amazement, my fears instantly dissolved. An inner knowledge assured me these were not burglars, but were ministering angels who had come to comfort me. I slipped out of bed and approached the one who entered the room. He gently embraced me. A sense of peace flooded over me. Then I backed away to look up at him. I stood momentarily transfixed, amazed at how tall he was. He had dark hair, brown eyes, and was youthful, but I was so enamored with his height that I wasn't trying to get a description. Being consoled, I slipped back into bed and slept peacefully the remainder of the night.

The following morning I had to ask myself if it had only been a dream. I was so certain I had been awake. Whatever the case, God had comforted me.

It was never determined what caused Bob's crash. As time passed, stories flooded in concerning people, who as a result of Bob's life and his death, had surrendered to the Lord. We knew he had not died in vain.

> "I tell you the truth, unless a kernel of wheat falls to the ground and dies, it remains only a single seed. But if it dies, it produces many seeds." (John 12:24 NIV)

Less than a month after Bob's death, we were leaving on an overseas tour to South Africa. Our hearts were still heavy. One evening we sang in a village church for an all-night meeting. When a Scripture reading was announced, I reached for my Bible. It flipped open to where a photograph of Bob and Sharon Peaker lay between the pages. I was dumbfounded. Instead of Bob's face, I saw that of the angel—the one who had comforted me in Wyoming. Throughout the night I would turn to the photo, and the angel's image was there rather than Bob's. That was the only time that phenomenon occurred. I won't attempt to explain it or to theologically pigeonhole it. But I thanked God, as it served to be a touch of His love.

On a day when no singing was scheduled, missionary Alice Fishback drove us to the coast. The beach was deserted. Alice suggested we go for a walk while she remain at the truck to study a lesson. With her sympathetic nature, she had sensed that we needed some time alone.

Waves of a heavy surf crashed onto the rocky shore causing us to think of the lyrics, "When sorrows like sea billows roll...." We paused to gaze toward the horizon. Somewhere far over that Indian Ocean lay Papua New Guinea. We longed to be there, wishing we could have attended Bob's funeral. It was fitting that the "pastor pilot" Peter van Zanen had preached at the memorial service. With his compassionate nature, he was a great comfort to all the families who were grieving. But we felt alone in our grief. My chest heaved with a sigh. For both of us, emotions that had been put on hold, broke loose and tears flowed freely.

Based on, "Weeping may endure for a night, but joy comes in the morning," (Ps. 30:5b), a song poured from our aching hearts.

THE DAWN WILL COME

The heart is heavy, the pain is deep, ♪ ♪
In empty silence my spirit weeps,
My eyes stare vacant, their radiance gone,
The endless night holds back the dawn
    and joy which comes with the morning.
The memories linger to plague my mind,
I point no finger, no fault to find,
But turn to Jesus, He'll heal the ache,
    I trust the dawn will break.

Jesus speaks softly, "Come if you're distressed,
Come unto me, I will give you rest,
I care, I have been there, I will help you now to
    make it through the night,
Hold on, 'til the dawn, when I'll scatter all your
    darkness with my light."

The heart though heavy, and tinged with grief,
Now waits in silence for full relief,
The Lord gives peace so profound and real,
With hope rekindled I truly feel that joy will come
    in the morning.
The memories Jesus now brings to mind,
Help me to see what is good and kind, ♪ ♪
So through His strength I will carry on,
And trust He'll bring the dawn.

We stood before a crowd of ladies in Johannesburg. The blacks sat to one side, the whites to another. Those of Indian origin sat to themselves, as did those who were racially mixed.

"Have you ever felt like you're not accepted—like you're not welcomed by some?" Janice asked. "Even we, though treated wonderfully as guests, can sometimes feel like we are on the fringes. Maybe you haven't been unkind or cruel to anyone, yet neither have you made an effort to welcome others into your home or into your heart." Relating the incident of Bob Peaker's telephone call to us, Janice concluded with, "Let us seek opportunities to say, 'You are IN. We love you.'"

There were tears in some of the ladies' eyes. Publicly, some declared their new resolve to reach out. It started with a wealthier Caucasian saying, "Here is my phone number. You who live in Soweto where there is fighting, please call me if you need help. You can take refuge in our home." Others followed the example of openness.

The meeting ended with a mingling of races as they joined hands in a circle of prayer. The example of Bob's life was helping people on another continent. He was still "tipping his wings."

Bob also spurred the writing of another song. It stemmed from a time when we were flying with him and saw a glorious rainbow—not just the arch, but the full circle. It appeared as though we would fly through the ring. Bob turned and said, "Write a song about it, girls."

Later, when on a flight with Peter van Zanen, we again saw a full-circle rainbow—a reminder of Bob's suggestion. When the song did come, it was more through inspiration than from our own efforts.

♪ ♫ AS BEAUTIFUL AS A RAINBOW ♪ ♫

Light is kindled in a heart when you give a smile,
Gratitude is deepened
    when you go the second mile,
And if sincere compassion will motivate your day,
You will find, love multiplies,
    as you give it all away.

CHORUS:
Reach out and touch a life,
Make dreams come true,
Strive on with heart and soul, God's will to do,
And when you've given all,
Then you'll know why,
Life is as beautiful as a rainbow in the sky.

Rainbows are a contrast in a dark and stormy sky,
You can be that contrast on which others can rely,
So rise on wings as eagles, and you'll begin to soar,
You will fly, to greater heights,
    than you've ever flown before.

Speaking of soaring—Janice had a dream one night that caused profound reflection.

"In my dream, we saw Bob again, and he asked if we would like to go for a flight. We eagerly climbed aboard the Cessna. Once airborne, Bob turned and told us to get out, explaining that we would be able to fly. We complied. Soon we were floating spread-eagle on either side of the airplane. Bob turned his head from side to side, smiling at each of us. Our joy and elation knew no bounds. Then he said, 'I must go now.' With that, he disappeared. Fear gripped me as I stared into an empty cockpit, assuming the plane would crash, and we would die! Like a movie replaying a scene, a Bible story flashed through my mind—that of Peter walking on the water, becoming fearful, then beginning to sink.

"In my dream, I reached up and took hold of a wing support. You did the same. Then the airplane glided to a soft landing. There on the ground was Bob. I was ready to berate him for deserting us, but before I could utter a word, Bob asked, 'Why didn't you keep flying?' With chagrin I replied, 'I guess our fears brought us down.' Bob nodded. His face took on a tender, understanding expression. 'It's hard while on earth to hang onto that strong faith for very long, isn't it?'"

Although it was only a dream, it is true in life. Despite good intentions, we often fall short of facing daily stress with an attitude of confident faith. Memories of Bob Peaker have since given us the incentive to go out of our way to make eternal touches on others' lives.

37

Behind Bars

∼ by Janice ∼

———————◖▭◗———————

Large keys dangled from the jailer's belt as she strode with heavy man-like steps down the dimly lit corridor. When we all reached the room at the end of the hall, the sound of her clanking keys ceased. She turned and directed her comment to George Bajenski so he could translate. Her eyes registered little emotion as she spoke.

"Seventy percent of the inmates are serving time for murder." George talked with her in his usual optimistic, uplifting manner. He has the heart and drive to make the most of every opportunity. Four years earlier he and his wife Vera had lost their only son. Fifteen-year-old Benjamin had been struck down by a passing motorist while he was crossing a street. We marveled at the Bajenskis' attitude of acceptance as they focused on God's purposes. In fact, it appeared that the tragedy had given George an increased burden for souls, as evidenced here in his native Poland.

In contrast I berated myself for the rebellious spirit with which I struggled. I didn't even want to be here. Why does Satan always use our minds as a battleground? Our two-month schedule in Europe had been full, singing every day. We had felt relieved when we had been told that this Saturday would be a free day. The morning had dawned gray, cold, and rainy—all the more reason to relish staying in, relaxing, and writing a few letters. Then during breakfast a local preacher had come and asked if we would sing a couple songs at the women's prison.

This type of opportunity doesn't come very often, yet we felt reluctant—it being our "day off." I wanted to say, "No, not today. Any other day, but not today." But Jesus' words came to mind to chastise my selfishness.

"I was…in prison and you did not visit me." (Matt. 25:43b)

With that we had pasted smiles on our faces and agreed to go. The pastor said he would come for us at 11 A.M. After he was gone, we returned to our room.

"Oh well, what's two songs. It won't take much preparation, and we still have plenty of the morning free," Faye said. The real battle in spirit came when the pastor arrived at 9 A.M.

"Will you come now and give an hour-and-a-half concert?"

My human nature was pressing the panic button. We knew our preparation necessitated more than merely choosing songs. The most essential preparation would be of the heart. We needed to surrender our plans and wishes, being willing and eager to serve. By the time we left our cozy quarters, umbrellas and instruments in hand, we thought we had our bad attitudes under control. But now standing in the drab room, facing incoming inmates, I wasn't so sure.

One woman met my gaze with a cold calculated stare. Another young punk with orange spiked hair had a hard expression. Satan tried to bring me down with judgmental thoughts and feelings of insecurity. How can I relate with these criminals? What will they think of

Christian songs? What if they ridicule our pronunciation of Polish? I had to rebuke Satan again. God had called us to this task. We had to determine to do our best.

The warden introduced us, and we proceeded to sing. During our second song, we noticed tears in the eyes of a couple of the inmates. By the fourth song, nearly a third of the audience was weeping. One, sobbing uncontrollably, received permission to leave the room temporarily.

At the close, George Bajenski, in his gentle caring manner, urged everyone to join in a prayer circle. The one who had been sobbing rushed forward and threw her arms around Faye. Her name was Beata, a twenty-five year old. The youth with orange hair hurried across the circle to cry on my shoulder. One of the guards expressed surprise.

Twenty-five-year-old Beata was remorseful. We have since learned she is back in society.

"We've never seen such an emotional response before. We are pleased to see it." With permission from the guards, following the prayer time the inmates went to their rooms and returned bearing gifts for us: delicate handwork on small pieces of cloth and intricately carved boxes made from bars of soap. It was our turn to weep. We were deeply touched. We both had to admit we were glad we had come.

Once outside the prison, we asked George if we could stop at the old folks' home. We had sung there the previous day, so we knew it was nearby. We wanted to take a picture of Babka Olzewski. George, who had known her for years, agreed.

The door to Babka's room was ajar. We quietly slipped inside. The 100-year-old woman sat, head bowed, hands folded in prayer. None of us cared to interrupt the solemnity of the scene. But Babka, sensing our presence, looked up.

"You have come back," she said with a toothless smile. "I have been praying for you. I asked God to touch lives through you, and He told me He was blessing your singing this morning." She couldn't have known we had just sung at the prison. Now we knew why the hearts of the women had melted with repentance. A dear elderly saint had been praying, unleashing a power far beyond our human efforts. We had better not be heady when great things happen, knowing that God has done the work through the power of prayer.

Since then, when additions to an already busy schedule tend to overwhelm us, one of us reminds the other, "This might be a special blessing like the Polish prison."

We want to be more willing servants, following the same motto by which young Benjamin Bajenski had lived, "All I am, all I have, all I ever hope to be...I dedicate to the Lord, Jesus Christ."

38

We See Jesus
in a Blue Shirt
~ by Janice ~

Which is better—to have a voice or a heart? To sing effortlessly with tones clear and beautiful, yet just be going through the motions? Or to yearn with a hungering desire to praise, yet vocal chords refuse to cooperate? If put to the choice, I would surmise that God would prefer we would choose the heart. When I am in good voice, I tend to take it for granted. Perhaps sometimes God allows voice problems to get our hearts in the right place.

"I will praise you, O Lord, with my whole heart; I will tell of all Your marvelous works." (Ps. 9:1)

Rain fell, a steady drizzle on the big tent, while a bitter wind sought entry by angrily flapping the canvas walls. I shivered, pulling my cardigan tightly around me. It was an exceptionally cold spring in Europe. It had snowed in April when we were singing in France. Icy fingers of arctic air had touched us in Norway. Now we were enduring this bone-chilling dampness in Poland. Despite the cold weather, a good crowd had filled the tent for the evangelistic services every night. People were attentive as we stepped onto the platform and sang in Polish, yet inwardly I tensed. I was losing my voice. When we took our seats, I whispered to Faye that my throat felt raw.

"Mine, too," she confided with a worried expression. It is difficult enough when one of us is in bad voice —but both! What would we do?

The following day we were to cross into what then was the Soviet Union for another month of singing. We had been to the USSR two years earlier when churches were initially gaining freedom. I recalled how exhausted we had become, even though it was a good kind of exhaustion. Church services lasted three or four hours. Often we were up well into the night listening to the believers tell of their experiences and trials they had faced under communism. With little sleep, we were rejuvenated daily through the deep faith of the Christians. Even unbelievers had an amazing receptivity of hearts, such as we had never before witnessed. Amid this bankrupt society, people hungered for truth and answers.

1991: The Rostvit Twins travel to former Soviet republics with George Repetski, well known there for his years of Christian broadcasting over shortwave radio.

We wanted this visit to be a special blessing, but our singing voices were giving out. A deep longing persisted—a desire to fulfill I Corinthians 14:15b "…I will sing with the spirit, and I will sing with the understanding also." We prayed, "Lord, when we are weak, we know that You can be our strength. Although we are in poor voice, please help us to give of ourselves, to sing with heart."

The following day we boarded a train bound for the Soviet Republic of Belorussia (now Belarus). The train was packed with Russians who had crossed into Poland to sell a few items, then buy goods not yet available in their own shops. We were scarcely out of the Warsaw station when a lady, who was fascinated to meet Christians from the West, pumped us with questions. For this portion of our tour, we were traveling with Canadians, including preachers Allan Dunbar and George Repetski. Mr. Repetski, who speaks both Russian and Belorussian, did the majority of the talking. He turned to us and asked us to sing a Belorussian song.

Our voices cracked on a few notes, yet the passengers in the compartment and those standing in the aisle listened intently. The message of the song was about the love of Christ. The inquisitive lady who had initiated the conversation wiped her tears and requested a copy of the lyrics. As people often do after we have sung in their language, the lady directed a question to us, assuming we spoke Belorussian. George translated her question.

"She asks if you had become believers on your own, or did you grow up attending church."

"Our parents are Christians. Yes, we attended worship services each Sunday, but that in itself does not make one a believer. We each needed to make our own personal decision—a time when we admitted to God that we had sinned and needed Him in our lives."

"When we were thirteen, our church was having a special week of preaching meetings, and the nightly sermons were about Jesus. Although he was God Himself, Jesus came to earth in human form." I remembered how evangelist Leroy Herder had made graphic word pictures, conveying the exhilaration of the triumphal entry, the agony of Gethsemane, the injustices and mockery of the trial, and the suffering and humiliation of the cruel execution on a cross." We did not know how much of the Gospel this Russian lady knew. With George Repetski translating, we talked of the crucifixion and our reaction.

"As I heard about Jesus' death, my heart was broken. We had heard the story many times before, yet the reality had not previously touched my heart. I could not blame others for murdering Jesus. My sins had nailed Him to that cross.

"At the close of each service, an invitation was given, asking people to publicly acknowledge their desire to accept Jesus as Savior and Lord. I wanted to step out, yet I was shy. Night after night we heard the preaching, and I felt convicted, but I still hesitated. Then Sunday came. The sermon was about Jesus' resurrection from the dead. The church building was packed. I even recognized some schoolmates in the crowd. Would they ridicule me in school? I was determined to make my decision public that day. I would give my life to Jesus, no matter what others might think."

While recounting my conversion to the lady, I remembered how eager, yet nervous I felt that Sunday morning so long ago. Heat had surged through my chest as I had anticipated walking forward, and I applied the Scripture about the two on the road to Emmaus, "Did not our heart burn within us...while He opened the Scriptures to us?" (Lk. 24:32) The lady was leaning forward, listening intently.

"When the invitation was extended, I walked down the aisle, tears blurring my vision. I became aware that someone else was walking beside me and was surprised to see that it was my twin. My first thought was, I hope she's not doing this just because I am. I wanted her conversion to be genuine also. Then I saw her tears. She, too, had been struggling with the decision for days. I should not have been surprised that God was convicting both of us at the same time. We were also jointly immersed in the waters of baptism, a beautiful picture of a death, burial, and resurrection to a new life. Being twins who had shared our physical birth, was it any wonder that we should also experience our second birth, our spiritual awakening, simultaneously?"

As I concluded my testimony on the train, I felt humbled that I didn't have a more dramatic story to tell. To my surprise the Russian lady's face was a picture of captivated wonder.

"It sounds like a fairy tale to me." She shook her head, sighing with hopeless resignation. "How can we be expected to reach that point of believing when we have never had the opportunity to hear?" Her words called to mind Romans 10:14.

"How then shall they call on Him in whom they have not believed? And how shall they believe in Him of whom they have not heard? And how shall they hear without a preacher?"

George and Allan continued to witness to the lady during the five-hour journey to the border. Eventually Faye pulled a Russian Bible out of her flight bag and handed it to the lady. She stared.

"How much will it cost?"

"Nothing. We want to give it to you."

Clutching the cherished gift to her heart, she sighed. "I have always wanted a Bible, but never dreamed I would have one. There are some for sale on the black

market, but it would have taken three-weeks' wages!"
Pictures flashed through my memory of the many times
on this European tour when we had dreaded carrying
the heavy box of Russian Bibles: getting into a subway
beneath Paris, scurrying to catch a ferry to Norway's
coast, checking in at airports, or transporting our luggage to a taxi. To see the delight on this one woman's
face made it worth it all. As we reached our destination
and busied ourselves getting luggage off the upper
racks, the lady tapped George's arm.

"Thank you for giving me my first lesson about
God."

As on our previous trip, the Russian people were
eager and curious to hear visitors from the West. No
matter what the size of building, it was packed. People
stood in the aisles or in the staircases. Children sat on
the platform, filling every inch of floor space. Still others
gathered outside the windows, even in the rain.

Faye and Janice use deaf signing with a song.

Faye and I were to sing several times through the services. When we were not singing, we sat on the platform, gazing at the sea of faces. It was not like an American crowd where some people's expressions may register boredom, indifference, or apathy. Instead, their eyes communicated deep hurt, despair, and general hopelessness. Some, hanging on every word, showed a genuine hunger, as if grasping for hope. When I would spot them, I would silently pray for their hearts to be open to God's message.

Following our first songs in a small but crowded church in Rogachov, we sat down. I felt exhausted from the pressure my diaphragm had to keep to maintain my notes on pitch. Oh to be in better voice! As I looked up at the crowd I thought of the verse, "…since we are surrounded by so great a cloud of witnesses…let us run with endurance the race that is set before us." (Heb. 12:1b)

I thought of our friend and brother, Bob Peaker, who had died nine months earlier. I silently prayed, "Lord, if you would give another special brother like Bob was to us, it might help us to sing with heart. Forgive me for this selfish request. All I need to do is fix my attention on You."

After praying that prayer, I scanned the audience in search of persons to pray for. Suddenly my heart leaped at the sight of a man in the middle of the crowd. It wasn't a physical attraction to handsome features. My spirit was bearing witness at the sight of a Godly man. His eyes, the windows to the soul, exuded peace. My initial reaction was to think as Jesus did of Nathanial, "Behold, a man in whom is no guile." (Jn. 1:47b)

I thought of the verse, "Let us fix our eyes on Jesus, the author and perfecter of our faith…." (Heb. 12:2 NIV) I determined then to pretend the man in the audience was Jesus. It would help me to sing better. When it came our turn to present more songs, my heart welled up within me and the message poured forth as from my whole being. The tones still lacked in quality, but I sensed our songs were touching lives. I seldom dared meet the gaze of the man wearing a blue shirt. Just to know he was there gave me that deep longing and drive to do my best.

When we took our seats, my exhaustion was lifted. I glanced toward the man in the blue shirt. His attention was on Allan Dunbar who had stepped to the pulpit to preach. His expression communicated more than words. As singers, we often look for those faces in the crowd that register an obvious love for Jesus. It's like food for the soul to be encouraged by their expressions. Immediately following the service, Faye slipped her instrument into its case.

"Did you notice the man in the blue shirt?" she asked.

"Did I! He was like a light shining in darkness."

"I pretended he was Jesus seated in the audience. It helped me to sing better."

She had done the same thing as I had. Slipping my brown cardigan from the seat back, I commented wistfully, "Oh that others at first sight of me would say, 'I see Jesus.'"

Anatoly

Moments later George Repetski approached, together with the man we had seen in the crowd. "Girls, I'd like to introduce you to someone."

I felt like saying, "We know him. We call him Jesus." But I only smiled.

"Janice, Faye, this is Anatoly. He will be our driver during the remainder of our time in the republic," he said. Our "blue-shirted Jesus" would be in every service, an ever-present lift.

In each new location, we would search the faces of the crowd until we could locate where Anatoly was sitting. If we couldn't find him, one of us would whisper to the other, "Where is Jesus?" The answers were varied each night. "Sitting by the left wall," "standing in the foyer," or "in the balcony." At one place when we spotted him, his expression read, "Here I am." It appeared that he knew we always looked for him.

In yet another service, we searched but could not locate him. The church was packed; people were standing in the aisles. Then I looked out the window beside us. There he was, standing with those who were out in the rain. He had no umbrella. Water dripped from his hair. He smiled as I met his gentle gaze. Then with hand signs he indicated, "I'm praying for you." I moved my lips to form the Russian word for "Thank you."

When we stood to sing, we felt a strength in the spirit. After being seated, I scanned the vast crowd in search of one to pray for. A lady in the fifth row sat as one transfixed, intensely listening to the preaching. I spent much time in prayer for her. At the close of the service when an invitation was extended, she inched her way past others who crammed the aisles. Tears stained her cheeks.

"Now I know what has been missing in my life. I need God to fill the void. I don't know what is expected of me, but whatever it takes to become a Christian, I'm willing to do it," she said.

After the service, George Repetski told us this was the woman's first time to attend a church service. She said our songs in Russian deeply touched her heart, causing her to want to hear what Christianity had to offer.

We thanked God that our songs, in spite of our bad voices, had helped. Because we were singing as unto Jesus, the Holy Spirit could communicate more than simply the melodies and lyrics.

We hungered to tell Anatoly how much his presence inspired us to sing wholeheartedly, yet we could not converse with each other. Despite the communication barrier, we shared a kindred spirit, which was mutually understood and appreciated. We worked to learn some Russian vocabulary, and we took Anatoly by surprise when we said, "Anatoly, we see Jesus in your eyes." He was thrilled to hear us speaking Russian, but when it dawned on him what we had said, he dropped his gaze in humility.

Anatoly then took on the role of teacher, helping us learn more Russian. When we reached Minsk, Anatoly's hometown, we were pleased to meet his family. His wife Vera had the same gentle heart that Anatoly possessed.

Near the end of our month in the republic, Anatoly requested that George Repetski translate something he wished to tell us. "I had two sisters. One has died. The other has recently gone through a bitter divorce and has little to do with the family. I feel as though I have lost both of them. Please tell the twins I praise God that He has given them to me as sisters."

Our good-bye was difficult. Anatoly drove us to Vilnius, Lithuania where we would part company. We had plans of speaking our gratitude to this brother, having rehearsed in the car what we could communicate in Russian. However, when we reached our destination, there was a hubbub of activity. As luggage was unloaded from the van, Faye and I stood to one side, awaiting an opportunity to speak with Anatoly.

A cold wind whipped our hair. The bronchial cough that had been plaguing me for weeks again let loose.

Suddenly a strong hand brusquely whirled me around. A broad-shouldered woman was taking both Faye and me by the arm. Like prisoners, we were being escorted toward the nearby block of apartments. I caught enough words in her husky voice to know she meant well.

"We must get you inside out of the cold. The driver must return to Minsk before dark. We do not need to delay him with good-byes."

Faye and I felt powerless, wanting to break away, yet not wishing to offend. At the last moment before entering the darkness of the apartment building's stairwell, we peered with desperation over our shoulders. Anatoly had just caught sight of us. His expression was one of questioning bewildered pain. We were all being denied a formal farewell. We groped our way up the dark stairs, knowing we would need to suppress our deferred hope and be sociably pleasant. The apartment faced the back of the building, so we couldn't even wave from a window. We knew we would not see Anatoly again.

When we were finally left alone that night, we both stood by the window, staring into the grayness of the night. Tears rolled in our silent pain. We prayed, asking God to care for Anatoly as he drove the long way back to his home. We also thanked Him for the joy of having gained this treasured brother, even though the parting had been painful.

During the ensuing ten days in Lithuania, we managed, with the help of an English/Russian New Testament as well as a dictionary, to write a long letter in Russian to Anatoly and Vera. We knew we would not get all the verb conjugations, nor the numerous case endings correct, but we prayed that the letter would reach them.

The Rostvit Twins were the first ones from the West to sing in the auditorium of a large school. After each song, several of the children would step forward and hand the twins flowers. By the end of the concert, the edge of the stage was piled with lilacs, roses and tulips.

When we returned two years later, we had another prayer on our lips, "Lord, please work it out for us to see Anatoly's family again." The only problem was that this tour would take us nowhere near the city of Minsk. Our final singing engagement was in the town of Kobrin, near the Polish border. From there we were to travel west into Poland. Minsk lay five hours to the east.

When George Repetski went into the station to purchase tickets, my gaze took in the tracks to the east. I sighed, wishing we could head that way. George returned bearing news that we could not catch the westbound train. All trains into Poland were booked solid, filled with Russian merchants.

"What can we do?"

"They said we will have to travel eastward to Minsk to find room on any train to Poland."

To Minsk!?? God had answered our prayer in a most unusual manner. Surely we would see our brother

Anatoly. We did not consider how improbable our chances were of finding him. George Repetski had to part company with us, so he contacted an acquaintance, Tonya Kravetz, to meet us at the Minsk station. She was to arrange our tickets for our westward journey to Poland. But Tonya spoke no English, and we understood very little Russian. How could we expect to locate Anatoly in a city of 2 to 3 million people, when we had no address nor telephone number? We also did not realize that phone books were not public property. Only government agents were allowed to have them.

Again we were to see God's hand in the matter. Since Mr. Kravetz was a member of the Secret Police, they just happened to have a phone book. With much difficulty in our effort to use Russian, we communicated our desire to contact Anatoly's family. Tonya, being a new Christian, was eager to meet them. She telephoned Anatoly and Vera and invited them for a visit with some American twins. By Tonya's facial expression, we could well imagine Anatoly's surprised reaction.

Before long, he and his wife were entering the apartment, reaching to grasp our hands. Tears of joy filled their eyes and ours. Words weren't needed as we each savored the eternal moment and God's love shared in this special reunion. We nodded as we understood Vera to say, "This is a big gift from God." The feeling was mutual.

Although our Russian was limited, we seemed to have no problem communicating. Anatoly related that during years under Communism, when Christians were imprisoned for their faith, he had a ministry of writing to encourage incarcerated Believers. He kept a box of letters he had received in return from them. Then he showed us a bundle of letters, indicating these were his real treasures. Among them was our letter, the one we had written in Russian.

"You got it," I squealed with delight. "Could you understand it?" I asked in Russian.

"*Da,*" he nodded, though his smile betrayed amusement. With the kindred spirit we shared, we had assumed correctly that he would figure out what we intended to say, despite the lack of good grammar in our writing effort.

⸙

The relationships established by the Lord are rich blessings. Little did we know that God was preparing to establish another friendship back in America—an unusual answer to a prayer.

We had plans to climb Pikes Peak shortly after returning to Colorado. God had His own plans for the adventure we were to experience on that mountain.

Pikes Peak, elevation 14,110 feet.

39

Mountaintop Experience

∿ by Faye ∿

———————◖▬◗———————

"Stop, I'm out of breath." My chest heaved as I took deep breaths of the brisk morning air. As yet the sun offered no hint of warmth. I leaned against a boulder and whispered a prayer, "Lord, make the way clear." Janice, who seemed to have more energy than I, didn't rest as long as I had hoped and started trekking onward.

"Come on, we've got to keep moving," she said. We had hiked the first seven miles up the mountain the previous day and had stayed for the night at a rustic cabin for hikers. Today we were making the final six-mile ascent to the summit. We had left at 5 A.M. and reached timberline before dawn. Each time we stopped to rest, we would take the time to pray before pressing on.

Well above timberline, bitter winds blew across snow-fields still remaining in early summer. I tightened the drawstring on the hood of my jacket to fit more snugly around my face. Placing one foot in front of the other, we fought against the winds. "I need to take another breather," I called to Janice. Locating shelter from the wind, we huddled together behind a rock. For a few moments we sat in silence hearing only the thumping of our hearts. I considered the prayer we had been voicing all day, "Make Your way clear." The prayer was not for our safety. We were not lost; we had a clear trail to follow. We prayed for others, ones we had met on this mountain who we feared were lost—not physically, but spiritually.

I looked upward. With still more than a mile to go, the summit loomed above us. The sight of this famous mountain was not new to us. We had grown up in the shadow of Pikes Peak. Following each tour, this area was home. How many times had we peered from an airplane window and welcomed the sight of this snow-capped wonder that towers majestically above Colorado's high plains. Lifting my chin and closing my eyes, I basked in the kiss of gentle sunlight and silently slipped into prayer. After a few moments, Janice broke the solemnity.

"Let's go." We trudged on, feeling the effects of the scarcity of oxygen, yet encouraged by each step of progress. The higher we climbed, the more range of scenery came into view. Ultimately we reached the summit with a feeling of achievement. Taking in the spectacular panoramic views, we burst into song. "When high upon a mountain, my heart begins to sing. I thank the great Creator for making everything."

While singing, we scanned the wooded area far below, searching for the hikers' camp. That was precisely the focal point of our prayers.

The stay at the cabin had been interesting. The care-takers, Russ and Lisa Carpentier, had welcomed us warmly. Having endured a long lonely winter, they, along with their two daughters, had been eager to meet hikers. They were full of questions.

When they asked us what we do for a living, we simply told them we sing.

Janice, Lisa, Russ, Faye, and the girls, Katie, and Ashley.

"Sing for us," Lisa had said. We started with "Life is Like a Mountain Stream," "Reaching New Heights," and "Yodel Praises," some of our own compositions which might relate to their surroundings. Then Russ requested "Amazing Grace."

As we sang, he quickly slipped away. We could see he was fighting back tears. God was working in his heart drawing him to Himself.

> "No one can come to Me unless the Father who sent Me draws him…." (John 6:44a)

Later in the evening while we were all out on the deck, Russ admitted, "I always thought of myself as a man's man, but your songs bring me to tears. Did God put you in this kind of work?" We briefly told how the Lord had led us into a life of music.

"Well I think He had a hand in sending you up here," Russ said. He went on to share the story of their lives. Both he and Lisa had been bartenders but had taken this caretaker job to get away from the bar and develop closer family ties. Russ also hoped the distance would help curb his addiction to cocaine and alcohol. But it had not.

"You know, when I struggle up seven miles in deep snow with a heavy pack, I have to believe there is someone out there who can help me get home with the groceries." Pointing upward Russ added, "Seeing the stars each night, I know there must be a God." As if thinking out loud, he whispered, "I want to know more about Him." Those words had stirred within us a desire to show this family God's love. We had been able to share a few things that evening as opportunities arose naturally in conversation.

On our descent from the summit, I prayed, "Lord, should we stay at the hikers' camp again? If we do, will we have opportunity to share more about Your love? Or has enough been said for now? Will we do more harm than good if we stay? We don't want to turn them off. What should we do, Lord? Please make it clear." How could God make it clear? What did I expect—a hand-written message in the clouds? A tap on the shoulder? A voice from heaven?

As we neared the camp, Ashley and Katie came running. They asked how our hike went. Before we could answer, Lisa and Russ arrived.

"You'll stay another night, won't you?" Just then a deafening clap of thunder overpowered our reply. Wide-eyed, Lisa pointed down the trail.

"Did you see that? Lightning just struck!"

With the back of his hand Russ thumped Janice on the arm. "See, your Boss is giving you an ultimatum. You'd better stay!" We all made a dash for the log cabin, reaching it just as the downpour hit. And I had questioned how God could make His will clear? You can't get much clearer than a bolt of lightning!

We did stay the night, and a lasting friendship blossomed. Over the next six years, we hiked up the mountain many times, summer and winter. After countless six-hour treks to the cabin, we concluded God must have a sense of humor. We had prayed for non-Christian friends, so the Lord gave us a loving concern for a family halfway up a mountain. He must have known we also needed the exercise!

Gradually Russ and Lisa's search for God took root. Mark Wall, an acquaintance of theirs from the bar, came to live at the cabin for a year and a half. Mark was likable and helped chop wood or carry drinking water from the stream.

Evenings found us all sitting around the barrel stove talking. Mark often joined in, sprinkling the conversation with spicy remarks or profound thoughts.

During Russ and Lisa's growth process, the Lord also used several other Christian hikers to help answer their searching questions. After much inner struggle, Russ and Lisa did surrender their hearts to the Lordship of Jesus Christ. God freed them of their alcohol and drug addiction. When they hiked the seven miles down the mountain in deep snow to make their decision known publicly and to be baptized, we sang a new song. "My Prayer" reflected the thoughts of their broken hearts.

> Lord God above, I need Your love.   ♪ ♪
> You know the struggle I've been going through.
> I want Your peace. I need release.
> There's nothing that I can hide from You.
> Lord I give You my all. Help me Jesus lest I fall,
>   for I hate the darkness I've been living in.
> Keep me on Your narrow path,   ♪ ♪
>   so I need not face Your wrath,
> Make me clean and let Your Spirit dwell within.

In 1999 the Carpentier family moved off the mountain and became caretakers for a Christian camp. Russ began sharing his testimony with groups of troubled youth; Lisa spoke at women's meetings. The profound change in their lives influenced their former cocaine and drinking buddies. They led several to the Lord, including Mark Wall. His life took such a dramatic turn with an insatiable hunger for God's Word that he felt called to the ministry. He is now in Bible college.

> "For we are God's workmanship, created in Christ Jesus to do good works, which God prepared in advance for us to do." (Eph. 2:10 NIV)

We had climbed several other 14,000-foot peaks in Colorado over the years. Why had we waited until we were in our forties to climb our "home" mountain? Were we in the right place at the right time because it was God's timing?

40

God's Timing

～ by Faye ～

At various times God allows us a glimpse of His orchestration of events. Allow us to paint the picture from someone else's point of view.

Behind a Melting Iron Curtain

In 1991 the Soviet Union was going through both death throes and birth pangs of change. As restrictions were lifted, Christians clung to the glimmer of hope. Some, being skeptical that freedom would be temporary, hesitated to exercise boldness in their faith. Yet others, like Vasily, would seize the opportunity while the door was open. This preacher in his sixties yearned to share the Gospel with soldiers stationed at a Soviet military base near his home in Kovel, Ukraine. He was certain, however, he would face opposition if he were to ask for an opportunity to preach there. When Vasily learned that George Repetski, his Canadian friend, was coming to Ukraine with some twin singers, he determined that a concert might be the door opener needed to gain access to the military base. He would take the risk and inquire.

The uniformed officer, an imposing figure, towered head and shoulders above snowy-haired Vasily. Vivid scenes of 1946 flashed through Vasily's memory. The Soviet Union was oppressing its people under the tyrannical rule of Stalin. At age sixteen, Vasily had been bold in his faith and had been punished for it. He was caught sharing Christian literature with a friend at school.

Without his parents even being notified, Vasily was taken by police, interrogated for five days without sleep, then escorted to the train station to be sent to Siberia. Officials told him that they would see to it that he would never spread Christian literature there again. For seven years Vasily worked in a Siberian labor camp, barely surviving on meager rations. Not long after Stalin's death in 1953, Vasily was released. The emaciated twenty-three year old returned home to Ukraine for a joyous reunion with family.

Communism continued to imprison many Christians over the subsequent thirty-five years, yet Vasily never lost his fiery zeal to spread God's Word.

Now as he stood on the Soviet military grounds, Vasily's pale blue eyes sparkled with confidence as he met the officer's penetrating gaze. Without hesitation, he came to the point.

"Some American twin ladies who sing in Russian and Ukranian are coming to Kovel. Would you be interested in their presenting a concert on the military base?"

Janice and I were apprehensive when we were taken to the military base and escorted to this same commander's office. Without a smile, the man rose from his position behind his large desk, shook our hands, and motioned us to have a seat.

Folding his muscular arms the man leaned forward to direct his comments toward us. His booming voice equaled his intimidating size.

"For years we've been taught that religion is the

opium of the people." I thought he was going to put restrictions on what we could sing, but then his expression softened. "Now it seems that the whole mindset has reversed. Everyone wants to hear about God. Many have a craving for Christian literature. In fact, I personally would like to have a Bible to read."

Reaching into the bag I had set by my chair, I pulled out a Russian Bible and gave it to him. The commander's sober expression instantly transformed to that of wonder, reminiscent of a child receiving a present. He insisted we sign our names in the cover and have a picture taken with him.

There were no restrictions placed on our concert. The commander himself made the introductions. The audience's attention was intense, not only for our singing, but also as George Repetski preached a message.

Following the program, the soldiers gratefully helped themselves to the mountain of complimentary Christian literature Vasily had arranged on a table. The Ukrainian preacher was ecstatic.

"Just think of it! I once was sent to Siberia for having shared Christian Literature, and now the Soviet military is begging me for Bibles! I never thought I'd see the day!" [Since the "Iron Curtain" came down, Vasily who had once been told, "You will never distribute Christian literature again," has personally given away more than 70,000 copies of God's Word.]

We reflected on God's timing! The Lord had used us to help gain access to a Soviet military base. He who causes kingdoms to rise and fall also turns the hearts of men.

Philippine Rebel on the Run

Squatting at the water's edge, Mariana nervously scrubbed the faded army shirts. Suddenly, wary as a wild animal, her ears caught the rustling sound. In a flash she dropped the laundry and backed into the bamboo thicket. She cowered in the shadows scarcely breathing, yet aware of the wild pounding of her heart. Would the rebel forces find her?

As a youth, Mariana had joined the rebels with the intent to revolutionize the Philippines by helping the plight of the poor. She married another rebel, and they vowed a life of destruction. But two decades later they finally came to their senses. They realized they were nothing but a band of robbers—"rebels without a cause." When they deserted, Mariana and her husband knew they would now be on a hit list. They agreed to go their separate directions in hopes of not being caught.

Together with her four children, Mariana surrendered to the regular army of the Philippines. The military granted asylum, guaranteeing protection only if she and her children remained inside the army camp. Mariana's only available means of income was to do laundry for the soldiers. But she dreaded this task, as the stream was located outside the boundary of the camp.

Mariana waited—listening. The dense bamboo thicket shielded her from the tropical sun, but nothing shielded her from the ever-gnawing fear. Her dark eyes shifting nervously caught the slight movement in the foliage to her right. The rustling increased; then from the thick brush emerged a mangy dog. Mariana let out a sigh of relief. With caution she returned to the stream and feverishly scrubbed socks. She wondered how long she could continue to live this way. The wage she earned was scarcely enough to feed her family. Would they have to leave the safety of the military's protection and go to a town to find a better paying job? That's it, we'll leave, Mariana determined. We'll leave tomorrow.

However, when Mariana awoke at dawn, she felt a strong inner urge to stay at the army camp two more days. Why two days? She didn't recognize that the nudge was from God, yet she obeyed the instinct. On the second day, two large trucks pulled into the open field near the camp's main entrance. With curiosity, Mariana's children peered through the fence. Several men were setting up a big tent. News filtered through the camp that there were to be gospel meetings. The children begged to attend. Initially Mariana refused, afraid to leave the camp. They all sat in the darkness behind the fence, listening as loudspeakers carried melodies up the hillside. Mariana relented. Together they slipped out the gate and joined the happy crowd.

They all listened with rapt attention as American twins sang several songs in the local language. Then missionary Charles Littell preached. The message from God's Word touched Mariana's heart. It spoke of life free from guilt, sin, and fear. Mariana wanted that more than anything. Following the sermon, the twins again stepped onto the platform. They sang a message in Cebuano. "Life passes like smoke, or like a flower that withers. No matter how careful you are, there is always an end. So remember God while you still have breath." Tears blurred Mariana's vision as she thought of her daily fears of being killed. When Mr. Littell invited people to give their hearts to Jesus, Mariana was the first to step to the front.

While Janice and I were singing, we had seen Mariana, her expression conveying deep turmoil. During the following days she attended teaching sessions, eager to learn. On the afternoon of the eighth day, she joined others at the river to be baptized. When she emerged from the water, she smiled. A look of peace softened her large dark eyes.

"Maybe the rebel forces will still find me. If I die, I die. I'd rather face death as a Christian than as a rebel," she said. God's love had reached out to a rebel who was tired of running. We felt blessed to be a part of His perfect timing.

Voice Problems

On our tenth tour of Australia, I was plagued by voice loss three times, and each time received prompt answers to prayer. The first occurred in Taree, New South Wales, in the home of longtime friends, Joy and Al Billingham. Janice and I had joined Joy and her sister Doreen Halfpenny on the back porch for a cup of tea. We watched the sunset over the Manning River.

"I think I should go in. My throat is feeling a bit raw." I reluctantly excused myself. Soon I felt feverish, so headed off to bed early.

During the night I had a dream involving the Brompton family, friends back home. The Bromptons live on a ranch high in the Rocky Mountains. We have often visited them, appreciating their high ideals. Jim and Twila who home school their four daughters, make the application of God's Word a top priority. While doing ranch chores, the teens love memorizing entire chapters of Scripture—an example that motivates other youth in their country church to do the same. The family also traditionally celebrates a Spiritual Birthday to demonstrate that their second birth is more important than the first.

Above all, their humble, loving, and non-judgmental attitudes confirm their deep desire to be like Jesus. Scripture tells us, "note those who so walk." (Phil. 3:17) Friends like these, truly "family" to us, make tremendous prayer partners.

Twila and Jim Brompton and their family have often been in prayer at the precise time when the Rostvits had a specific prayer need.

L.-R. Holly, Heather, Hazel, Heidi Brompton

In my dream I was simply seeing their faces, one after another: Jim wearing his black cowboy hat, Twila with her long braided hair, each of the daughters: Holly, Heidi, Heather, and Hazel, and grandmother Doris. I blinked my eyes, discovering I was awake. It was 3 A.M. I wished the dream could continue. Suddenly I swallowed and realized that my throat was no longer sore. My fever was also gone. I lay there praising the Lord.

Later we telephoned the Bromptons and, taking into account the sixteen hour time difference, learned that they all had been praying for us at the very time of my dream. That was God's timing again.

My second voice problem occurred in Victoria. I woke up one Sunday with laryngitis. I considered staying home from church. We were with the van Zanen family, the "pastor pilot" from Papua New Guinea who now resides in Australia.

At breakfast, Peter and Simone offered to pray for me. Prayer with this couple always draws us into God's presence. Although my voice remained a mere whisper, I prepared for church, trusting I would improve. We chose songs in which Janice could sing my soprano part, but by service time God had restored my full voice range. My praises that morning were all the more heartfelt.

The third time struck as we arrived in Adelaide, South Australia. A flu virus threatened to take serious hold, settling heavily into my lungs. I feared it would develop into bronchitis. Janice insisted I rest while she unpacked the luggage. Not long after we had settled in, we learned that the next two weeks' schedule was to be relatively heavy. Feeling weak, discouragement set in. God's Word exhorts us, "Let us not grow weary while doing good." (Gal. 6:9)

We sent an e-mail message to our parents and to our church in Colorado requesting prayer. Although it was night in North America, we rejoiced that within a matter of hours, people would be praying. Little did we know that God would also use His even faster method to get the prayer need to one who had no e-mail.

Twila Brompton, on the ranch high in the Rockies, was awakened in the middle of the night with a gnawing sense that we needed prayer. She was in tune to the Holy Spirit's nudging. That same day in Australia, the heaviness in my chest, as well as the discouragement, completely lifted. We faced the busy schedule with renewed zeal, thanks to the prayers of others, even ones whom God awakened in the night.

Help for Border Crossings

During a 2001 trip to the former Soviet Republic of Belarus, we asked friends to specifically pray for our border crossings. Each time we had been there, customs officials gave us a hassle about our instruments. As they are costly items, they want to make sure we are not smuggling instruments for resale.

We traveled by bus, arriving at the border at 11:30 A.M. We filled out declaration forms, on which we mentioned the instruments. A customs official came to the bus, our declaration form in hand.

"Who has instruments? Let me see them." After making his brief inspection, we were surprised that he simply nodded, indicating we were free to go.

Weeks later we received a letter from the Brompton family. Again Twila, who usually is a heavy sleeper, was awakened in the night with an urgency to pray for us. It was 2:30 A.M. in Colorado. With the nine-hour time difference, that was the very moment we had arrived at the border. No wonder the border guard had not harassed us. A definite answer to prayer.

How many times are we empowered or protected because someone is praying?

Two Quarts of Blueberries

One December as we and our parents drove eastward to spend Christmas with our sister's family, Mom gasped, "Oh no! I forgot the two quarts of blueberries." It had become a tradition for her to give blueberries to her grandson, Shannon. Each year he eagerly lifted packages under the tree, trying to determine which held Grandma's home-canned berries.

To our surprise, shortly after arriving in Roanoke, Virginia, a package came from Greg Rostvit, a cousin in Minnesota. It was two quarts of blueberries! Mom happily gift-wrapped the jars. When we telephoned Greg to

thank him, we asked why he had sent them.

"Each morning I meet with some other Christian guys on the job. It was during a prayer time with them that I felt a compulsion to send you blueberries and that it needed to be two quarts," he said. When we told Greg of our Christmas tradition, and that we had forgotten our jars, he said, "I guess I'm in tune sometimes." Does God smile when we recognize His fingerprints creating precisely-timed events to give us joy?

The following summer in Minnesota while picking blueberries with Greg, we enjoyed swapping stories of God's goodness. We reflected on the difficulties our grandparents must have faced when they first emigrated from Norway. What would it have been like to leave home, country, relatives, and friends, knowing you'd never see them again. They sacrificed for the sake of their descendents. Now we were reaping the benefits.

Living in the jet age, we are able to make that voyage back to the "old country." Anticipation gripped us as we thought of our next trip to Norway. This time we'd be going way north, above the Arctic Circle.

41

To the Arctic Circle

∼ by Janice ∼

In 1998 we were returning to Norway for our seventh tour. On our journey, we spent a week in England with Eric and Dawn Batteiger's family. Eric, who for some years has been the minister of our home congregation, was on a nine-month leave to help establish a new work near Birmingham. During the days with them our bond of kinship deepened. Their love for each other, their well-behaved children, and their unselfish ways to help others were a tribute to their Christian faith. Some British families told us that the Batteigers' Christ-like example led them to faith in God.

> "You show that you are a letter from Christ, the result of our ministry, written not with ink but with the Spirit of the living God, not on tablets of stone but on tablets of human hearts." (II Cor. 3:3 NIV)

It was a reminder that the Lord reaches individuals not only through church services or concerts, but more often through personal examples in everyday circumstances. As we left Birmingham, we prayed, "Lord, help us likewise to mirror Your image, impacting those we meet." The next person we encountered was a taxi driver en route to London Heathrow Airport. He was from India, so we sang several songs in his language. He was both delighted and bewildered.

"I listen and hear ladies from India! But I turn around and see Americans," he said.

Faye (left) and Janice have sung in churches
and prayer houses of Norway.

Flights via Oslo and Tromsø took us to Vardø in the arctic region of Norway. We were filled with excitement to see a new area. The treeless terrain, land of the midnight sun, home of hardy Laplanders and weathered fishermen, fascinated us. Most treasured were the "soul touches" with people. Following a concert at a hospital, one man stood tottering on his new prosthesis.

"Please come to me. I cannot come to you," he said with tears in his eyes. Then he embraced us. "Your songs touched deep in my heart."

Not far from Vardø there was a camp where immigrants to Norway were processed. Several of them attended one of our concerts, so we sang in their various languages. One young lady from Colombia, South America was pleased that we understood Spanish.

"You have challenged me. Now I want to share my faith with others in the camp," she said.

One afternoon, Svein, (name has been changed) who had driven us to some of our concerts, took us to a private residence to sing for his friends. From the time we entered the home, we felt ill at ease. There were pagan symbols and new age decorations. Smoke from incense wafted in our direction, reminiscent of Hindu shrines in India. Svein was most eager for us to meet Salome (name has been changed). She had the airs and suggestive dress of a worldly woman. By her cold stare, her demeanor, and things she said, we surmised she dabbled in mystic practices. Our spirits bristled.

When Svein asked us to sing, their response was stilted. The husband stayed in the adjacent room, paying no attention. Their teenage daughters made excuses to leave. At first we assumed Svein wanted to witness to this family. But when he proudly told us that Salome could predict the future, we concluded he was under her spell.

"She has a sixth sense," he said with a glint in his eyes.

Sixth sense! Call it what he may, it is the same as fortune telling or divination, which is condemned in the Bible. "Do not practice divination or sorcery." (Lev. 19:26b NIV) As we were leaving the home, Svein told Salome that we would be going to Hammingberg the following day. He lingered while we went to the car. When he joined us, he had solemn news.

"Salome told me you shouldn't go to Hammingberg. There will be a tragedy! Something will happen on the road," Svein said.

"Svein, we're here to serve the Lord, not to cancel plans at the word of a psychic."

"But she uses her psychic abilities for good," he reasoned. I thought of the verse in Isaiah, "Woe to those who call evil good, and good evil." (Isa. 5:20a) We reminded Svein that the Bible speaks explicitly against these practices. According to Galatians 5, those who practice sorcery are among those who will not inherit the kingdom of God. When we suggested we pray about it, Svein was angered.

> "Let no one be found among you who practices divination, or sorcery, interprets omens, engages in witchcraft, or casts spells, or who is a medium, or spiritist, or who consults the dead. Anyone who does these things is detestable to the Lord," (Deut. 18:10-12a NIV)

Hammingberg, Europe's most northern town by road.

The following day a young couple, Roar and Lilja Berg, came for us. Roar bowed in prayer before we set out for Hammingberg. The Bergs were new in the faith, yet already very mature through their daily study of God's Word. Their love for Jesus was evidenced by their eagerness to share what God was doing in their lives. The drive paralleling the rocky coast was beautiful. As our conversation was uplifting, we gave no thought to Salome's prediction. Beside a quiet bay lay Hammingberg, Europe's farthest northern town by road. The church dominated the small community. There, Roar

played the organ, and we enjoyed singing, especially on songs where Roar chimed in, harmonizing with his rich baritone voice. On the return trip, our precious fellowship continued. We delighted in taking time out to walk across the tundra and rock-strewn landscape. We saw hundreds of reindeer, their racks giving them a top heavy appearance. Roar led us to a lake he and Lilja often enjoyed, to share in a quiet time of prayer. Our hearts were touched that they would take us to their special inspirational spot. We were reminded of Jesus' habit of retreating to the wilderness.

"He Himself often withdrew into the wilderness and prayed." (Luke 5:16)

Midway through the return trek, Roar paused and pulled out a compass. We were puzzled.

"Are we lost?" Faye timidly asked.

"No, it is just a precaution." Roar smiled, slipping the compass back into his pocket. "Since there are no trees, the landscape all looks similar. You can't tell direction or time of day by the sun either, as in summer its path simply circles the horizon. It is common to carry a compass since one can get disoriented easily if a heavy fog suddenly drifts in from the sea." We returned to Vardø. It had been a glorious day without mishap.

We also went with Roar to another coastal fishing town. Word had reached us that again Salome had predicted trouble, but we ignored her. We assumed if she told us not to go, then God probably had a blessing in store for us there! Sure enough, we sensed God's presence as one man wept through our entire concert and expressed that God's love had met his need. God was making significant changes in peoples' lives, and we were blessed to see His workings.

One afternoon we were invited into the home of Per and Solveig Olson. As we savored a dish of home-canned *multe* (cloud berries,) we also savored their fellowship.

"We Christians are few in number up here. It's like a spiritual ice age," Per said. "We feel that God sent you twins to remind us that we Christians need to put aside our denominational differences and work together in loving unity. We all can strengthen each other and be a greater witness for Christ in the community."

Several days prior to our leaving Vardø by ship, Svein gave us a word of caution. "Do not leave on the ship! Salome said, 'I see faces in the wake. The ship will sink!'"

"Svein, we know you are concerned for our safety, but you also know how we feel about Salome. We won't live in fear of everything she says."

"But her predictions always come true," he insisted.

"No, they don't! Nothing happened on our trip to Hammingberg or to the fishing village."

"If the thing does not happen or come to pass...the prophet has spoken it presumptuously; you shall not be afraid of him." (Deut. 18:22)

"Maybe God wants you to stay here longer," Svein said, meaning well.

"We'll pray about it," Faye assured him. "If even one of our contacts for future bookings telephones and asks us to postpone our arrival, we'll conclude that God wants us to spend the added time here. But we will not change our plans simply because of Salome's predictions.

The morning of our departure dawned gray, cold,

blustery. We tightened the cords on the hoods of our windbreakers as we stood on the dock with our suitcases. Svein was again trying to persuade us not to leave when Per, Solveig, and Roar arrived to see us off. An inner calm settled over us when Per offered to pray. As we boarded the ship, we clung to God's promise.

> If I take the wings of the morning, and dwell in the uttermost parts of the sea, even there Your hand shall lead me, and Your right hand shall hold me." (Ps. 139:9,10)

The waters of the Arctic were rough as the ship pulled out of the harbor. We remained on the windswept deck, praying as Vardø slowly faded from view, disappearing into the fog. Then we took refuge inside. Along with many others, we got seasick. Later the seas calmed, and so did our queasy stomachs. For three days we enjoyed the coastal scenes, the grandeur of mountains rising right out of the sea. One sunny afternoon when passengers crowded the deck, we gave a concert for our captive audience. Many of them were tourists, so we sang in a variety of languages.

At Bodø, we disembarked and journeyed southward by train. We detoured to Gaddede, a small town just across the border into Sweden. We were eager not only to meet some relatives there, but also to solve a family mystery concerning one of Mom's cousins. She always wondered why Johan did not immigrate to America with the rest of the family. Widar Anderson, Johan's son, met us and drove us into the wilderness of Sweden's north country. We were glad to see the home place of our grandmother, to get acquainted with these relatives, and to give a concert in their beautiful chapel. It was interesting to hear the family history that had unfolded nearly a century ago.

In 1903 when our grandmother Sanna was in her late teens, times were difficult. Sanna's parents made plans for the family to immigrate to America where homestead land was available in northern Minnesota. Sanna's married brother Andrew also planned to immigrate with his wife and children. However, at that time, Sweden was beginning to industrialize. The heads of government were feeling threatened that so many young men were leaving the country, as they were needed to work in the factories or to serve in the military. So officials put pressure on their local representatives, the parish priests, to detain young men. The Gaddede priest convinced Andrew and Sarah to leave their fourteen-year-old son, Johan behind. "At least until he has been through confirmation," he reasoned. That way he could record to the officials that Johan had been detained.

As it would be difficult for the family to change their departure date, they left as planned, promising to send money for Johan's passage later. The family went by horse and wagon westward over the mountains to Norway's coastal town of Trondheim. There they boarded a ship, assuming their separation from Johan was only temporary.

A couple years passed. Johan received the money for his ticket, so he set out. Since he had no means of transport to the coast, he trekked the more than two hundred miles to Trondheim. All passengers had to be examined by the ship's doctor before being allowed on board. Johan, exhausted and hungry from the strenuous hike, fainted, so the doctor refused him passage.

Heavy hearted, the youth trudged back to Sweden. He worked at various jobs, determined to catch a different ship later. Then he met a young lady whom he eventually married. Johan envisioned the two of them immigrating to the United States together. Then news reached them concerning the ill-fated maiden voyage of the Titanic—its sinking in the frigid waters of the north Atlantic. Another ship loaded with immigrants also sank about that time. Although all the passengers of that other ship were rescued, the news of two such tragedies was enough to deter the young couple's plans. Johan's wife insisted she would never set foot on a ship.

It is intriguing how events in history can alter the course of some lives. Like Joseph of old living in Egypt to fulfill God's plan, perhaps Johan's life in Sweden separated from family was a part of God's plan, for his descendants. We thought of Solveig, Widar and Elsa's daughter, who has a well-trained operatic voice. God's plan might spread her influence throughout Europe. Only He sees the full picture.

"You, O Lord, shall endure forever, and the remembrance of Your name to all generations." (Ps. 102:12)

In 2001 our sister, Laura Jean, traveled with us. She was seeing the land of our forefathers for the first time. While singing in Bergen, we watched Norwegians celebrate their Independence Day, the 17th of May. What a sight to see hundreds of people in their colorful local costumes. We took a boat ride on the Sognefjord. Many

tourists were on board, so we three sang as we enjoyed the magnificent scenery. Viewing one tiny community, its white church reflected in the deep blue waters, Laura Jean was excited to learn that Anne Kari Lia, our second cousin, was the church organist there. Later we were with Anne Kari's parents in Telemark, from where our ancestry stemmed in 1400. Einar and Gunnhild invited many friends and neighbors into their home where we shared our faith through songs and testimonies. Laura Jean, Faye and I were also privileged to sing in a nearby Stave church that has been in use since 1147.

We swell with a deep love for Norway, a land of unending beauty. It is a part of our physical and our spiritual heritage. Although we feel a sense of belong-

ing, it matters not whether we are Scandinavian or American, for "our citizenship is in heaven." (Phil. 3:20)

42

Double Curse
Double Blessing
~ by Janice ~

———————◖▭◗———————

Janice and Faye did not realize that their being in the country would influence people's views concerning twins.

Often, through means we cannot anticipate, God makes an impact on a culture. God does the work and He deserves the praise. For example, the gospel's influence in Papua New Guinea changed a peoples' attitude and treatment of twins. To clarify, I'll share it from their viewpoint.

A thick cloud lay like a rumpled blanket over the rugged highlands. Dawn's muted light struggled to penetrate the woven walls of the village hut. Senik stirred, stiff after the night on her mat. The cool mist added a sense of foreboding to her anxious thoughts. Awkwardly she struggled to her feet, one hand supporting the small of her back. This pregnancy was particularly cumbersome. Her sister Lipu had commented she was big and would have a healthy baby.

But a stab of fear had plagued Senik's mind. How would her people react if she were to have twins? She shuddered at the thought. As long as she could remember, they considered multiple births to be a bad omen. Now she dreaded the possibility of facing that shame.

Feeling the chill, Senik set about to rekindle the fire. Wood had been stacked near the fire pit where it could dry overnight. She stirred the bed of coals and placed a handful of crooked sticks on top. A whiff of smoke curled upward adding soot to the already blackened palm-thatch. Senik rubbed smoke-irritated eyes with the back of her hand. She reached for the string bag of vegetables that her sister had carried from the garden. Finding some *kaukaus* wrapped in leaves, she placed them in the edge of the embers. The roasted sweet potatoes would give her needed strength. Just then a little one in her womb stretched. Senik grimaced as she placed one hand on her swollen abdomen. *I do hope you are not twins!*

A mangy dog crept out of the shadows and drew near, sniffing the sweet potatoes. Senik struck it across the back with a stick. The mutt let out a yelp and scurried for the doorway, tail between its legs. Senik's gaze followed the dog's retreat. A dog! It was a painful reminder of the condescending words she had heard the previous day. An insensitive woman, with a furtive glance toward Senik, had muttered, "Only dogs and pigs should have litters."

Turning her attention back to the fire, Senik mechanically turned the *kaukaus*. She could not dismiss the ceaseless parade of unpleasant recollections, like the haunting face of young Pendiap. Only two moons earlier she had given birth to twins. When twins were born, it was thought that only one was the true child—the other, an impersonating spirit come to destroy the family. Pendiap was horrified by the timing, as there was a funeral in the village that day. She wondered if the dead man's spirit had entered one of the babies, or if others would blame her for the old man's death. She feared their reaction. In her panic, the young mother frantically snatched up her newborns. Like a crazed fugitive, she staggered along the narrow path leading to the outhouse. Not pausing to give her act of desperation a second thought, Pendiap, with trembling hands, thrust both infants into the pit. The babies' muffled cries faded in the darkness of their putrid tomb.

Senik let out a sigh. She stared at the fire pit while she vividly recalled Pendiap's face, a mirror of numbed horror and inconsolable grief. Senik wished to be freed from the images of Pendiap. Of dogs. Of litters. Of twins! Hunger pangs brought her back to the present. She reached with her bamboo tongs and extracted one of the roasted *kaukaus* from the coals. The nourishment would be needed for the day's trek. Senik had determined to cross the ridges to the mission hospital at Kudjip. If she were to have a big baby, she would need help with the delivery. The hike was an arduous journey, but Senik endured without complaint, grateful that her sister had volunteered to join her. Lipu had led the way, her string bag heavily laden with garden produce. She would cook to help supplement what the hospital would provide.

When the time of delivery came, Senik's greatest fears were realized—a multiple birth. Was it a look of concern or disgust she detected in her sister's eyes when the second girl was born? Then to compound their disgrace, a third one came. Lipu turned away, her expression downcast. Senik, too, was despondent, unable to hide her shame. She did not want to dispose of her babies as Pendiap had done, yet feared the reaction of others if she kept them. She glanced toward the incubators where her tiny daughters lay, being fed intravenously.

A week later two other women in the maternity ward gave birth to twins. There may have been some consolation for Senik, as she was not alone in her dilemma, yet she sat stone-faced. In her troubled state of mind, she still had not produced any breast milk. One morning when the triplets were three weeks old, a nurse announced that American twin ladies would be singing in the ward. Senik, Lipu, and the other mothers of twins perked up with intense curiosity.

As my twin and I were singing, we were unaware that Senik and Lipu's thoughts spun in a whirlpool of questions. Who are these ladies? How can they sing in our language? They are twins, but which is the impersonating spirit? How can either of them be evil when both are praising God?

Lipu's countenance was the first to change. Gazing pensively toward the incubators, her former expression of disgust transformed into a smile of genuine acceptance. Senik noted the difference. It sparked a resolve in her own mind. Perhaps twins or triplets were not a curse after all. She would keep her daughters and face whatever reaction may come at the village. The following morning Senik sent word that she wanted to see the American twins.

When we entered the ward, Senik looked up, greeting us with a smile. She sat cross-legged, one infant on her lap, another held to her breast. Lipu cradled the third one. The change in Senik's attitude was evident. She was now producing milk for her premature triplets. It was no accident that we should sing in this hospital on that particular day.

❦

As told in the chapter "On the Ramu," an unusual reaction to us as twins occurred in the village of Garati in 1984. The church was then very new. Ruri, a village leader, had been the first to accept Christ. Upon his example of being baptized in the Ramu River, others

also surrendered to Jesus. Their zealous faith was fresh, open to God's leading. Ruri admonished them, "Now that we've left the worship of ancestral spirits, we must be very sensitive to God's Spirit. He will show us what belonged to Satan's old ways that must be forsaken."

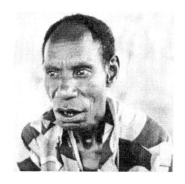

His conviction caused me to reflect on our American society. What do we change when we become Christians? Are we sensitive to the Holy Spirit when He convicts concerning our conduct, the way we dress, what we watch, what we read, or what we do? Do our standards change to the extent that the world can see a difference?

When we sang in Garati, the Christians began to rethink their treatment of twins. "Here are twins who are doing good, not evil. Perhaps we are wrong to separate our twins," one had observed. Shortly after that tour, twin boys were born in Garati. The parents planned as customary to send one of the infants to a distant village. Missionary Sharran Pryor was distressed.

"Remember the Rostvit Twins, how they loved doing everything together? Twins are not a bad omen. They are a blessing from God. Don't deny your sons the joy of being raised together." The family took Sharran's advice and were glad they did. On subsequent tours, we have seen those twin boys, and others also. Parents in various villages are proud to show us their twins. They explain that because they saw us both serving God, they are now raising their twins together.

When we returned to Garati in 1996, the whole community buzzed with excitement. Everyone was eager for us to meet two toddlers—twin granddaughters of Ruri. They had been named after us. The mother said, "When our little Janice and Faye grow up, we hope they will praise God like you do." What a double blessing— an honor to be in the center of events that God has obviously orchestrated. God had us in New Guinea not only as singers, but also as TWINS.

"That they may see and know, and consider and understand together, that the hand of the Lord has done this," (Isa. 41:20a)

The Rostvit Twins with their namesakes, little Janice and Faye.
L.-R. Janice with Janice, and Faye holding Faye.

[Since then, David and Sharran Pryor have completed the translation of the New Testament for that language area. We will be in Garati in 2002 to sing for the dedication celebration. It will also be a joy to see our twin namesakes again.]

Many have asked us what it is like to be twins. Our reply has often been, "What is it like NOT to be?" It is trite but true. We have known nothing else. It is more than having a sister the same age. It is better than having a best friend with you at all times. It's a bit like an extension of yourself. We share a unique bond. Being twins is even a mystery to ourselves. How can we explain the times when we come from opposite ends of the house and discover that we are humming the same song in the same key, the times when we have identical dreams, or the times when we feel each other's pain? Twinship defies description.

Faye and I are "mirror-image" twins. That is, we are identical, yet alike as we face each other—one right handed, the other left. The crown of our hair is on opposite sides. Dental records verify cavities in corresponding teeth. These things are common among "mirror-image" identicals.

One time we went through a "mirror maze." Walls were either panels of glass or were mirrors. Each of us had difficulty finding our way through. Seeing my own reflection in some distant mirror and assuming it was an open passage to my twin, I kept banging into glass panels. Others found our dilemma quite amusing. Our life has been a mirror and a maze—a maze of experiences in a unique ministry. If God had revealed our future when we were shy teenagers, we probably would have reacted, "You want us to go WHERE? And do WHAT?" But the Lord has guided one step at a time, one tour at a time. Our travels, whether exhilarating or tiring, joyous or fearful, have been challenges we could face, together. We are grateful God made us twins. More important than being mirror twins, is that we should mirror God's image.

> You are a mirror, reflecting God's face,
> Reflecting His mercy, reflecting His grace.
> Is the image clear, or is it dim?   ♪♪♪
> When others see you, do they see Him?

It was autumn. Autumn is a short season in the Rocky Mountains where snows can invade the high country with howling fury, or can sneak in early with quiet serenity to politely blanket the landscape. In September, before winter sets in, aspen trees display their color, making mountainsides awash with glimmering yellow gold. To be in the mountains always leaves us marveling at God's handiwork.

The early hour was crisp cool when we drove into the valley where a lake mirrors the twin-like peaks called The Maroon Bells. Parking our van, we struck out walking with camera and tripod in hand. Drawing near the lake's shore, a sense of awe silenced us. All was still! A dark shadow engulfed the entire valley, as dawn's early light only lit the tops of the peaks. We set up the camera and waited for sunlight to bathe the scene.

Faye and I reflected on our years together. Much had changed in the world and in our society over the past four decades. On the political scene, Communism, which was on the rise in the 1960s was no longer a threat. The Iron Curtain had long rusted away, and the Berlin Wall had crumbled.

Now it was September, 2001. A new threat loomed like a large shadow over our land. We could despair if we focused only on terrorism or on the moral decay in our society. But if we trust in God and set our minds on things above, we will see that good does triumph over evil. God IS still in control. When everything seems like a huge shadow around us, we can remember that Jesus never changes.

"Jesus Christ is the same yesterday, today, and forever." (Heb. 13:8)

We can trust in Him, the rock of our salvation.

Despite my circumstances now,
contentment fills my soul, ♪♪ ♪
To mirror Your reflection Lord,
has been my highest goal.

The sun rises over the valley, shrinking the shadow, and creating a picturesque scene of mountains perfectly reflected in the lake. The moment is right. We set the timer of our camera and leap on stepping stones to reach a rock out in the water. The sun shines on us and we know we have become a part of the mirror image.

God had said in the beginning of time, "Let Us make man in Our image" (Genesis 1:26a) Now as new creations we are told to "put on the new man who is renewed in knowledge according to the image of Him who created him," (Col. 3:10)

"For whom He foreknew, He also predestined to be conformed to the image of His son." (Rom. 8:29a)

Oh that we would daily run to the Rock, allowing the SON to shine on us, so that we may mirror HIS image!

We have faced more adventures not included in this book, but we hope that the emphasis of the stories we did share will encourage you to reflect on God's wondrous works, not only in our lives, but especially in your own. Our prayer is that you may also be a "mirror image," not in a twin sense, but a perfect reflection of the character of our Lord Jesus Christ.

And now as I behold this beauty, may I reflect Your image, too, Jesus my Savior, I now surrender. Oh Lord, I give my life to You.

Rostvit Twins CDs, Cassettes, and Songbooks

JESUS (22 songs) Twenty-one songs are composed by the Rostvit Twins
CD— $15.00
Songbook (21 songs)—$15.00
Cassette (12 songs)—$8.00

TREASURES FROM THE HEART (11 songs) All songs are written by the Rostvit Twins
CD—$10.00
Cassette—$8.00

NATURE'S VOICE OF PRAISE (11 songs) Ten of the songs are written by the Rostvit Twins
CD—$10.00
Songbook—$10.00
Cassette—$8.00

To Order CDs, cassettes, and songbooks, send check to The Rostvit Twins, 1441 Northview Drive, Colorado Springs, CO 80909-3028. Add $2.00 shipping. Colorado Springs residents, please add 6.4% sales tax; all other Colorado residents, please add 2.9% sales tax. Indicate amount enclosed. _____

Name: _____

Address: _____

Phone Number: _____

Items: _____